Nitya Yoga
The Yoga of Constant Communion

Krishna

Aum Sri Krishnaya Paramaatmane Namaha!

Nitya Yoga

The Yoga of Constant Communion

(Second Revised Edition)

Essays on the
Sreemad Bhagavad Gita

by

*V*anamali

Aryan Books International
New Delhi

Nitya Yoga: The Yoga of Constant Communion

ISBN: 978-81-7305-273-6

Copyright © Vanamali Gita Yogashram

All rights reserved. No part of this book may be reproduced or transmitted in any form or by any means, electronic and mechanical, including photocopy, recording or any other information storage and retrieval system or otherwise, without written permission from the author and the publisher.

First Edition: 2004

Second Revised Edition: 2015
Reprinted: 2025

Published by

Aryan Books International

Pooja Apartments, 4B, Ansari Road, New Delhi-110 002 (India)
Tel.: 23255799, 41099562
E-mail: aryanbooks@gmail.com
www.aryanbooks.com

Jacket Design and Frontispiece: Anjali Kamat
All Other Illustrations: Sandra Schweppe

Designed and Printed in India by
ABI Prints & Publishing Co., New Delhi.

Aum Sri Krishnaya Paramaatmane Namaha!

To Thee O Partha's Sarathy,
To Thee the Saviour of Draupadi,
To Thee my Love, my Vanamali,
To Thee I make my Prostrations.

Aum Sri Krishnaya Paramaatmane Namaha!

Dedicated to

My darling grand-daughter

NITYA

The beloved of Krishna

Aum Sri Ganeshaya Namaha!

Vakrathunda mahakaya soorya kotih samaprabha
Nirvighnam kuru me deva sarva karyeshu sarvada

O Lord with curved trunk and huge body, as effulgent as a thousand suns, I beseech you to remove all the obstructions in all my undertakings, at all times.

Kayena vacha manasendriyairva,
Bhudhiathmanavath prakrite swabhavath,
Karomi yadyat sakalam parasmai,
Sri Narayanayeti samarpayami.

Whatever I perform with my body, limbs, speech, mind, intellect or my inner self, either intentionally or unintentionally, I dedicate everything to that Supreme Lord Narayana.

Aum Sahanavavatu, Sahanau bhunakthu
Saha veeryam karavavahai
Tejasvinavadheethamastu
Ma vidvishavahai

May He, the Supreme, protect us. May He nourish us. May we work together with energy. May our study prove to be effective and fruitful. May we never have cause to dislike each other. May peace be upon us, forever!

CONTENTS

Introduction   *xi*

1. **Arjuna Vishada Yoga**   1
   The Yoga of Arjuna's Despondency
2. **Sankhya Yoga**   21
   The Yoga of the Wisdom of Sankhya
3. **Karma Yoga**   57
   The Yoga of Action
4. **Jnana Karma Sannyasa Yoga**   82
   The Yoga of Knowledge, Action and Renunciation of Action
5. **Karma Sannyasa Yoga**   99
   The Yoga of Renunciation of Action
6. **Atma Samyama Yoga**   114
   The Yoga of Self-Discipline

7.	**Jnana Vijnana Yoga** The Yoga of Knowledge and Discernment	128
8.	**Akshara Brahma Yoga** The Yoga of the Imperishable Brahman	145
9.	**Raja Vidya Raja Guhya Yoga** The Yoga of the Sovereign Knowledge and Sovereign Secret	165
10.	**Vibhuti Yoga** The Yoga of the Divine Manifestations	183
11.	**Viswaroopa Darshana Yoga** The Yoga of the Vision of the Cosmic Form	200
12.	**Bhakti Yoga** The Yoga of Devotion	217
13.	**Kshetra Kshetrajna Vibhaga Yoga** The Yoga of the Distinction between the Field and the Knower of the Field	238
14.	**Gunatraya Vibhaga Yoga** The Yoga of the Distinction between the Three Gunas	262
15.	**Purushottama Yoga** The Yoga of the Supreme Person	280

16.	**Devasurasampath Vibhaga Yoga** The Yoga of the Distinction between the Divine and the Demonic Qualities	297
17.	**Sraddhatraya Vibhaga Yoga** The Yoga of the Three- Fold Faith	310
18.	**Moksha Sannyasa Yoga** The Yoga of Liberation and Renunciation	325

Summary of the Gita's Teachings   375

Glossary   393

The Call of the Divine

INTRODUCTION

Aum Sri Krishnaya Paramaatmane' namaha!
Aum Sri Parthasarathaye' namaha.

PART-I

In India we begin everything with a prayer. Whether we are taking a bath or naming a child, whether we are taking our food or going to bed, building a house or looking at the new moon, everything is an act of worship, because everything is imbued with the divine Spirit. Nothing is mundane or common and no act can be relegated to the purely material. In fact, there can be no division between sacred and secular, because everything is sacred. Everything is divine. Everything is permeated and saturated with the divine Spirit. The Upanishads say *Isaavasyamidam sarvam*. Everything here is nothing but Iswara, the Supreme Lord.

We start our study of the *Sreemad Bhagavad Gita* with a prayer to the book itself—the *Bhagavad-Gita*, which is in the nature of a dialogue between Narayana, the Supreme Soul, and Arjuna, the embodied self, whom he wished to enlighten.

The script was transcribed by no less a personage than Vyasa, an ancient sage, noted for his wisdom. The dialogue occurs in the middle portion of the mighty epic of the *Mahabharata* and showers on us the nectar of the immortal Advaita philosophy, which dispels the sorrows of mortal existence.

Next our obeisance is to Lord Krishna, who was God incarnate, the son of Vasudeva, destroyer of evil forces and the preceptor of the whole universe. Therefore, he, Lord Krishna, is the universal Guru. It is because of his grace that we can study this sacred scripture and it is because he is the very stuff of our consciousness that we can understand what is being read. He alone is the narrator and the listener. He permeates and enfolds our entire being. So we begin every chapter with a prayer to him, the Supreme Consciousness, who enacted the role of Arjuna's charioteer.

In the following pages we will be studying this book, the *Sreemad Bhagavad Gita*. Many of us may have heard of it, but before discovering its specific message, it may be good to have some idea of its unique place in the history of religious scriptures.

Introduction

THE GITA'S PLACE IN SACRED LITERATURE

The world has seen many scriptures both sacred and profane, both profound and shallow, which men at different times have clung to, as if they and they alone contained the entire truth of life. Time has been the touchstone on which most of them have been tried and found wanting, thus sinking into oblivion. The *Bhagavad Gita,* however, has stood the test of time and today more than any other scripture that the world has produced, it has a message for suffering humanity. It brings not just a ray of hope but a burst of blinding sunshine into the dejected mind of humanity, which stands upon the brink of a catastrophic war, which it thinks is not of its own making. None of us can claim to be totally innocent, since anything that happens in the world has its roots in the negativity created by all of us. But we are not prepared to accept this and find ourselves projected willy-nilly into a battlefront for which we are totally unprepared. The readymade answers given by science and technology have failed us. Our youthful dreams of a Utopian society based on love and peace have crumbled to dust. Humanity is aghast to find that the meek scientific robot of its own creation has turned into a veritable monster—a Frankenstein who is ready to gobble up its own maker.

The history of religion has been a history of the fanatic clinging of the human mind upon one or other of many creeds to the exclusion of all others. Thus, religion, which should have been a unifying force, became a force for dissension and hatred. All scriptures and all religions are after the same truth. Truth is one and eternal. The human mind from the dawn of civilisation has been seeking for it through many different channels. So how does the disparity between religions arise? The fact is that this truth, though one and eternal, expresses itself in Time and through the mind of man.

So every scripture must contain two elements, one temporary and perishable, the other eternal and imperishable, and applicable to all ages and countries. Even though the *Bhagavad Gita* has a temporal and local setting, its spirit is so profound and universal that its message has been appreciated by all humanity through the ages. When we compare the *Gita* with other great religious books of the world, we find that it does not stand apart as a work by itself, as the message of the spiritual life of an enlightened soul like Christ, Mohammed or the Buddha, nor is it the product of a spiritual age like the Vedas and the Upanishads. It is given as an episode in the epic history of the country called Bharata or India and arises out of a critical moment in the life of one of the leading personages in that episode. It represents not only all the facets of Hinduism but of religion in its universality without limit of time and space. The suggestions given by Krishna in the *Gita* have to be understood by everyone today for saving our world, which has become totally materialistic. It is both metaphysics and ethics and the practical application of both in the world. True spirituality is never cut off from life. The transcendent and the empirical are closely connected. The opening chapter of the *Gita* raises this important question of how we can live in the spirit and continue to act in the world.

The *Gita* is set in the middle portion of the great epic, the *Mahabharata*, and its setting is essential to understanding its import. The background makes us realise that the teaching of the *Gita* is not just another spiritual philosophy or ethical doctrine but a treatise on the practical application of this philosophy in our daily lives. It gives us a lesson on the practical application of ethics and spirituality in human life. It is the only scripture which tells that we are completely responsible for our lives and therefore we should take control of our life and act to the best of our ability.

Inscrutable are the ways of God. The cosmic purpose is simple and single-pointed. It aims at the total annihilation of the individual ego in order to attain unity with the Supreme. Through the intricate web and often bizarre design of our individual existence, this purpose is steadfastly adhered to, even though we may not be aware of it. Very often before we become the ego less and perfect instrument we have to pass through a cleansing period of an inner evolution, which has to be brought about by an outer and sometimes physical revolution. We find that the faster the evolution, the more violent the revolution which triggers it. The stab of pain is often more potent than the caress of love, to goad the *jiva* towards its goal. The more advanced the seeker, the more severe the tests he or she has to undergo. Fortunate indeed are those who are called upon to participate in the hastening of the cosmic purpose! The message of the *Gita* is addressed to the indomitable Spirit in the human being which will not let her rest till the final battle is won and the divine status achieved. In this there is only one thing, which we have to remember that Life is a drama in which the Eternal Spirit manifests itself as the *atman* in the human being in order to participate in the marathon race of its own pilgrimage to itself! Birth and death are but milestones on the way and all the different bodies one has to inhabit are the guesthouses on the road. The different circumstances in which one is placed have to be used as goads to help us in our ascent. We have eternity at our disposal and immortality as our goal and God himself as our one and only travelling companion!

Introduction

MESSAGE OF THE GITA

The message of the *Gita* is to make us understand that God is our only friend, sole relative and perfect guide, ever present, ever ready to help us, nay carry us if need be. The only condition is that we should choose him with our own free will—admit that the greatest aim in life is to find him, to seek union with him, and to become one with him. Once that has been given top priority, the rest of the jigsaw puzzle of our lives will fall into place.

But it must be remembered that the action it urges is not human action but action done for the Divine and by the Divine. Its ideal man is not the emancipated social worker but the God-man, who having emptied himself of his ego becomes merely an instrument in the hands of the Divine, for the upliftment and welfare of the world. If civilisation is to have a future, it can be only through the production of such enlightened souls and not through the production of more nuclear weapons.

The Karma Yogi does not perform social service but impersonal service for the sake of God and as a continuous offering to him who stands behind both humanity and society. It is not that the *Gita* decries humanity. The God-man of the *Gita* does indeed have the highest ideals, which we may expect any person to have, but he has these ideals, not due to his humanity but due to his divinity. The *Gita* like a loving mother embraces all these ideals in her all-encompassing arms and opens not just one door but also many doors to the Life Divine. All those who have the heart of an Arjuna can enter therein. No one is abandoned, none cast out. It is not meant for the Brahmin or the intellectual or for the initiates alone. The only condition for studying the gospel of the *Gita* is a burning desire to lead a spiritual life, a burning desire to know God and be one with Him. Once this has been recognised as our one priority, we can begin the study of the *Gita* and the meaning will be clear to us; we will then be able to find an answer to every predicament. Otherwise, we will find only a meaningless jargon of an impossible theory.

A PRACTICAL GUIDE

To such a one who has fixed her sights on the highest goal of life, the *Gita* offers an immediate and practical guide to extricate herself from the pangs of everyday living, into the glories of a Life Divine. If there is any meaning to life, it has to be found in and through the world itself. If there is a Heaven, it has to be discovered on this earth or else it is of no use to us. If God is not just some unjust monster, incarcerating himself in some other world, then he should remain with us every moment of our lives, helping, guiding, and comforting us, so that we can find a way to unravel ourselves from these mortal coils and reach the goal of Supreme Beatitude in this very life. Our study of the *Gita* thus begins with this affirmation. It is not a book that one can read, to while away an idle hour in the afternoon. It is a book with a divine purpose—to make the human divine—to turn the human being into God and for that God became man—the Absolute took on a human form as Lord Krishna or the *avatara* of the age to give the message of spiritual life to Arjuna—the prototype of all humankind. Whenever Lord Krishna speaks in the first person, he is not referring to Himself as a historical personage but to himself, as the *Purushottama*, or the Supreme Person, descended into the human body in order to help the human being to ascend. May that divine charioteer deign to descend into the hearts of each one of us so as to enable us to extricate ourselves from the horrors of the age we are living in and take us into the sunshine of a divine epoch!

The meaning of the *Bhagavad Gita* is so deep that the more we read it, the more we get out of it and the more we live according to its teachings the more our level of consciousness increases. Its message is of eternity and thus it has a timeless significance. The vicissitudes of life have no impact on this message because it arises from a source, which transcends the transitions of life.

Each chapter of the *Gita* is termed *yoga*. The word *yoga* has many connotations but the primary meaning is union. Thus, any activity which enables us to obtain union with the Divine, can be called *yoga*. The *Bhagavad Gita* has eighteen chapters, all of which have been called *yogas*; hence we can say that it gives eighteen different methods of union with the Divine. At the end of every chapter is given a short description of the significance of the book. It is ranked as one of the Upanishads, which are the foremost spiritual texts of Hindu philosophy. They come at the end of each Veda. The subject matter of the *Gita* is *Brahmavidya* or the knowledge of the Eternal Brahman, the Supreme Reality that cannot be further transcended. It is also *yogashastra* or the practical method of living in constant and loving unity with the Supreme Beloved in eighteen different ways. That is to say, it combines within its comprehensive grasp both the Science of Being and the Art of Living. Above all, it is *Krishnarjuna Samvada* or the dialogue between Krishna and Arjuna, Man and his Maker—between Man and God.

As the message is imparted by the Eternal Godhead to the Eternal individual, the teaching is also eternal. It is not a message conveyed in mere temporal language to suit a specific occasion, but the occasion has been taken to convey to the eternal human nature the knowledge of its relationship with the Eternal Absolute. The *Gita* integrates and synthesises all the different systems

Introduction

of Hinduism which were prevalent at that time—the sacrificial portion of the Vedas, the transcendental teaching of the Upanishads, the theism of the *Bhagavad Purana*, the dualism of the *Samkhya* and the *yoga* of Pantanjali. Krishna shows how all these different lines of thought converge to the same end. The *Gita* is recognised as one of the three orthodox scriptures of Hinduism along with the Upanishads and the *Brahma Sutras*.

METHOD OF STUDY

The union of the individual with the Absolute is the final consummation of the *Bhagavad Gita*, the Song of God. It leaves nothing unsaid. The Sanskrit language in which the message is conveyed is known as Devanagari, or the language of the Gods. It is impossible to translate it into any other language. A mere reading or translation will not give us the full benefit. In the study of this book, we will have to make use of the ancient Vedic method of studying the scriptures. They used three steps—*sravana, manana, niddidhyasana* (listening, contemplating, practicing)!

Our first step is therefore to listen to the chanting of the Sanskrit verses. The second is to contemplate on the meaning. The third is to put the teaching into practice. The inner message of the *Gita* can only be understood when you delve deeper and deeper into the depths of your own soul. It is not a scripture, which one reads every day and keeps aside reverently in the hope that the very reading can bring you some spiritual benefit. The *Gita* has to be assimilated into the very core of your being so that one lives the *Gita*. The word *Gita* means song and the *Bhagavad Gita* is the song of God and therefore the Song of Life, of existence, and omniscience leading to Bliss—*Sat*, *Chit*, and *Ananda*!

The first two questions that arise in our minds when we read the *Gita* are why such a great spiritual message should have been given on a battlefield and why Krishna, the protagonist of Hinduism which upholds the law of *ahimsa* or non-violence, urges his disciple, Arjuna, to fight! These questions will be fully answered during the course of the first two talks on the *Gita*.

Before entering into the actual text of the *Gita* we should have some idea of the historical background in which it is placed, as well as a brief knowledge of the spiritual history of India leading up to it.

THE VEDAS

The most ancient scriptures of the Hindu faith are four in number and are known as the Vedas. In fact, they are the most ancient records of spiritual philosophy known to man.

Each Veda is in turn divided into four parts. The first three portions need not concern us here but the last portion is known as the Upanishads and is collectively called the *Vedanta*, which means the end of the Vedas. Veda itself means knowledge. Thus, the end or culmination of all knowledge is the realisation of the Supreme and that is the subject matter of the Upanishads.

The language of the Vedas is strange, mythical and clothed in allegory. It is difficult for the ordinary mind to grasp in its entirety. It is an esoteric teaching meant for the initiates alone. It is generally believed that the Vedic seers or *rishis* recognised the truth and experienced it, while in a state of transcendental consciousness enabling them to have supra-mental vision. Their language is clothed in mystery and cannot be understood by the ordinary human, who lives on a lower plane of consciousness.

The Vedas are called *anaadi* or without beginning. They contain the knowledge of the Supreme, which is without beginning and without end. But the study of the Vedas is a lifetime endeavour. The child has to be initiated at a tender age and spend many years with a competent Guru in order to master the chanting and even more years to understand their meaning. Thus, a special class of people called the Brahmins was created in the Vedic society to specialise in the study of the Vedas alone. The rest of the society had a moral obligation to protect and look after the needs of these people for they were the custodians of this Supreme Truth. The world owes a great debt to the Brahmins for having kept alive this amazing knowledge for more than ten thousand years. If this caste had not existed, this esoteric teaching would have sunk into oblivion long ago. Since it was an oral tradition, many elaborate rules were laid down in the Vedic book on phonetics called the *Shiksha* in order to ensure the absolute purity of tone, pitch and modality, which the Vedas demand. The sound is the most important thing in the chanting of Vedic *mantras* because even if one does not know the meaning, the correct intonation guarantees the expected results. Hence, we find that the Vedic seers took elaborate precautions to ensure the purity of the sound. It is an amazing fact that unlike other languages, which change with the passage of time, the Vedic language has not changed and the *mantras* are chanted today in exactly the same way as they were more than ten thousand years ago!

Even if we approach the Vedas from a purely historical point of view, it can be said that they are the ecstatic expressions of the experience of our race at the dawn of civilisation. The earliest historical evidence in the world is provided by the Vedas. They are more valuable than copper-plates or stone inscriptions. Every Veda ends in a set of books known as the Upanishads. They contain the highest philosophical truths ever to be grasped by the mind of man, the highest spiritual truths which the human intellect is capable of conceiving.

The Vedic age was surely the Diamond age of Indian spiritual life; perhaps of human spiritual life for we find that the rest of the history of the Hindu religion draws its inspiration and sustenance from this vast storehouse of spiritual power.

After the Vedic age, there appears to be a lull in Indian spiritual thought. The highest peak that could be scaled by the spiritual mind had already been conquered, so there was nothing more to be said. This stands true even today. If one can master the Vedas and live according to their suggestions, there is nothing more to be done. But these truths are too lofty for the ordinary human mind to grasp; thus, we find the Golden age of Hindu thought called the Puranic age.

THE PURANAS

Without the Puranas, the Vedic religion however sublime would have slipped into oblivion like the ancient Egyptian mysteries, the Macedonian and Cretan cultures. Although these cultures had attained high levels of spirituality, they have been wiped off the face of the earth because they had no communication with the masses.

If religion is to serve any purpose, it must have its head in the Heavens and its feet planted firmly on the earth. The authors of the Puranas were also *rishis* but of a different type. It was their foresight and compassion that brought the truths of the Vedas to the level of comprehension of the common man. It may be difficult for the human mind to conceive of abstractions like truth, beauty, nobility etc., but even a child can appreciate a noble man, a beautiful woman, or a truthful person.

The Puranas projected these abstract truths in the lives of the great *avataras* as well as through the lives of the sages and saintly kings. Those who read the Puranas were moved to emulate the example of these noble souls and thus change their own materialistic lives and imbue them with grace and nobility.

THE EPICS

The *rishis* Valmiki and Vyasa, who were the mighty intellects of the Puranas, wrote these books in a form that was best suited for the simple mind—the form of a story. The sage Vyasa was the author of the eighteen Puranas as well as the mighty epic—the *Mahabharata*. The sage Valmiki was the author of the *Ramayana*, the first epic poem ever composed in the world. He was himself a contemporary of the great *avatara*, Sri Rama, and wrote about the exploits of that incarnation, in a way that has inspired generations of Indians for well over ten thousand years. These two epics were written in a story form with a special purpose. A deep inner message was hidden between the leaves of the story so that both listener and narrator ascended the spiritual ladder while listening and narrating.

The Puranas are of many types and they teach the highest standard of ethics and morals to satisfy every type of devotee—the intellectual, the philosophical as well as the emotional. They portray through their characters every type of virtue that we must strive for and every type of vice that we must avoid. Can there be a better example of truth than Harishchandra, of righteousness than Yudhishtira, of gratitude and charity than Karna, of mortal perfection than Sri Rama, of chastity than Sita and Savitri, of *bhakti* than Hanuman, of renunciation than Bhishma and Bharata, of lust than Ravana, of arrogance and envy than Duryodhana? The examples are endless and they all point us the way to moral perfection in a far more telling way than commands. The stories also tell us that though fate seems irrevocable, it can be reduced and perhaps overcome by prayer and penance and the grace of God. There are numerous such moving episodes in the Puranas that strike home these messages with great clarity and charm. In other words, the Vedic truths were embedded in the Puranas so that consciously or unconsciously, the listeners imbibed these truths.

The Puranic stories were usually told to the Hindu child while it was still in the mother's lap, so easy and simple are they. Yet through these stories were woven the mighty truths of the Vedas, sometimes spoken through the mouths of the characters, sometimes in examples given from the animal and bird kingdoms. Thus, these truths were woven into the very fabric of the daily life of the Hindu child so that he or she lived the Vedic life whether they knew it or not. That is why it is said that Hinduism is a way of life and not a religion. In fact, the word Hinduism is itself a misnomer. The religion followed by the Hindus is known as the Sanatana Dharma—The Eternal Law of Righteousness. It propagates the eternal truths that reveal themselves to the purified mind and intellect of the human being from age to age and civilisation to civilisation. It is not the sole prerogative or exclusive property of any one nation or country.

By this compassionate act of theirs, the Puranic sages ensured that the Vedic way of righteous living, the Sanatana Dharma, crept into the life of every man, woman and child in ancient India and was not reserved for the chosen castes alone as was the study of the Vedas. The *Bhagavad Gita* comes in the middle of the great epic The *Mahabharata*. It is the fully ripened fruit of the mighty tree of the Vedas. However mighty the tree, it is only the fruit which has the practical

Introduction

value. The *Gita* is the twice-distilled essence of the Vedic Dharma.

> *Wealth and power pass like a dream,*
> *Beauty fades like a flower,*
> *Long life is gone like a wave.*

PART-II

THE MAHABHARATA

For a better understanding of the *Bhagavad Gita* we have to know something of the story of the *Mahabharata*. The epic touches on all the true values of human society—religion, ethics and morality. These values are displayed in the saga of the Kuru dynasty that ruled India about ten thousand years before the birth of Christ.

The capital of the Kurus was known as Hastinapura and was situated at a spot a few kilometres away from the modern town of Meerut. Their other capital, built later by the Pandavas, was known as Indraprastha. Modern Delhi is built on its ruins. The main characters that appear in this epic are Bhishma, the grandsire of the Kuru clan, who was born as the son of the great king Santanu and his wife Ganga. Bhishma was heir to the throne of the Kurus but he gave it up and took a vow of celibacy in order to help his father. He had two nephews called Dritarashtra and Pandu. The former was born blind and, therefore, though he was the eldest, his younger brother Pandu inherited the throne. Dritarashtra had a hundred sons, who were collectively known as the Kauravas, the eldest of whom was Duryodhana. The sons of Pandu were known as the Pandavas. The eldest was Yudhishtira, who was a personification of all virtues. The second was Bhima, who was a mighty man of strength. The fourth and fifth were the beautiful twins Nakula and Sahadeva. The third or the middle Pandava was Arjuna, to whom the discourse of the *Bhagavad Gita* was given. He was a brilliant archer. An archer must have great concentration and determination so that he can hit the mark and these qualities are seen in Arjuna.

Since Pandu died before Yudhishtira came of age, the Pandavas were brought up together with the Kauravas in the city of Hastinapura, under the loving guidance of their grandfather, Bhishma and the excellent tutelage of their preceptor Drona. They excelled in everything they did and were of a noble and obedient nature so they were well loved by all. Their cousins, the Kauravas, could not brook this. Aided and abetted by their wicked uncle, Shakuni, they plotted to kill the Pandavas and snatch the kingdom for themselves. However, due to the grace of God they were foiled in every murderous attempt, ranging from arson to felony.

When Yudhishtira was crowned as heir apparent, Duryodhana tried to burn the

Pandavas to death in an inflammable palace especially made for the purpose. Their uncle, Vidura, warned them of this dastardly plot and they escaped into the forest where they went into hiding and were thought to have died by the exultant Kauravas. However, they managed to form a marital alliance with the powerful kingdom of the Panchalas when Arjuna won the hand of Draupadi, the Princess of Panchala due to his prowess in archery. It was at this time that Lord Krishna made his entry into the Pandavas' lives. He was their cousin and a staunch friend. He was also God incarnate. From that time onwards he took the lives of the Pandavas into his capable hands and guided them through the stormy course of their lives to come. Backed by him and the kingdom of Panchala, the Pandavas returned to Hastinapura in order to demand their rightful inheritance. After a lot of persuasion Duryodhana was forced to give them half the kingdom. Keeping the capital for himself, he gave them a portion of the wasteland and jungle to the south. However, since Lord Krishna supported them, they got the aid of the divine architect, Visvakarma, who transformed the jungle into a wonderful city, which they called Indraprastha as a tribute to Indra, the king of the gods. This is the location of the city of modern Delhi.

PLOT TO OUST THE PANDAVAS

Yudhishtira was a wise and just king and the land flourished under his rule. At a magnificent ceremony called the *Rajasuya Yajna*, Yudhishtira was proclaimed as Emperor of India. The Kauravas who were present could not bear to see the affluence of their cousins. After their visit to Indraprastha, Duryodhana could neither eat nor sleep; so sick was he with jealousy. In order to help him, his uncle, Shakuni, devised a master plot by which the Pandavas would be deprived of their entire wealth without shedding a drop of blood or any expenditure of money! At a gambling match, which was arranged by Shakuni, Yudhishtira lost everything he possessed including his four brothers whom he staked and lost one by one. At last when he had nothing to lose, Duryodhana taunted him and challenged him to a final throw. The stake was to be his wife—Draupadi. In order to tempt him to this terrible act, Duryodhana promised to give back everything he had won so far if he won this final throw. Tormented and confused as he was, the poor king agreed to this and of course lost his beloved wife. Duryodhana then ordered Draupadi to be forcibly brought to the court.

The scene which took place then is one of the most highly charged spiritual scenes in the whole epic. Draupadi was dragged into the court where she courageously faced the assembly and asked them to tell her whether her husband had staked her after he had lost himself in which case he had no right to stake her at all since he was already a slave to the Kauravas. The entire Kuru assembly remained silent and her own husbands hung their heads in shame. Duryodhana ordered her to be publicly disrobed. Draupadi looked desperately around for help but there was no one who dared to raise a finger to save her. Duryodhana's brother Dushhasana was already tugging at her *sari*. She tried desperately to cover her breasts with her arms and begged the elders in the assembly for help. Then the dreadful realisation dawned on her that no one was prepared to help her, not even her husbands who were the greatest warriors of those times. Dropping all pretence of trying to save her honour, she lifted up both her arms to the heavens and begged Lord Krishna to save her. To the amazement of the crowd, though Dushshasana pulled and tugged at her *sari*, all that happened was that the pile of cloth next to him grew and grew but he was unable to disrobe her totally! In fact, his gargantuan frame was totally exhausted and he fell to the ground but Draupadi continued to sing and chant to Lord Krishna immersed as she was in a state of ecstasy. She realised that God is the only one capable of saving us in every situation. This of course is a great lesson for all of us.

This miracle seemed to have brought the assembly to its senses and Dritarashtra ordered that the Pandavas should be given back their kingdom. Of course his sons refused to do so and at last it was agreed that the Pandavas, along with their wife, were to be banished to the forest for a period of twelve years. The thirteenth year was to be spent incognito at some well-known town. If they were discovered during that year, they would have to repeat the whole punishment. If they managed to complete it successfully, Duryodhana promised to give back their share of the kingdom.

DECLARATION OF WAR

The Pandavas spent their twelve years in the forest accumulating spiritual wealth while the Kauravas accumulated the hatred of the citizens. The thirteenth year was spent successfully in the court of a neighbouring king and at the end of it they sent a message to the Kuru court asking for their share of the kingdom. But true to his nature Duryodhana did not keep his word. Yudhishtira was anxious to avoid war at all costs and begged Krishna to go to the Kuru court to seek reconciliation and avert war if possible. In fact, Yudhishtira was prepared to go to any lengths for the sake of peace so he sent Krishna as ambassador to the Kuru court with instructions to opt for peace even at the cost of honour. He told Lord Krishna to ask for half the kingdom, which was their right, and if that was refused, to ask for five towns and if even that was refused, to ask for five villages and if even that was unacceptable to Duryodhana, he, Yudhishtira was prepared to settle for five palaces for himself and his brothers. Duryodhana laughed in scorn at these weak efforts at conciliation, or so he thought. He derided the Pandavas for their cowardice and told Lord Krishna that he wouldn't give them five pinpoints of land.

"I'm against all giving," he said. "Go and tell those cowards that if they want their kingdom they can fight for it like true Kshatriyas". Thus, war became inevitable much to Yudhishtira's sorrow. Though he and his brothers and wife had been unbearably humiliated in public and cheated out of their just rights, he had been prepared to give in but now, he had no option but to bow to the will of destiny and start making preparations for the war.

PARTHASARATHY

Duryodhana had decided on war as soon as he saw that the Pandavas had gone through their banishment successfully and he had already amassed an army, well before the Pandavas had even thought of war. It so happened that the

Yadava army belonging to Lord Krishna had not been promised to either party. Of course Duryodhana knew that Krishna would side with the Pandavas but he thought it well worth a try to go and ask for his help. Both Arjuna and Duryodhana went to Dwaraka, to see Lord Krishna. Krishna offered them a choice. They could have either his army or himself. Duryodhana objected to this and said that the arrangement was fair only if Lord Krishna agreed not to take up arms. Krishna laughingly agreed to this blatantly unfair proposal but gave the first choice to Arjuna since he had seen him first. Much to Duryodhana's relief, Arjuna unhesitatingly chose Krishna—alone and unarmed—and Duryodhana grabbed the crack regiment of the Yadava army, known as the Narayana Sena, which contained many of Krishna's own sons. Krishna then told Arjuna that since he had agreed not to take up arms, he would take up the reins of Arjuna's chariot and become his charioteer! This is how he got the name of Parthasarathy or the charioteer of Partha or Arjuna. The two armies met on the battlefield of the Kurus, which was known as Kurukshetra. It is about hundred kilometres from modern Delhi. The battle lasted for eighteen days, by the end of which the Kauravas were completely routed and the empire came to the Pandavas. The *Sreemad Bhagavad Gita* is the discourse between Lord Krishna and Arjuna when they were already seated in the chariot and about to commence the battle.

At the time when the two armies met in Kurukshetra, Vyasa went to Hastinapura and met Dritarashtra, who was sitting alone with his personal minister Sanjaya and told him of the ominous portents which were a prelude to war. He hinted at the dire consequences of the war, "Do not grieve over what will happen to those who have now camped in those beautiful tents." Dritarashtra did not say a word.

Vyasa said, "I will give divine sight to Sanjaya. Let him go to Kurukshetra. He will meet no harm and he will know everything that happens by day or night, even that which is only thought within the mind."

"Go then O Sanjaya!" said Dritarashtra, "stay in our camp and return to me when it is over. Then tell me everything."

Sanjaya bowed to the blind king and he and Vyasa left the king. Vyasa returned to the forest and Sanjaya to the battlefield.

Sanjaya returned on the tenth morning and found the king sitting in a dark room all alone. Sanjaya brought a lamp and said, "Sire, I have come to tell you everything."

This is the beginning of the *Sreemad Bhagavad Gita* when Sanjaya began his narration.

ॐ *Hari Aum Tat Sat* ॐ

Aum asato ma sad gamaya,
Tamaso ma jyotir gamaya,
Mrityor ma amritam gamaya.

Aum Shanti! Shanti! Shantihi!"

From the unreal lead us to the real,
From darkness to light,
And from death to immortality.
Aum Peace, peace, peace.

My bow Gandiva slips from my hand and my skin burns.
My mind reels and I am unable to stand.

Chapter I. Verse 30

I

ARJUNA VISHADA YOGA
The *Yoga* of Arjuna's Despondency

Aum Sri Krishnaya Paramaatmane' namaha!
Aum Sri Parthasarathaye' namaha.

The first chapter of the *Gita* was told to Dritarashtra, the blind king, the father of the Kauravas, by his wise minister called Sanjaya, who had been given the gift of television by the sage Vyasa, the author of the *Mahabharata*. Sitting in their palace at Hastinapura, Sanjaya described to the blind king in graphic detail all the happenings on the battlefront, much in the way of the modern cricket or football commentator.

However, since all able-bodied men had to take part in the war, Sanjaya departed to the battlefield after describing the layout of the battle. The rest of the narration was given to the king after the tenth day, when Bhishma fell. Dritarashtra, the king of the Kurus, was born blind. This is an indication to the fact that when the leader himself is blind we can only expect his followers to be equally blind to their duties. His wife Gandhari had purposely blindfolded herself. This is a hint to show us that though she recognised the inequities of her husband and children, she wilfully turned a blind eye on them as indeed we see in the epic.

An important aspect of the *Gita*, which we should always bear in mind, is that it is addressed to the fighter—the man of action and not to the philosopher, the seer or the saint. Hence, it has a wider range of applicability, since in life most of us are called upon to act, rather than contemplate. Those who can turn away from the world and take to the life of a hermit are few indeed; not that the *Gita* decries contemplation; far from it. But since it is the law of Nature that we must act, then the most useful thing for any teacher to tell us would be the technique of action, and this is what the *Gita* stresses in the first few chapters. We have already touched on the profound truths of spiritual life, which were declared in the Vedas, and the Upanishads, which were later synthesized in the Puranas. In the *Gita* we find another synthesis, of its great doctrine of *Karma Yoga* with the *advaitic*

Arjuna Vishada Yoga

or non-dualistic philosophy of the Upanishads and the theism of the Puranas.

The *Bhagavad Gita* starts on the morn of the fateful day before the commencement of the great Mahabharata war. The *Gita* opens with Dhritarashtra's request to Sanjaya to describe the scene of the battle. The two armies had drawn up in battle formation. The horses were fresh and restive, the men were tense and eager, trumpets and conches were blowing, men were shouting orders, flags were flying, drums were clamouring and the stage had been set for the final scene in the mighty drama of their lives, the grand climax for which the two factions had been expecting and preparing, for the major portion of their lives. This is the opening scene or setting for our spiritual book, the *Bhagavad Gita*, the song of the Lord. He has chosen to sing his song in the middle of the battlefield and not in the silence of the forest or the sanctity of a temple or the peace of an *ashrama* or the sylvan glades of a forest but in the midst of the noise and clamour of a battle. What is the reason for this peculiar choice of location? Was it deliberate or accidental? The Lord's doings though mysterious are never accidental. Everything has a plan and purpose. Nothing comes by chance or is left to chance. So what is the divine purpose in choosing such a location? Before going into this, let us go one step further into the first chapter and see what transpires.

Before leaving for the battlefield, Sanjaya gave a swift portrait of all the generals on either side and the various activities, which were going on. Suddenly his narrative was arrested by the arrival of the main characters on the scene—Arjuna seated in his chariot eager and ready for the battle with Krishna holding the reins in his steady hands, controlling the four milky steeds, who were straining at the bit, eager and ready to charge into battle. They made a striking picture. The rays of the morning sun produced a blaze of glory round the golden chariot and created a halo round Krishna's head. He held the four, fiery, white horses in a firm grip in his left hand and a small whip in his right hand, as he turned around to give a quizzical look at his friend. Arjuna stood behind him, tall and handsome, holding his famous bow, Gandiva, firmly in his left hand with a confident smile playing about his lips as he ran his eyes over the two armies. He told Krishna to take the chariot to the middle of the field between the two armies so that he could observe and get an overall picture of the opposing army before the battle commenced. Obedient to his role as a charioteer, Krishna, the Lord of all the worlds, acceded to the command of his friend and devotee and drove the chariot to that no man's land

Arjuna Vishada Yoga

between the two armies. He stationed their magnificent chariot strategically, just in front of Arjuna's grandsire, Bhishma and his Guru, Drona. He then said to Arjuna: "Behold all these Kurus assembled here."

Had Krishna placed the chariot in front of Duryodhana and the other Kauravas, the discourse of the *Gita* would never have taken place. The Lord's strategic placement of the chariot had a definite purpose. Arjuna, the mighty bowman of his age, turned round to survey the opposite army and saw not his enemies but his grandsire, Guru, cousins, friends, relations, teachers, and nephews. Suddenly a drastic change seemed to come over him. Before the astonished gaze of the onlookers, his lips quivered, his face crumpled and his mighty bow slipped from his nerveless grasp and fell with a thud to the bottom of the chariot. He seemed to be in the throes of some mortal ailment and was earnestly questioning the Lord about something.

Arjuna had always been the invincible warrior, never shying away from a righteous battle but now when placed in the un-enviable position of having to fight with his beloved grandsire and *guru*, he found himself unable to keep up his warrior's role.

A tremendous psychological revulsion welled up inside him, making his whole body tremble with the weakness of his emotions and he told Krishna that he could not fight. His bow fell from his nerveless grasp and he himself crumpled to a heap at the back of the chariot, a useless specimen of humanity, weakened through emotion and incapable of correct thought or correct action. It was to this warrior, this man of action who was now a wreck of his former self that Krishna, his friend, philosopher, guide and God, delivered the message of the *Sreemad Bhagavad Gita*.

Thus, the first few stanzas of the *Gita* are in the nature of an overture before the commencement of the drama.

WHY THE BATTLEFIELD

There are two questions that perplex the mind of the reader at the very outset. The first is why such a great scriptural instruction like the *Gita* should have been given on the battlefield. Surely the Lord could have chosen a more fitting background. Why not an *ashrama* or a forest or a temple or any place other than a battlefield? The second question is why a great spiritual preceptor like Lord Krishna should have urged his disciple to such a violent action rather than encourage him in *ahimsa* or non-violence, which is the foundation of Hinduism.

Let us take up the first question. The world is a *dharmakshetra* or field of righteousness in which the Lord, who is the protector of *dharma*, is actively present. Life is made up of dualities—good and bad, joy and sorrow, light and dark, beauty and ugliness all go together. These are counter correlatives and one cannot exist without the other. We know joy only because we have experienced sorrow, we known light because we have lived in darkness. A person who lives in the sun will never know the meaning of light because he has never experienced darkness. The human mind, however, seeks its happiness by attaching itself to the so-called positive half of each of these dualities and denying the other. But life is a coin with two sides. To accept one side and deny the other is being impractical. All religions teach us to shy away from the bad and seek only the good. But since they cannot deny the existence of evil, they create a being called the devil on whose head all evil, is placed. This immediately detracts from the omnipotence of God since the devil appears to be more powerful than God since he can undo most of God's work. In the history of religions, Hinduism is unique since it does not seek to teach an ethical sentimentalism which loves to look on nature as good and beautiful but refuses to face her grim and terrible mask—which dwells lovingly on the beauteous form of Lakshmi and recoils from her visage as Kali. In fact, it is not a facile philosophy meant for the kindergarten student, but for the post-graduate in spiritual life who has the courage to admit that both good and evil come from God.

The philosophy of the *Gita* is not for the weak or the coward who is afraid to face life as it is.

Unless we have the courage to face existence as it is, we will never be able to arrive at a solution to its conflicting demands. Harmony has to be achieved in and through the discord, which we cannot deny. War and destruction seem to be the principle of not only our material lives but also our mental lives. Life is a battlefield of good and evil forces and the human being is placed in the centre as it were of this field, now swayed by the good, now drawn by the evil. The evil forces as in the Mahabharata war appear to be far stronger than the forces of good. Like Arjuna we stand in this no man's land between the opposing forces wondering how best to drive our chariot between them so that we can emerge victorious. Every moment we are forced to make some decision or other. Perplexed and torn between these warring forces in our own nature, we know not what we should do. Even within the physical body there seems to be a mighty war raging between the attacking forces of germs, disease, old age, and death and the defending organism, which manfully tries to preserve the citadel and succeeds in the beginning and succumbs at the end. No one can claim to be totally non-violent if he has not experienced violence.

The universe as well as our bodies is a field of tremendous activity, conflict and warfare. The world we live in is a fierce, dangerous and destructive world. In this devouring world, the human being moves forward, precariously balanced between the evil and good forces within her and outside her. With every step, something is crushed or broken whether we will it or not. However great our belief in *ahimsa* or non-violence, every breath of life is also a breath of death. The chances are that any breath we draw may well be our last. And with every breath we kill a million, microscopic bacteria. As a baby, we enter this Kurukshetra of life with a cry, having passed many hours in the narrow uterine passage and many months cramped and twisted inside our mother's womb. Having come out we play our role in the drama of life on a stage that is not of our own making and a script that is not of own choosing! Eventually, we make our final exit, with a cry of pain and fear, not knowing what is in store for us. This battlefield of life is shown to Arjuna in all its terrifying proportions in the 11th chapter—'Viswaroopa Darshana'. The Pandavas and the Kauravas represent the conflict between the two great movements, the centrifugal and the centripetal, the divine and the demonic, which Krishna describes in the 16th chapter. *Dharma* leads us into spirituality while *adharma* leads us deeper into materialism. The two are not irreconcilable as they spring from the same source. The Pandavas and the Kauravas are cousins and have a common ancestry. The world is also called *tapakshetra* or the field of austerity or discipline. God is at once the judge the and redeemer. He creates and destroys. He is both Shiva and Vishnu.

Now let us have a look at the birth of our external world. From a clash of mighty material forces, everything in the world including this earth has come into existence. There seems to be no construction here without a preceding destruction. The eater eating, being eaten seems to be the formula of existence. But surely this cannot possibly be the only picture of life. This repellent aspect must hold within itself the secret of a final harmony. The *Gita* tells us that though the outward aspect is that of existence advancing through struggle and slaughter, yet there is an inward aspect, which is that of the Universal Being fulfilling himself in a vast creation in and through the destruction. Kurukshetra is also a *Dharmakshetra* where righteousness shall prevail. But before we reach this *Dharmakshetra*, we will have to struggle and fight our way through Kurukshetra. How can one do this without staining our hands with blood? How can we battle without incurring sin, for battle we must, on a thousand different fronts before we can achieve the Utopia of our dreams. It is not enough to preach universal love when we are incapable of loving even our neighbours. It is not enough that our own hands remain clean for the law of strife and destruction to die out of this world.

The love that we preach about has itself been constantly a power of death in the history of the world. Even the love of God when deflected through the medium of the human ego has been responsible for so much slaughter and destruction. In the name of the Prince of Peace, the bloodiest wars in the history of mankind have been fought. So unless the human being learns to realise the divinity within him and in all beings, no amount of preaching about love and non-violence can save him from the nightmare of hate and violence he has created for himself. The *Gita* teaches us how to discover this divinity, thus turning the Kurukshetra into a *Dharmakshetra*. There is a law that operates in the external world just as there is a law that operates in the field of our bodies which integrates the apparently conflicting powers outside, as it integrates the cells of our body into a whole. Every cell in our body is different from the other, every thought is different from the other, yet there is a law that integrates the psychic structure as well as the physical structure both individually and universally. This is the cosmic *dharma* or law of righteousness. So while there is activity, movement, destruction and transformation, there is also organisation, balance and harmony, right from the atom to the solar system and even beyond that. When we come to think of it, the miracle of life is the fact that the human being continues to maintain his balance despite the overwhelming forces of destruction arrayed against him and this is because Kurukshetra is first and foremost a *Dharmakshetra*. The battlefield of life is first and foremost a field for the play of the divine justice. So long as we are willing or even unwilling warriors on this battlefield, we are pulled hither and thither by the restive horses of our chariot over which we have no control, not knowing our true goal or nature or destiny, helpless victims in the hands of the blind mechanism of nature, enmeshed in her threefold strands of *sattva, rajas,* and *tamas,* prey to every passing mood and whim, unable to control our thoughts, our bodies and our lives. The *Bhagavad Gita* shows us the way out of this slavery into the freedom of the Life Divine.

ALLEGORY OF THE CHARIOT

The battlefield is thus an allegorical representation of life. No other setting could have been more suitable for a gospel, which teaches us how to survive and evolve spiritually, even in the midst of the battlefield of life. The famous pictorial representation of the *Bhagavad Gita* is that of a

Arjuna Vishada Yoga

chariot drawn by four restive horses in which are seated Arjuna and Lord Krishna. The latter is holding the reins and turning round to face the despondent Arjuna. The chariot stands for the body of man and Arjuna is the embodied soul seated within. The horses are the four aspects of the mind known as *manas, buddhi, ahamkara* and *chitta,* rushing headlong into the field of sense objects, which is beckoning to us from all sides. Arjuna is the representative of the evolved man faced with a violent crisis in his life, which seems quite incompatible with his aspirations for a spiritual life or even for a moral life. But he has sense enough to realise that, by himself he is helpless to combat the enormous forces of evil that threaten to overwhelm him and destroy the very foundations of his social and spiritual life. Therefore, he has given over the reins of his chariot into the capable and willing hands of his divine master, Lord and friend, who restrains the straining steeds with a firm grip of his capable hands and guides the chariot through the dangerous battle with ease, protects him and takes him, who has thus surrendered his ego, to a glorious victory. This is the symbolism behind the famous picture of the chariot on the battlefield. The setting was not chosen at random. It has a great purpose and role to play in the understanding of the gospel.

FIRST TWO WORDS

Now let us take the first two words of the *Gita* – *Dharmakshetre, Kurukshetre*. The former means a field of righteousness and latter was the battlefield of the Kurus. How can a battlefield be a field of righteousness? By its very nature a battle is founded on the rock of unrighteousness. Then what is the point in bringing these two words in close proximity to each other! In ancient Sanskrit literature, every word as well as its position was chosen with care so these opposites coming next to each other at the very outset of the teaching must have a special message. To understand this we have to know the meaning of the word *kshetra*. It means field and in the 13th chapter Krishna says that the whole of cosmic nature is the *kshetra* or field for the play of God. There are many fields but only one knower of all fields and he calls this the *kshetrajna,* who is none other than the Lord. He tells Arjuna that our body itself is known as *kshetra* or field. On a large scale he says that this entire universe, which is the field of action for all creatures, is also a *kshetra*. It is the Divine Spirit, or *kshetrajna,* the knower of the fields who uses these fields for its divine sport. The body is the individual field of action of this Spirit and the universe is the cosmic field for the same Spirit. In the beginning these fields are *Kurukshetras* or fields of battle but the evolved man can turn them into *Dharmakshetras* or fields of righteousness.

Arjuna Vishada Yoga

THE YOGA OF SORROW

The first chapter of the *Gita* is known as 'Arjuna Vishada Yoga' or the "*Yoga* of Arjuna's Despondency". The title seems to be contradictory. How can sorrow be called a *yoga*? The word *yoga* is derived from the Sanskrit word, *yuj*, which means 'to unite'. Any action which can unite us with the divine can be considered 'a *yoga*'. When the whole world is joyful and everything goes our way we hardly feel the need for God, but when everything is against us and we are beset with problems and filled with sorrow, then we begin to feel the necessity for God and that is the time when most people turn to God. God is usually the last resort when our doctors and our lawyers and bankers have washed their hands of us! Thus, sorrow itself can become a *yoga* if it unites us to God. Sorrow if left to feed on itself is a *tamasic* attitude, eventually bringing ruin to the person who indulges in it, but righteous sorrow if used in the proper way may well prove to be a goad for further evolution. Krishna used this opportunity to turn Arjuna's sorrow into a *yoga* to further his evolution.

The arguments, which Arjuna presents in the first chapter, seem very plausible to us. It appears as if he has a feeling of strong disgust for all killing and a great desire to escape from these terrible realities and take to a life of seclusion. He feels that he can no longer participate in this fight for survival. Far better to be killed unresisting by his relations, than jump into the fray and kill them in order to save himself, is what he says! This is the deep sorrow which overwhelms Arjuna so that he falls into a mood of terrible despair from which he cannot arouse himself and which if left to itself would grow and take him farther and farther from the spirituality for which he is craving. This is the picture of Arjuna at the beginning of the *Gita*—the picture of a man filled with revulsion for the action he is being forced to do since he thinks it to be devolving. But Krishna knew Arjuna well and understood that these ethical arguments, which seem so appealing to us, actually stemmed from a totally different source.

Arjuna was a Kshatriya—a warrior who had never had any doubts about his duty all his life but at that psychological moment when he saw his relations and especially his grandsire and teacher on the opposite side, he suddenly felt unsure of his stand and begged Krishna for a solution to his dilemma. At the outset it must be remembered that Arjuna was not a conscientious objector who was against all violence. He was first and foremost a warrior, who had fought many wars and was prepared to fight many more wars including this one. What put a break to his combative attitude was not because he had become a pacifist but because his psyche had weakened due to the fact

Arjuna Vishada Yoga

that he suddenly realised that by agreeing to this war he had put himself in a position in which he would have to fight and perhaps kill his dear grandsire and *guru*. No doubt he had known all this before but perhaps he had chosen to ignore it since the war was a righteous one, which he had to fight to free the citizens from the tyranny of the Kauravas and uphold the Kshatriya *dharma*. The Lord can read into the minds of all and discover the true motives behind our words, which are often a mask for what we want to hide, even from ourselves. Human motives are very mixed. We can never be sure even of our own motives. Non-violence is very often made a mask for weakness and detachment, a name for what is really escapism. Luckily for Arjuna, the Lord who had been his constant companion since youth was ready at the opportune moment to raise him out of his lethargy of self-pity. Arjuna had never thought of turning to Krishna for advice in all the years of their friendship because he had been riding the crest of the wave, ever the hero and unexcelled bow-man, but now when his make-belief citadel had crumbled to his feet, he turned to Lord Krishna, his charioteer, hitherto unrecognized as the Lord and asked him humbly for advice.

Krishna allowed Arjuna to pour out all his arguments without interruption and then in the second chapter he answered him in a way that was best fitted to bring out the best in him and raise him up the ladder of evolution.

"My mind is tortured by doubts about my duty. I'm turning to Thee for advice. Pray instruct me for I have surrendered to Thee." This was Arjuna's plea.

The Lord waits patiently for us to play out our game of make-believe that we are the heroes of our life's drama, waits patiently till we stumble and fall and turn to him for help and then like the wise and loving mother, he rushes to our aid and points out to us the clear-cut path of duty by following which we will emerge victorious.

We know only the surface part of our being but there is a lot beneath the surface, which affects our personality all the time even though we are not aware of it. When we are overcome by our emotions like love or hatred, we find that involuntary and instinctive emotions and actions overrule our reasoning power. We are not even aware of how the subconscious mind affects us since it collaborates with the conscious mind most of the time. It is only when we get off the track of instinctive behaviour that we realise how powerful the subconscious is. Unless mind and body are in perfect balance, we can never be masters of ourselves. It is only when the conscious mind surrenders to the Supreme in us that we experience perfect freedom. Thus, when Arjuna consciously surrendered to Krishna, he

Arjuna Vishada Yoga

became the perfect recipient for this great wisdom.

Arjuna's distress is actually an ever recurring theme in the life of the human being. The evolved person feels disappointed with the glamorous world and yet clings to them. He forgets his divinity and is attached to his personality. He has to be restored to this divinity before he can proceed. It is the evolution of the human soul that is portrayed here. The chapter ends in the darkness of the soul, which is an essential step in the progress to spirituality. Most of us go through life without facing such ultimate questions. If we are fortunate enough we may face a crisis when we regret the mess we have made of our lives. Our ambitions lie in ruins and we have no one to turn to but God. Draupadi went through such a crises in the Kuru Assembly when she realised that there was no one to help her except Krishna and now Arjuna goes through the same experience. There has to be a revolution before a new growth can take place. This can happen to anyone at any time. There are no limits of time and space in it. The battle takes place every moment in every mind.

As has been said before, life is a battlefield like the field of Kurukshetra, which each one of us has to learn to face and fight our way through, before we can reach the other side, which is *Dharmakshetra*.

ॐ *Hari Aum Tat Sat* ॐ

Thus, in the Upanishad of the *Bhagavad Gita*, the knowledge of Supreme Brahman, the Scripture of *Yoga*, the dialogue between Sri Krishna and Arjuna, ends the first chapter entitled 'The *Yoga* of Arjuna's Despondency'.

2

SANKHYA YOGA

The Yoga of the Wisdom of Sankhya

Aum Sri Krishnaya Paramaatmane' namaha!
Aum Sri Parthasarathaye' namaha.

In the first chapter of Arjuna's despondency, the question as to why the *Gita* should have been given on the battlefield has been answered. In the second chapter or the *Yoga* of Integral Knowledge, the second question as to why the teacher should advise his pupil to fight will be taken up. In the whole of the first chapter and up to the eighth verse in the second chapter, Arjuna expounded the ethical arguments against the war to which the Lord listened patiently without interruption since he knew that Arjuna was cracking up under the load of a great emotional upheaval for which speech itself was an outlet.

> How can I shoot arrows at my Grandsire Bhishma and preceptor Drona who are worthy of reverence. Far better for me to live on alms than enjoy the bloodstained pleasures which will be our lot after killing them. My mind is tortured by doubts and bewildered as to my duty and therefore I surrender to you. I am your disciple. Pray instruct me as to what is best for me. Even if I win, I do not see how I can remove the sorrow which is threatening to overwhelm me.

Arjuna thinks his problem is purely ethical and has stated the dilemma of the man of action, a struggle on the physical plane between the powers of right and justice against the powers of wrong and injustice. The ethical sense condemns the act and insists on *ahimsa* or non-violence as the highest law of spiritual life. As Arjuna states, he can fight the battle either on the ethical plane of non-resistance or he can take the ascetic path and shun the action altogether. The *Gita* does not reject either of these two paths. It recognises *ahimsa* as part of the highest ethical ideal and admits that ascetic renunciation is one of the ways to spiritual salvation. But it takes its stand over and above these positions. It justifies all life and existence as we know it with all its discrepancies as a manifestation of the One Divine Being and insists that a complete human action can and must be made compatible with a complete spiritual life

Sankhya Yoga

lived in union with the infinite. Not by shutting one's eyes to the disparities of life can one attain this, but by boldly marching forward through the din and clamour of life as we see it now in our present state of consciousness.

YOGA

This march of the *jiva* or individual soul towards Godhead if done with knowledge and purpose is called *yoga*. The Sanskrit word *yuj* means to unite and thus any method employed by which one can unite with the infinite can be termed as *yoga*. The eighteen chapters of the *Bhagavad Gita* are known as *yogas*. Each one of them can lead us to God if used with knowledge and sincerity of purpose. Knowledge is the keystone to all *yoga*. The *Karma Yoga* of the *Gita* insists that any action if done with knowledge and a burning desire to attain union with the Divine can itself be termed a *yoga*. Thus, in the second chapter at the very outset, the Lord expounds to Arjuna the highest knowledge, which is the knowledge of the Self or the *atman*. It may seem strange that this knowledge should be delivered at the very beginning, since it is very difficult to grasp, but the Lord does this with a special purpose. The knowledge of the Self cuts at the very root of the human problem, which was Arjuna's problem. The root cause of our unhappiness lies in our inability to know who we are. This might seem a strange statement to make but the fact is that we do not know who we are, in truth. We may know many things like the distance to the moon, the depth of the ocean and the theory of relativity but this basic fact of who we are, we do not know, not even the cleverest of us.

WHO AM I

We think we are the body but it does not need much analysis to discover that this body that has changed so much from babyhood to this present condition cannot be the one, which produces such a strong sense of identity in us. Even though my body has been ravaged by time, I myself am in no doubt as to my identity. So how can this changing body be the final truth of me? Now let us see if my mind or intellect is my true being. This is even less plausible. The body at least seems to remain the same for a period of few years but the mind is changing every minute and the intellect also keeps changing even though more slowly. The intellectual opinions held in my teens are certainly different from what I hold now. But the 'I' who knows these opinions remains the same. So who or what is the 'I'! 'Who am I?' is the million-dollar question. The answer to this question was discovered by the *rishis* or seers of the Vedas through a process of meditation and enquiry into the nature of the Supreme Reality. They proclaimed that our unshakable belief in the existence of an unchanging entity in us was perfectly correct since it was based on the super-conscious knowledge of the unchangeable Spirit within us, which they called the *atman*. So the very first words of Lord Krishna to Arjuna in the second chapter, which many people believe to be the actual beginning of the *Gita*, is the confirmation of this great truth.

> You are grieving for that which should not be grieved for, yet you speak like a man of wisdom. The wise do not grieve either for the living or for the dead.

Totally depressed mentally, his body also became weak but in that moment of utter misery, he heard the divine voice of his Master talking to him with a lilt in his voice and a smile on his lips. We worry and grieve for people because we consider them to be mere bodies, lumps of flesh and skin held together by a skeleton of bones, but he who knows the truth underlying these lumps of flesh, will not grieve if something happens to that body either through disease or death. These people arrayed on the battlefield were not to be considered as mere bodies but the eternal, immortal Spirit embodied in various human forms. The Spirit is eternal and unborn. Samkhya *Yoga*, which is referred to here, is not the traditional school of Samkhya by the sage Kapila but to the Advaitic teachings of the Upanishads.

> There was never a time when you or I or these kings did not exist,

said Krishna,

> Nor is it true that we shall cease to exist in the future. Just as the body passes through childhood, youth and old age so also it takes on a new body after it casts off this one.

Death and re-birth are like a man casting off his old clothes to don new ones. What is there to grieve over this? If anything we should rejoice. The phenomenon of life is the progress of the *jivatma* from individuality to immortality, with births and deaths as the means to its progress and the final goal of unity with the Divine. Unable to see the existence of the *atman*, which is our reality, we impose reality on the body, which is only a temporary phenomenon. Our sorrow for ourselves and for others arises from this original mistake. We do not realise that what gives a semblance of reality to this body is the Spirit within. The house has no life of its own. It is the person who lives in it that gives life to the house. The house of the body is only an empty shell made out of the five elements and one day it will revert to the elements from which it came. But the person or the reality within is not bound by the house and can easily shift to another of its own liking.

Sankhya Yoga

> That by which all this is pervaded is imperishable and no one can destroy that immutable reality. Weapons cannot cut it, fire cannot burn it, water cannot drown it and wind cannot dry it.

Thus spoke the Lord about *atman*.

This is the greatest truth of our being—that we are the *atman*, the immortal and indestructible Spirit which was never born and thus can never die and the body is only an outer covering. But this truth is hard for the mind to grasp and even harder to experience. And therefore Krishna goes on to the next point.

> Even if you consider yourself to be the body, you should not become over-attached to it, just as you should not become over-attached to any material possessions because the destruction of that which is born is certain, just as its rebirth in another form is also certain. This being an inevitable fact, a wise man should not grieve over it.

A pot falls and breaks and returns to the earth from which it was made and perhaps another day it is re-made in another form, another shape, even more beautiful than the last. So the Hindu philosophy asserts that this body is only a cloak for the Spirit and will one day revert to the earth from which it was made and then another day re-combine in another form for the continuation of its spiritual journey.

The Lord says:

> These bodies were unmanifest in the beginning before birth, will become unmanifest in the end after death and are manifest only for a short period of time in the middle. How can we postulate reality to these and why the attachment to them?

DEATH

So the very basis of grief is false. We grieve for that which we should not grieve and mourn for that which never existed. Once we know the reality in us and in all things, there will be no further cause for grief since we would see that all this is the one immutable, deathless and shining Spirit! Something that is real in the ultimate sense cannot die and that which passes away cannot be called real. The real has always 'been' and will always 'be' and can never cease to 'be' while the unreal cannot come into being at any period of time! So when a person is said to have died, it is his impermanent body which can be called dead and never his reality or *atman*. The destruction of the existent is unthinkable because that which is existent, by the very laws of nature, cannot be destroyed and that which can be destroyed can never, except in a very temporary sense, be said to be existent. We grieve over the phenomenon of death because of a mix-up in standpoints, or super-imposition of the reality of the Spirit on to the body. The process

Sankhya Yoga

of death is only a transition and not destruction. A change of condition is what we call death. The law of evolution of the universe requires this. In fact, we die every moment. Every moment all the cells in our body are being renewed. Normally, change external to ourselves is perceptible but in the case of our own body, we are never aware of its changes. This is because there is something in us which never changes and on which all change is superimposed like a movie on the white screen. The flitting pictures have meaning only because of the unchanging white screen behind. But this change is only a condition and not a substance. Therefore, this body, which is a changing phenomenon, is not real. Our basic reality is the *atman,* or the Self, which is infinite and unborn. So all change and evolution is a progress of the finite towards its reality, the infinite. This is the reason for birth, death, transmigration and re-birth. The fear of death is due to a misunderstanding as to its necessity. We are not punished by death. We are only educated by it.

The *Gita* gives a simple analogy to bring home this point. We cast off one garment when it has become useless and put on another, which is new. Who would grieve at such a delightful exchange? Old clothes for new! Likewise, in the death of the body we should not imagine that there is a real loss. All change, whatever be its nature, is a requirement of cosmic justice. Birth and death are parts of this requirement. The *atman* does not move from place to place but the *jivatma* or the embodied soul moves from one abode to another taking along with it the causal body of its *samskaras* and *vasanas*. This is the reason for its taking on of another body. Arjuna's sorrow stems from the fact that his vision has been limited to the picture of life given by the senses and he is unable to see the higher requirements of the laws of the cosmos. Arjuna's idea and ours that death is an undesirable consequence that follows the battle of life is false. In the twenty verses beginning from verse eleven, the Lord enunciates the highest and the most transcendent philosophy of *advaita* or non-dualism, which is found in the Upanishads and which was later actively preached by Adi Shankaracharya.

SWADHARMA

The arguments given to Arjuna in the second chapter proceed from many levels. The first and the most important level is the metaphysical one. But Arjuna like the rest of us could not grasp this level or even if he could grasp it intellectually, he had not reached the state when it was a living experience. So the next argument of the Lord is from the social level in which we all stand, and from which we all have to proceed in order to reach the metaphysical truth of our eternal Spirit. The third great teaching of this chapter is the need to perform our *swadharma*. We have already seen that the word *dharma* is the very first word of the *Gita* and like most ancient scriptures, the first word is meant to give a clue to the purport of the entire book. The word *dharma* has been translated in many different ways—as law, religion, morality, duty, etc. It means all these and even more. It comes from Sanskrit root *dhr*, which means to uphold or to protect. So *dharma* is that cosmic law, which can protect us, provided we uphold it. It is the law of Being in each thing, which makes it what it is rather than anything else. For instance, we can say that the *dharma* of fire is to burn, the *dharma* of water is to moisten, etc. In the higher species and in the human being in particular, it is not immediately apparent what our *dharma* is. We may have many *dharmas* or duties since we are called upon to play many roles. A woman has one *dharma* as a daughter and one as a mother and still another as a wife or an official. So what is her real *dharma*? This difficult question is answered in the *Bhagavad Gita*.

If the first word of the *Gita* is *dharma*, its last word is *mama*, which means 'my'. In a nutshell the gospel of the *Gita* is an exposition on 'my *dharma*' or the *dharma* of each human being! An animal has only a single role to play in life. So it has only a single law, which it has to obey. It cannot help but obey the law of its particular *dharma*. There is no dilemma for it. It has no choices and therefore no obligations. The human being, however, is on another plane. There is no hard and fast rule in life which can be given to the whole of humanity, which it can follow at all stages of life and find fulfilment. At every stage and in every station of life there is a separate *dharma*. This is the greatness of the *Gita*'s teaching: Be true to your *swadharma* or the rule of your particular being and then evolve and progress spiritually. As you evolve you will find that your *swadharma* seems to be changing in which case one has to change. To force a *dharma* or rule of conduct on oneself just because it appears to be superior is not being true to one's own nature and therefore cannot bring anything but unhappiness to oneself and to others. The *Gita* accepts the fact that values are relative and cannot be enforced on all indiscriminately. We cannot expect the same rule of behaviour for a child as for an adult. In spiritual life also this is true. To expect all people to follow the same rule of conduct in all walks and states of life and in all situations is as impractical as it is absurd, and leads to the typical guilt complex which is found in the faithful followers of most religions. The vastness of the *Gita*'s outlook and the all-embracing love which enfolds both saint and so-called sinner in the same divine embrace is so lofty that even to understand

Sankhya Yoga

it, one has to be evolved oneself or else it may be misunderstood as it has been by many.

THE FIGHTER

The *Gita* is addressed to Arjuna, the warrior, the Kshatriya hero whose duty or *swadharma* is that of battle and protection of the innocent. The *Gita* is not addressed to the Brahmins or the priest class in which case its message would have been totally different. In life most of us are called upon to play the role of the fighter far more often than that of a priest and hence the hero of the *Gita* is the Kshatriya, whose duty is to protect and uphold the law and deliver his people from the grip of the tyrant, through war if necessary. Unflinchingly he has to do his duty and thus uphold the universal law of *dharma* even at the cost of sacrificing his ego-filled bonds to his relations.

"Far better is it for me to be killed rather than kill!" is Arjuna's plea or "far better to leave the battlefield and take to the life of recluse."

To both these, the teacher gives a stern negative. Arjuna's dilemma is our dilemma, Arjuna's problem is our problem but the *Gita* does not give the obvious and easy ethical solution. The *Gita* does not tell us how to evade the issue but tells us how to surmount it and march forward to eternity. It tells us how to affect a resolution between the higher aspirations of our spiritual ideals and the horrifying actualities of our outer life. Most of the time we try to compromise. We are spiritual half the time and materialistic for the other half and thus carry on in this unsatisfactory fashion, hopping from one standpoint to another till the end of our lives. Such a progress can never be fully satisfactory nor is a compromise a final solution. The solution can only lie in finding that Reality in us, which encompasses all these differences and yet transcends them. Thus, the *Gita*'s solution to the problem is from the highest spiritual angle and not from the surface ethical point of view. The highest spiritual angle means, knowing and experiencing that Spirit which is the Supreme Reality in us as well as in the cosmos and serving him through all the activities of one's intellect, heart, and will. Only then can we solve the riddle of life. The secret of action according to the *Gita* is one with the secret of all existence. Life is not to be lived for the sake of the body but for God, and the living soul or *atman* is an eternal portion of the Godhead.

Existence is not just a blind machinery of Nature but also the constant manifestation of the Spirit. Action is for self-fulfilment and not for the apparent fruits of the moment. Arjuna was born and brought up in the Kshatriya caste. Physically and mentally Nature had made him fit for the role of a warrior. So to Arjuna the Lord said,

Sankhya Yoga

> You have a duty to yourself and you have a duty to the world and you have a duty to the deepest Self within you, which pervades the entire cosmos. This is your *swadharma* and only in the clear performance of it will you evolve and help society to evolve and thus achieve the cosmic purpose.

A KSHATRIYA'S DUTY

If Krishna had allowed Arjuna to run away from the battle, it would have been the downfall of his spiritual life. Arjuna in the forest would still have been Arjuna, the warrior. Though physically he might have restrained himself, yet mentally he would have been dwelling on the scene he had fled from, the patent duty he had neglected and the guilt of having condemned his people to a lifetime of misery under the rule of the tyrant—Duryodhana. Far from taking an upward trend, his spiritual life would have plummeted downward. True to his nature, he would never have been able to find peace and contentment, in the seclusion of the forest, leading the life of a hermit. Another point to be remembered is that Arjuna's refusal to fight did not stem from revulsion towards the taking of a life and a strong turning towards *ahimsa* or non-violence. He was not a conscientious objector. He was the hero of many battles in the past and he would as easily continue to be the terror of all evildoers in the future. On that day he was unable to face the battle, not because there was a change in his ideology but because of his emotional attachment to his relations. In the struggle between right and wron,g the one who avoids the confrontation due to sentimentality, weakness or cowardice is committing a fault.

His case was like that of the judge who had been condemning many people to capital punishment when they deserved it without a thought of the evils of such a system, and who one day is confronted with his own son who has been charged with murder of the first degree. Now we find that the judge starts talking about the quality of mercy. He insists that the system of capital punishment is a sin and should be abolished from the state, etc. The judge has had no actual change of heart and would just as happily have sent any other father's son to the gallows as he had been doing all these years, but today the judge desisted from the clear-cut performance of his duty because the murderer happened to be his own son and in order to mask this weakness, which he subconsciously recognises as a weakness, he bolsters up his case with the highly ethical arguments of humanity, mercy and kindness.

In such a case, when there is no actual change of heart, the truly spiritual action would be to adhere sternly to one's duty, regardless of one's personal and emotional preferences and

Sankhya Yoga

attachments. The *Ramayana* gives the classic example when Sri Rama, in order to uphold the *swadharma* of a king, was prepared to forsake his beloved wife in order to set an example to the citizens! In England, on the other hand, we find a king who abdicated at a time when his country needed him the most in order to fulfil his personal desire for a woman!

Next, let us consider the spiritual evolution of the citizens of the land whom Arjuna was bound to protect. If Arjuna desisted from the fight for whatever reason, the battle would not have been fought and the citizens would have been at the mercy of the tyrants they abhorred. Their state would have been pitiable indeed. Unable to pursue the laws of *dharma* of their calling, their spiritual life would have been totally in abeyance as can be seen from the history of all people in the thrall of a despotic rule. So Arjuna would have been guilty of a double crime by running away.

Lastly, let us consider the state of his cousins, the Kauravas, headed by Duryodhana. The latter had led a life of unbridled passion and violence. No one had ever tried to curb his arrogance from childhood. He had soared from crime to crime. If unchecked, his life would surely have regressed from man to beast. Being a Kshatriya his only hope of salvation was a warrior's death on the battlefield. So even when looked at from the standpoint of the Kauravas, it was Arjuna's bounden duty to enact the role of the chastiser and to allow himself to be used as an instrument in order to fulfil the cosmic plan. The *Mahabharata* says,

> There are only two types of men who can pierce the sun and reach the sphere of Brahman—the *sannyasin* who is steeped in *yoga* and the warrior who falls in battle!

RELATIONSHIPS

As has been said, Arjuna's objection to killing did not arise from a violent revulsion to all killing as such but only to the killing of his own relations. This is no doubt a natural human consideration but, as has been mentioned before, the purpose of the teacher of the *Gita* is to raise the disciple above the attachments of his body to a far higher level. Love for one's relations is no doubt one step in the evolutionary ladder but it is far from being the last one. Our mind clings weakly to some type of relationship. We feel good and secure if we have our own baker, doctor, lawyer and above all banker, apart from our mother, father, brothers and sisters. These relationships are what give us a sense of security in our own community and their lack makes us feel strange and insecure in a foreign country. But when we analyse the nature of these relationships, we find that they are ephemeral and afford a very poor basis for a lasting security. Your relations often let you down, your friends desert you, your lawyer fails you and your doctor washes his hands of you and when the stock market crashes, you no longer possess the wealth with which you thought to ward off the horrifying assaults of disease and death! So what is the use of these relationships on which we place our entire well-being? They are pitiable props indeed and merely act as a hindrance to our spiritual progress. The teacher of the *Gita* takes Arjuna to a height from which the true meaning of relationships emerges. Not that we should shun our relations but that we should so enlarge our narrow vision that we can embrace the whole world as being related to us. From the heights of this spirituality, the judge would find it impossible to condemn any other man's son as he would his own! This indeed is universal love. The teacher of the *Gita* also points out another angle to the question of relationships. We can accept the whole universe as being related to us or shun all relationships and accept only one, namely God alone as our father, mother, friend, guide, husband, wife or any other role we might thrust upon him. One who sees God as his sole relation, needs no other relation in the material world. With a little analysis we will find that both these viewpoints, though seemingly opposite, are actually identical. To see God as our only relation is to see everyone and everything as related to us, for God is in every creature. This is the great truth that the Lord leads Arjuna to accept. Towards this ideal does he steer him forward as masterfully as he guided the restive horses.

That Arjuna has to do his duty has been made clear. The knowledge has been given but the teacher would not be true to himself, if he did not give a practical guidance as to how this duty, fraught with difficulty should be done in order to gain the highest. Thus, the *Gita* is also a *yoga shastra* or the practical application of *Brahmavidya* or the knowledge of the absolute.

"Even a little of this *yoga* will save you from great fear." This is the promise of the teacher, since the knowledge of our immortality immediately removes from us the dreadful fear we have of death! We are afraid of many things—of sin, of suffering, of hell, of punishment, of God, of the world and even of ourselves. This is the great fear that besieges humanity, the fear of a world of whose true nature we are ignorant of, of a God whose true being we have never seen and of a cosmic purpose that we do not understand.

The undiscerning cannot discriminate true *karma* from the ritualistic piety of that portion of the Vedas known as 'Brahmanas' in which the Vedic sacrifices are performed for the sake of getting material benefits. The *Gita* asks us to give up all actions done for selfish reasons and hence condemns this particular portion of the Vedas. Ritualistic practices necessary for gaining anything from the world are dictated by the *gunas* or modes of nature—*sattva, rajas* and *tamas,* which will be dealt with later. The one who wants to attain perfection should go beyond these modes and direct attention to the Supreme. Therefore, Krishna asks Arjuna to go beyond the three *gunas*—become a *trigunatita.* For the single-pointed seeker of truth, ritualistic practices are of as much use as a pond during a flood!

The creed of the Kshatriya is to know one's own Self, to know God and to help humanity, to protect the right without fear or faltering in the battlefield of the world. Arjuna, the flower of Aryan manhood, has been given the Supreme knowledge that he is the eternal and imperishable Spirit, that life and death are but two sides of the same coin, that sorrow and suffering are to be disregarded for they are only the reactions of the senses to the unrealities of the world. Fight he must when by destruction alone the world must advance but without hating that which he has perforce to destroy or grieving for those who perish, knowing that the one immortal Self is in everything. He should do his duty, his *swadharma* with a calm, strong and equal spirit, for that is the action which God and his own nature have given him to accomplish. He has no other choice in this matter actually, for the individual is not merely a social unit living in the human atmosphere. The whole universe is our atmosphere and nothing in it is alien to us. Thus, from the point of view of the ultimate nature of reality, from the standpoint of one's connection with the society around, as well as in the interest of one's own Self, we have to realise that no one is free from some duty or other. Inaction is unthinkable. Even the decision of not to act is itself an action. Thus, the world compels everyone to act in some way or the other. Knowledge is precedent to action. Knowledge and action are inseparable. To know one's *swadharma* and act upon it, maintaining our mental equilibrium, poised in the face of difficulties, this is both *Samkhya* and *Yoga*.

YOGA OF ACTION

The forty-seventh verse of the second chapter contains the central idea of the famous *Gita* doctrine of *Karma Yoga*:

> Your right is only to the action and not to the fruits thereof. Do not be impelled to act for selfish reasons, nor should you be attached to inaction!

At the first sight, this appears to be an impossible command or at best suited only to a madman, for whom else but a madman would perform action without considering the fruits! On further analysis, however, we find that this command of Lord Krishna's is the only answer to perfect action. In it lies the secret of perfect action. To work without expectation of reward is something the modern mind cannot grasp because we are already sunk in the mire of expectation of fruit even before the tree has been planted. We are always after the rights we can demand from the world and oblivious of the duties we owe to it. Lord Krishna, on the other hand, states categorically that we have only one right and that is to do our duty, our *swadharma* and then automatically we will gain our rights. The very forces of nature will see to it that we get our rights since we are performing our *swadharma*—playing our part in the cosmic drama without the hope of reward. Those who have not actually experienced this phenomenon will find it hard to accept since we have been fed on the theory that might is right and only the fittest will survive.

This law is no doubt applicable to the lower orders of creation but in the higher order and in the human being in particular it is this very law that is condemning him. This is the law of the jungle and Krishna would have us liberate ourselves from this law. He would have us act in such a way that wilfully and consciously we would live by the higher law of the performance of an action without expectation of a reward. This is perfect action. We think we are being very clever when we grab the fruits of our neighbour's tree without even paying for it either with money or labour! But let us see how far this is correct. It will easily be seen that so long as the fruits of action obsess us, we will be incapable of producing a perfect action. The action itself takes a second place as our mind is totally concentrated on the results. It follows that the action need not be done at all or at best done in a very haphazard fashion. How much sweeter would the fruit have been had we planted the tree, watered and nourished it and then been blessed with the gift of a perfect fruit! Another example is that of a student to whom the results are more important than his studies and who proceeds to cheat in the examination, to bribe the examiners and to buy the papers and use any dishonest method to gain the desired results. This act will not benefit him either spiritually or even materially. He or she may get a diploma certifying his success in the examination but since he has wasted his time on the campus, he has no knowledge of the subject and can in no way have benefited from the time spent in the institution.

Now let us look at the results themselves. When we undertake any action, no doubt we expect results but are these results in our hands? Even with the very best and sincere effort on our part, it need not follow that the expected result will materialise. Many factors, which are totally

Sankhya Yoga

out of our hands, go to produce the result. The action may be in our hands but the results never! Our sorrow and suffering comes inevitably from the fact that we expect certain results that seldom accrue. We demand our right to get the best results and forget the fact that we have not performed our duty to the best of our ability. In fact, had we so performed it, that itself would have been our reward. When we do our work whatever it be whether ploughing a field or dancing on a stage, the action itself should be a source of joy, regardless of the consequence. This is the secret of perfect action that it is capable of producing a deep contentment not to be had by the ordinary worker. This is the only sane approach to action.

Take the case of the painter and the artist. The painter paints because of the pay packet he will get at the completion of every picture, or signboard. The artist paints because he loves to paint and lives to paint. The former work is trash and condemned to be obliterated by the next advertisement, while the latter's work remains for posterity. The former is always on the seesaw of success and failure, of elation and despondency while the latter is unperturbed by anything, having derived his joy from the work alone. We must work in perfect serenity indifferent to the results. We have to accept the fact that we are not the sole determining agent in the production of the result of even the least of our action. The whole universe has something to say in the production of the result. We are not the deciding factor. Things may or may not turn out as we expect them to and there is nothing we can do about it.

RESULTS CANNOT BE MANIPULATED

"You have a right to the action alone and not to its results," is what Krishna says. The results of every action are in the hands of a cosmic law and you have absolutely no control over it, so actually you are just wasting your time by worrying about them. Far better for you to worry over how best you can accomplish the task on hand, for that right has been given to you by Nature. The human being keeps demanding his rights not understanding that rights and duties go hand in hand and one who has not performed his duty has no right to demand his rights!

If on the other hand we choose not to act, even that would be going against the law of Nature, as the second part of the forty-seventh verse points out: "Do not be attached to inaction!" Actually we have very little choice even in this matter, for it is obligatory on us to act. The decision not to act is itself an action. The mighty machinery of Nature would force us to act and if this is the case, the only way out of a seemingly impossible situation would be to act in the correct manner. *Yoga* is the equanimity we maintain during the performance of an action, which accelerates the process of the action so that one becomes an adept in the performance of it, like the artist. "*Yoga* karmasu Kaushalam!"—*Yoga* is expertise in action! The more disinterested you are in the fruits, the more perfect your action will be and the more likely you are to get the very fruits, which you have not thought about. This is the strange story of successful and fulfilling action. The true *yogi* is not an escapist from the world of action nor is he or she an incompetent fool who has taken up *yoga* because of his inability to succeed in worldly life. According to Lord Krishna, the *yogi* is the adept in action and it is he who has mastered the secret of action and therefore the secret of life. Lord Krishna himself is known as *Mahayogi* or the greatest *Yogi* and his life is clear proof of the fact that he who has mastered *yoga* or balance of mind can be an expert in every walk of life.

LIFE IS A YOGA

The *yoga* of the *Gita* is thus very comprehensive. It regards all life as *yoga*. The way in which we live in the world is itself *yoga*. We have already noted that rights automatically follow the correct performance of our duty or *swadharma*. To ask for rights would therefore be redundant. They who ask for rights are demanding something for which they are not qualified. They must be labouring under a sense of guilt that they have not performed their duty properly or else there would be no occasion for anxiety about rights, since they would follow without fail.

> Mean and pitiable are they who beg for their rights from a world, which is unwilling to give them and who fight for their rights and perhaps even die for them. What a wretched state is this,

says the Lord. Fixed in *yoga* do your duty, and live like a Lord, uncaring of the results which might follow. Having done your duty you can rest assured that the whole of the universe will strive to see that you get your just reward. Why should you beg from door to door for your rights unless you have a suspicion that you have not done your duty and thus do not deserve the reward for which you are clamouring! What a wonderful idea? If we could only follow it, what a beautiful world we would create. The wise sage who practices this *yoga* is able to break himself from the bondage of *karma* or action in this very life. By taking our attention away from the fruits, the *Gita* multiplies both our concentration as well as our joy in action. A child plays for the joy of playing and does not think of the benefit. All her joy is in the game. So also life is a game, which can bring maximum joy if played according to the technique of *Karma Yoga*! This joy which is attained by playing our part in the game of life brings instant rewards. Even in

Sankhya Yoga

this life we are released from the bonds of action and reach a state untouched by sorrow. Such people are indifferent to what is said in the scriptures or by other people since they are fixed in the Self. *Samadhi* is not a loss of consciousness but the highest kind of consciousness.

The first part of the second chapter describes the nature of pure Being or pure existence. The second part gives us the art of living or how one can apply this pure knowledge in our daily lives so that every minute is lived in joyous harmony and the firm conviction that we are achieving the cosmic purpose. To complete the teaching, the Lord paints for Arjuna the portrait of the person who lives according to the ideals described in the previous verses.

THE STHITHA PRAJNA

Hinduism gives the four-fold stages of society. The first is Brahmacharya or studentship, the second *grihastashrama* or the stage of the householder, third is *vanaprastha* or the process of giving up life in the world, and the last is *sannyasa* or total renunciation of the world. The enlightened person of the *Gita* is known as the *sthitha prajna* or man of steady intellect. He may or may not be a *sannyasi*. The *sthitha prajna* or the man of firmly established intellect is the man in cosmic consciousness, who lives in perfect harmony with society, with God

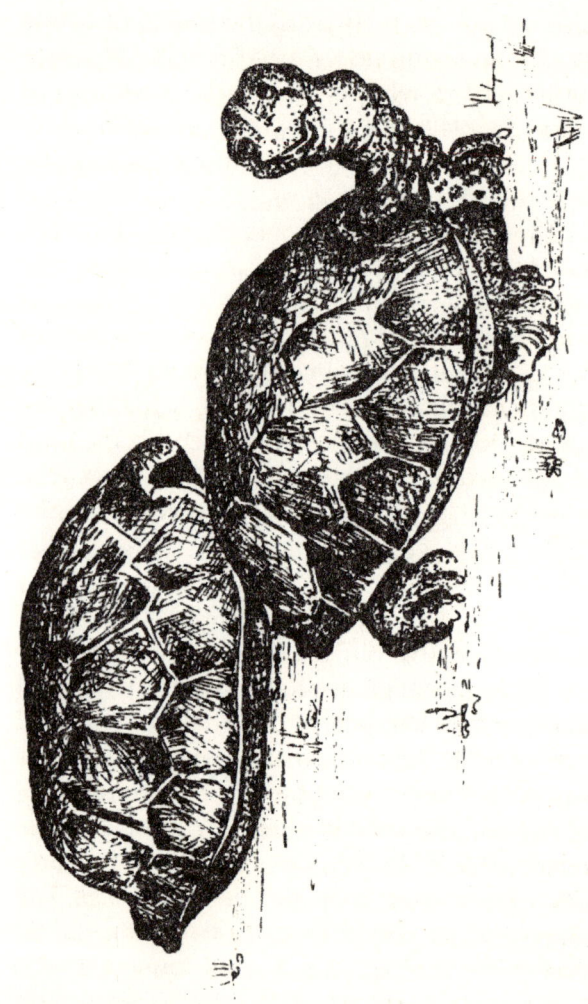

Secure in the Citadel of the Self

Sankhya Yoga

and the universe. In these eighteen verses, the essence of the eighteen chapters has been distilled.

All of us have some pre-conceived concept of how an enlightened person should look. He should be tall and talk with a resonant voice, have a beard, etc. Arjuna also asks for some external signs by which such a person could be known but the Lord's answer does not touch on any external sign. The first qualification of the ideal character of the *Gita* is that his or her mind has been withdrawn from the unreality of the world and fixed on the Reality within herself. Such a mind remains unperturbed in sorrow and does not hunger for joy since both these are aspects of the unreal and her mind is fixed in the Real, which is beyond both sorrow and joy. It has overcome anger, attachment and fear. It regards the activities of the world as a passing show so how should it be provoked by it? How can the mind form an attachment to that which it knows to be unreal and why should it fear death when it knows itself to be immortal?

The ideal person of the *Gita* is not one who runs away from life and hides in caves and forests. He or she wanders in the world amidst the sense objects but, like the tortoise, which withdraws its limbs within itself, he or she is capable of withdrawing her senses from the objects outside. She has perfect control over herself. This is not an easy task. It is much easier to shun the objects altogether and take shelter in the fastness of a mountain cave where it is possible to avoid all contact with temptation. To leave the senses free to roam as they like, and be able to withdraw them like the tortoise when necessary, is possible only for the truly evolved soul. The *Gita* wisely says that by abstinence alone the senses can never be controlled. We may be able to starve them to submission but they would remain docile only during the period of abstinence. The craving would still be there and would spring to life as soon as the proper food was made available. Not to sin in the absence of temptation is easy enough but to abstain from falling even in the midst of temptation, needs something more than self-control. It needs pure knowledge based on experience of the Supreme Bliss within us. Krishna makes the difference between outer abstention and inner renunciation. We may reject the objects but the desire for them will still remain. The hankering after sugar will persist only so long as we have not tasted honey. Once we know the sweetness of honey, the ordinary lump of sugar offered by the world will have no attraction for us. This is the secret of the imperturbable exterior presented by the *Sthitha Prajna*. He cannot be tempted because he knows and has experienced the source of bliss within himself.

When passion overpowers the mind, memory is lost, intelligence obscured and the person falls into delusion. We are not asked to unyoke the horses of the senses from the chariot of the body but to control them with the reins of the mind. The *sthitha prajna* moves about the world of senses with his senses under perfect control. He accepts everything without attachment or repulsion. He covets nothing and is jealous of none. He has no desires and thus makes no demands! Such a person is soon established in the peace of the Self. This is the way to end all sorrow.

What about the other picture? The person without self-discipline is like a boat on the waters, carried hither and thither by the wild winds of desire, now after one thing, now after another. With such a frenzied mind, how can one have peace and without peace how can one have the happiness for which our mind is constantly craving! Even from the point of view of material happiness, the wavering mind has to be harnessed to a particular goal and naturally from the point of view of supreme happiness, the mind has to be attached to the supreme goal! Self-discipline is a matter of the will and becomes easy when the vision is fixed on the highest.

The worldly person and the sage are total opposites. What is night for one is day to the other. Daytime is the time for waking, when the senses are alert and busy with their work of running after sense objects. The fruitless activity of the worldly person is night to the sage, for his senses are withdrawn from the objects and may as well be asleep. Day for him is when his total being is absorbed and awake to the Reality within, when he delights in the joy flowing from within, totally independent of the waking world of the senses. This day of the sage is night indeed to the sensual man since he cannot see any point in such a joy and does not understand the source from which it flows!

Just as the ocean absorbs and unifies all the waters that enter it, so the mind of the *sthitha prajna* remains unruffled whatever be the billows of passion that might buffet him. The ocean remains the same and maintains its own equilibrium regardless of the waters of the rivers entering into and regardless of whether the waters are full of mud or sparkling clear. The total quantity of the waters of the ocean is not dependent on the waters, which may or may not flow into it. The ocean is thus not dependent on the rivers since it is the source of all waters. It maintains its balance and equilibrium under all circumstances. Such also is the case of the realised sage, who has tapped the source of all bliss and is therefore unconcerned with the delights that ensnare the worldly person. On the other hand, we are like the small, muddy puddles of the monsoons, inflating and expanding when the waters of the senses enter into us and shrinking and drying in their absence, thirsting for the delight, which streams from the world of the senses, deprived and starved when they are denied. The *sthitha prajna* is the all-absorbing ocean of bliss, whose mind does not flicker or waver even when the waters of worldly desires flow into him. The worldly person, whose mind sways with every passing emotion, is like a rudderless boat on the waters at the mercy of every passing wind! How can such a person ever attain peace, is what the Lord asks.

Knowing the world to be one of duality, the enlightened soul does not cling to the good and recoil with disgust or fear from the bad. Equilibrium of mind in all situations and experiences and equality towards all whether good or so called bad, freedom from attachment and absence of egoism are the hallmarks of the realised soul. This is not the freedom obtained by shunning the world and remaining in seclusion, nor is it the so-called freedom, which comes from doing whatever the ego demands, but it is the freedom that comes from the complete annihilation of the individual ego because of its complete absorption in the Cosmic Ego. The *sthitha prajna* wanders about in the world without the feeling of 'my' and 'mine' and is ever at peace with himself and the world.

At the time of death, he or she attains *Brahma Nirvana* or absorption in the Brahman naturally and easily. Such a person is not an ordinary person but a cosmic person and her actions are not individual actions but cosmic actions and there is no question of her ever performing a wrong action because whatever she does is in obedience to the Cosmic Law. No one can judge her for she is beyond human law and no one can deny her for she is the essence of all that is. She is a walking God, clothed in humble form. In her, Nature has fulfilled herself and attained the goal and pinnacle of her spiritual evolution!

The *nirvana* of the *Gita* differs from the *nirvana* of Buddhism. The latter is *shunya* of void whereas the former is plenum or *poorna*.

ॐ *Hari Aum Tat Sat* ॐ

Thus, in the Upanishad of the *Bhagavad Gita*, the knowledge of Supreme Brahman, the Scripture of *Yoga*, the dialogue between Sri Krishna and Arjuna, ends the second chapter entitled 'The *Yoga* of the Wisdom of Samkhya.'

> Be established in Union (with Him) at all times and then perform action.
>
> *Verse 61*

3

KARMA YOGA

The Yoga of Action

Aum Sri Krishnaya Paramaatmane' namaha!
Aum Sri Parthasarathaye' namaha.

The previous chapter ends with the picture of the *Sthitha Prajna*, the man whose intellect and will is placed firmly in the Brahmic state of cosmic consciousness. This Arjuna could understand and appreciate because he was familiar with this idea as enunciated in the Upanishads. The usual teaching of the age pointed man to the path of knowledge, to the renunciation of life and the world as the only way to perfection. He was well aware of the Law of Karma and the fact that it was one's actions which make us revolve endlessly on the wheel of *karma*. He would have understood and accepted Krishna's command to turn away from all action but his urging him to this dreadful action was something he could not understand or appreciate. Action is the opposite of knowledge according to him. Its seed is desire and its fruit, bondage. Yet Krishna insisted on action as a type of *yoga*. Perhaps some kind of work could persist, but surely it should be the minimum and it should be of the most inoffensive kind, not this terrible action of killing. This was most puzzling to Arjuna and his first question in this chapter shows this.

The *Gita* is a mandate for action. It does not dismiss the world as an illusion and action a snare. Krishna recommends a full and active life in the world with his mind anchored in the Supreme. The view at that time was that the human being is bound by action and released through knowledge and *sannyasa* or renunciation of action is the highest ideal. Krishna, however, tells us that it is not possible to abstain from action and therefore the best thing would be to understand the technique of action. Arjuna's dilemma was not of whether violence or non-violence was better but how use violence against his own enemies? Krishna does not support the validity of violence and warfare but simply uses the occasion to indicate the sprit in which all work including war should be performed.

In the present day, there is a tendency to subordinate the elements of knowledge and devotion or *jnana* and *bhakti* and assert that the *Gita* is only a Gospel of Action, since we find action or *karma* to be the recurring theme. Undoubtedly this is so, but it must be kept in mind that the action of the Karma Yogi begins and ends in *jnana* or spiritual realisation and not in action as understood by the modern mind. The action of the Karma Yogi is saturated with *bhakti* or love for the divine—a conscious surrender of one's actions and very life into the hands of the Divine. This is not the type of action we are used to, which is dictated by egoistic and perhaps even altruistic ideals, of service to humanity and so on. The action to which the *Gita* urges its master *yogi* is not human action but the action of the Divine working within us. It is not the performance of social duties, which it encourages us to do, but an abandonment of all duties as dictated by the personal ego to a selfless expression of the Divine working through us.

Before we enter the portals of the three chapters dealing with *Karma Yoga*, we should have some idea of the Law of Karma on which this is based. The Law of Karma and reincarnation are two of the basic ideas of Hinduism. The microcosm is a reflection of the macrocosm and the laws dealing with the cosmos are also to be found in the human being. The laws of nature have their reflections in the human system. The law of *karma* is actually what Newton called the 3rd law of motion: every action has its equal and opposite reaction. Even though this refers to physical actions, in the human being as Lord Krishna says, mental action is more important than the physical. What this means on the human plane is that every time we perform an action, the motivation with which we do it is what binds us to the 'Wheel of Karma'. This motivation is what ricochets back to us as the 'opposite reaction' mentioned in Newton's Law and which we experience as the fruit of the action. When a mother reprimands or even beats a child in order to correct it from some dreadful mistake, she does it with love and the action does not have a negative result. If, however, a stranger beats a child, he does it with hate and thus it will bring a strong negative reaction on him. It is this law which governs the balancing of energy within our evolutionary system. However, we should understand that the Law of Karma is not a moral dynamic. Morality is a human creation. Nature does not judge. It only governs the balancing of energy within our system of morality. It serves as an impersonal and universal teacher of responsibility. Hinduism connects the Law of Karma with reincarnation. One small life of perhaps even a hundred years is hardly enough to balance our *karmic* debts incurred even during that lifetime. So where does the balance go? Nature does not like to keep anything dangling. Every cause has to have an effect and that effect has to be experienced by the person who started the cause. Very often the body falls before the *jivatma* or the embodied human being has experienced the effects of all its action. This is where Hinduism brings in the theory of reincarnation. What is it that makes the *jivatma* to project and confine itself into this space-time capsule known as the human body? This is because we have set into motion numerous intentions or causes which according to the Law of Karma must come to a conclusion known as the effect. Every action, thought and feeling is motivated by an intention and that intention is a cause that is incomplete without coming to the end of its energy cycle by producing an effect. If we participate in a cause, we have to participate in its effect. Every cause that has not yet produced its effect is an event that has not yet come to completion. It is an imbalance of energy that is in the process of becoming balanced. This balancing need not always occur within the span of a single lifetime. Your *karma* is created and balanced by the activities of many births and personalities. A person who does not understand the law of reincarnation and *karma* will not be able to understand the significance or meaning of the events in this life.

Someone who takes advantage of others creates an imbalance of energy that can only be balanced by having the experience of being taken advantage of by other people. If this happens in this life, he or she will react from a personal point of view rather than from the point of view of his *karmic* debts. The person will become angry or vengeful or depressed. He or she will lash out or grow cynical or become sad. Each of these reactions in turn creates further *karma* and further imbalance of energy, which in turn must be balanced. Thus, though one *karmic* debt has been paid off, another has been created. Hinduism says that each individual is totally responsible for his or her every action, thought and feeling, which is to say for our every intention. We ourselves have to partake of the fruit of our intentions. This is where reincarnation comes in. All of us are given innumerable lives in order to perfect ourselves.

If a child dies we do not know what *karmic* debt is being paid by it to its parents. Of course we have to be sympathetic towards their sorrow but we cannot judge the event. If we or the parents do not understand the impersonal dynamics of this event, we will react with great anger at God or our fate or the doctor who failed to save the child or our own negligence in not having done our best. All these reactions will create more *karma* and more lessons for the personality to learn.

Every experience can be considered from the point of view of your divine self or from the point of view of your personality. What does this mean in practice? Since we cannot know what debts are being repaid by every experience, we should not and cannot judge what we see. If we see a drunken driver ramming into a child, we do not know what sort of cruelty he had engaged in another lifetime and has now chosen to experience the same energy from a different point of view. Of course we have to respond with compassion and rush to the aid of the child but we should not judge or blame the drunken driver or rant and rave at him and think it all to be grossly unfair because it is not. We really don't know why some people are selfish and hostile and negative. This does not mean that we do not recognize negativity when we see it but we should not judge it. That is not our job. We may break up a fight but we should not judge the participants because we don't know what *karmic* debt is being repaid. A cause which took place in one lifetime with the conscious intention of the personality has to be balanced in another lifetime if it had not been balanced in the same lifetime. Even though we are not aware of the deeds which had caused a certain thing to happen, the fact is that we cannot judge it. When we judge we create negative *karma*. Judgement is a function of the physical personality. Nature does not judge. Everything is carried on by the purely impersonal functioning of the natural Law of Karma, which is only a metaphysical co-relate of a physical law—the third law of motion. What this means is that the law reacts to our intentions and not just to our actions.

An angry person will respond to the difficulties of his life with anger and thus he will bring to himself the necessity of experiencing the results of anger if not in this life then in another. A person who is always loving and kind naturally will find that he or she is put into such experiences in which he will experience love and kindness from others.

When we pass judgements like "She is worthy or she is unworthy", we create negative *karma*. This does not mean that we should not act appropriately to the circumstances in which we find ourselves. If we act from the standpoint of the higher self, we must cease from judging even those events that seem so cruel like the inquisition or the holocaust or the death of an infant or the prolonged agony of cancer. We must learn to understand and accept the fact that Nature is neither cruel nor unjust. It neither condones nor blames. It just keeps going forward with the absolutely impersonal system of justice known as the Law of Karma, which categorically states that you shall reap what you sow. If we allow ourselves to judge any event, we create negative *karma* for ourselves, which must be balanced and we become participants in what is known in Hinduism as the 'Wheel of Karma,' which forces us to take new births.

The Law of Karma ensures that everyone gets his or her just deserts. No one can say "I do not deserve such a fate". So also you cannot say "That poor man does not deserve such a fate". Nature sees to it that everyone gets what they deserve; neither more nor less. Natural laws cannot be bribed or biased. The fire will burn the hand of an innocent child as much as the hand of a criminal. It does not judge. It simply carries out its own duty. This is called non-judgemental justice, which is a point of view which allows you to see everything in life with clarity but does not allow your negative emotions to come up. Nothing escapes the Law of Karma.

In fact, the Puranas give a name for the person who accounts for every action of every creature. He is known as Chitragupta in Hindu mythology. The meaning of this word is 'hidden pictures'. It is only in the 20th century that we have heard of hidden cameras but obviously our ancient sages knew of these since they created a person who was meant to record faithfully without judgement or exaggeration every single event in the life of every single person. Thus, the Law of Karma is infallible. By going through life with compassion and charity, without allowing yourself to be overwhelmed with feelings of critical judgements, you will evolve and become more and more like your divine Self. Christ did not judge even those who spat in his face or crucified him. He only asked God to forgive them for their ignorance. Hence. Hinduism says that the only sin is ignorance.

This then is the reason for our many births, which are part of our evolutionary process. So we have to accept the fact that there is a continuous reincarnation of the impersonal energy dynamics of nature in the form of a physical reality in order to balance and pay off our debts which have been incurred in other lifetimes. It is only by understanding and appreciating this that we can become fully balanced and fulfilled individuals who are no longer bound by the meagre framework of their personalities but have merged with the eternity and infinity of their highest self. This background has to be known before we can appreciate the science of *Karma Yoga*. Arjuna knew all this—that actions bind us to the Wheel of Karma, that is why his first question to the Lord in the 3rd chapter was "Why do you urge me to this dreadful action"?

Krishna replied that there are two apparently contradictory means of salvation in the world— one, the *yoga* of knowledge and the other, and the *yoga* of action (Jnana *Yoga* and *Karma Yoga*). The former implies the renunciation of action and the latter accepts action as one of the means to salvation. Actually to consider these two viewpoints as contradictory is due to a misconception in our mind regarding the nature of action. Modern psychologists also distinguish between introverts and extroverts. Indian thought always adhered that it is action which causes bondage to the wheel of *samsara* and that we will attain spiritual perfection by renouncing action.

> This is not so,

says the Lord,

> for no one can remain inactive even for a minute. All are impelled to act through their very nature. So inaction is unthinkable for any creature.

We are also prone to think that all action is personal and dependent on the individual's volition. But this is far from being the case. Action is part of the total purpose of the universe as a whole. Bondage is the consequence that follows from action, which arises from the non-understanding of this truth. We do not realise that we have a vital connection to the whole universe. Every cell within us vibrates with the pulse of the universe. Any action, which is preceded by this knowledge, cannot create bondage. We are under the mistaken supposition that if we refrain from physical action we can be said to be non-active. Krishna tells Arjuna that the physical renunciation of action is a myth, which has existed in our mind from ancient times to this very day. None can stand even for a moment without action. The embodied human being cannot cease from action. Our very existence here is an action. The whole universe is an act of God. Living is itself his movement. The universe is ever active. It can never be inactive. An individual or anything else for that matter, which is a part of this active universe, has no freedom to maintain independence over the ordinances of the cosmic laws. The insistence that we have to act has been decided by the law that operates in the universe as a whole, and for us to say that we shall act or shall not act is mere wishful thinking for we have no choice in the matter. The universe is not separate from the individual. The microcosm is part of the macrocosm. In as much as there is nothing inactive in the universe, so also no individual can remain inactive. *Naishkarmya* is a state in which we are unaffected by our work since we work without desire for fruits.

Our physical existence, its maintenance and its continuance itself, is a journey, a pilgrimage of the body, *shareera yatra* and that cannot continue without action. The idea that we can be inactive arises on account of our misunderstanding of the nature of action. We feel that if our hands and feet do not move, if our mouths are silent, we are inactive. But action does not mean only the movement of the physical organs. Every cell of our body is active and the mind itself is never inactive. To think is to act and to be really inactive one would have to cease to think. Even in the mental inactivity of deep sleep, the mind is subtly active. So there is no occasion when we can be totally inactive, until we are dead. A person may have controlled her organs of action and closed her eyes and blocked her ears and shut her mouth like the three monkeys with the message "see no evil, hear no evil and speak no evil", but she gains nothing if her mind keeps dwelling on the very objects which she has physically shut out. Arjuna sitting in the forest and dwelling wrathfully on the iniquities of his cousins, the Kauravas, would be both a hypocrite as well as a fool. He would be a fool because he would be deluding himself that he was a non-actor who was rising up on the spiritual path, and he would be a hypocrite since he would be fooling others that he was a renunciate who had given up all worldly life.

On the other hand,

> He who performs action with his physical organs unattached mentally, he is the true yogi who excels,

says the Lord.

ESSENCE OF *KARMA YOGA*

The essence of *Karma Yoga* is thus unattached action, as has been said in the second chapter, and not inaction, which in any case is impossible. Though the Lord says that knowledge is greater than action, he does not mean that inaction is greater than action. In fact, the contrary is the truth, for knowledge does not mean the renunciation of works, but non-attachment to the personal gain to be got from the action. Jnana *Yoga* has to be fulfilled in *Karma Yoga*. The *yoga* of the intelligent will finds its fulfilment in the *yoga* of action done without expectation of reward. Thus, we see that inaction is a misnomer, and the absence of physical action cannot be regarded as inaction. To be thinking actively and to be inactive physically is forcibly condemned by the Lord. Mental action is real action. Your bondage or freedom lies in the way in which your mind works, and not in the movement of your physical body.

How to control your mind and produce action without desire? This is the difficulty, which is solved in the next few verses. The universe gives us one right and that is to do our duty—our *swadharma*. But even in the performance of our *swadharma*, a certain amount of desire is bound to creep in. The value of the performance of any action lies in the extent of unselfishness behind it. Even in *swadharma* there can be traces of selfishness. In comparison with the higher stage, the lower may appear selfish. Hence, in the advance of the consciousness through the process of its evolution, we will find that there is an ascending degree in the concept of selflessness until at last there is an utter selflessness or total annihilation of the ego behind the performance of any action. Such an action becomes inaction. This can be called 'cosmic action'. So we can't become impersonal by going outside ourselves but only by rising to the highest in ourselves, into our own free soul, for that is the only part of us that is truly free. How can this be brought about? Now the Lord brings in the beautiful concept of *yajna*, which is another of the unique ideas given in the *Gita*..

YAJNA

A *yajna* is a Vedic ritual in which certain types of prescribed articles are offered into a big fire along with the chanting of *mantras* in order to bring about certain results. The Vedas describe various types of *yajnas* which will bring about results, which are desired by the one who performs the ritual. The word *yajna* is usually translated as sacrifice and this has an unhappy connotation in English. We immediately imagine the painful and unpleasant duties that are imposed on us and the joyful things that we are forced to give up. But the word *yajna* or sacrifice as given in the *Gita* has a very beautiful meaning. Using the beautiful imagery of the Vedic *yajna*, Krishna says that in ancient times, the *Yajna Purusha* or the Supreme Being sacrificed himself in order to create the world. Thus, the Creator created the individual along with the idea of *yajna* or sacrifice implanted in him. Any action which is performed without this spirit of *yajna* and with the selfish intention of the fulfilment of a personal motive, will only bring sorrow to the individual. This is because we would be going against the rules along with which we were created.

The whole of Nature is continuously offering her entire merchandise as a sacrifice to the Supreme—the secret soul within her. The rains fall, the flowers bloom, the sun shines, and the rivers flow in a continuous offering to the Supreme Soul, quite uncaring for the fruits of their action. The human being thinks that Nature has spread out her bounties only for his sake and thus he has the right to grab everything for himself. Amidst Nature's orgy of gift giving, the human being stands selfish and adamant that he should be the sole benefactor of the results of his or her action. Is it surprising that in the midst of the abundance and ecstasy of life one finds in Nature, we stand alone, desolate and depraved. So long as we act, without the spirit of sacrifice, for personal enjoyment alone, utterly selfish, we miss the true aim and meaning of life. "Vain indeed is such a life," says Krishna. It is only when we begin to realise that our life is a part of the divine drama and not a separate thing to be pursued only for our own selfish reasons that we start to evolve. Then nature starts giving us of her bounties like the proverbial cow of plenty called

'Kamadhenu.' The fruit of our desires is a part of the cosmic sacrifice, which Nature offers to her Lord, and though we are allowed to participate in this divine *yajna*, we are not allowed to pursue them selfishly as if they could be seized from life by us, by our own initiative, without giving anything in return, not even gratitude.

The whole of the *Gita*'s gospel of *karma* rests on this idea of sacrifice and the Vedantic truth that all is Brahman. All existence is the Divine movement opening out from him and returning to him. Action is rooted in Brahman. But for him the world would not exist. Everything is the joyous activity of *Prakriti* or Nature, which itself is a part of the Brahman. It is for his satisfaction that Nature descends into the numerous forms of life and eventually returns again, through the evolution of mind and self-knowledge, to a conscious possession of the soul, which pulsates within her. All action must in its inmost reality be a sacrifice— a *yajna* offered by *Prakriti* to the Supreme Person— Nature offering to the Infinite the desire of the finite within her. Life is an altar to which she brings the fruits of her works and lays them before whatever aspect of divinity the consciousness in her has reached. When sacrifice is not willingly given, Nature extracts it by force, and thus satisfies the law of *yajna*. The *devas* are the subtle forces present in the universe, which are ready to help human beings provided they are cared for in return by the human. When we destroy nature for our own selfish interests, the *devas* will continually put obstructions in our paths. A mutual giving and receiving is the law of life. The world progresses because of this co-operation between the divine and the human. One who performs actions only to satisfy his own superficial ego eats (experiences) the fruit of sin. Unhappiness alone can accrue from such actions.

The universe is his dominion and house of worship and not a field for the self-satisfaction of the ego. It is a field for the discovery of the Supreme. To seek him through actions which are done as a sacrifice, ending in a total surrender or offering of the individual ego, is what the experience of life is intended to lead. But the human being sees himself as the sole actor and the enjoyer and ignores the laws of sacrifice, and seeks to grab all he can for himself and gives Nature only what he is compelled to give.

"Such a man is a thief," says Krishna, "who takes without giving in return"! The real evolution begins when we see a law other than our own desires. The real sacrifice is the one done with knowledge when we perceive that all forms are the one form of the Supreme. This is the *Purushottama* of the *Gita* to whom all sacrifice is to be offered, not for the sake of the benefits but

Karma Yoga

as a gift to him who is the Supreme Soul. In other words, our way to liberation lies through an increasing impersonality.

Karma Yoga is the doing of all actions as a *yajna* to the Supreme, who is within us and outside us. The action is an offering, rather than a means to an ulterior and selfish end. When anything is offered to a deity, the left-over is known as *prasad*. This *prasad* is always distributed to those who have made the offering. Devotees normally accept this *prasad* as a divine gift and will never dream of enquiring into the nature and quality of the *prasad*. Thus, the person who has got into the habit of offering all his or her actions to the Supreme will become totally satisfied, in fact replete with whatever she gets as the fruit of the action. That is to say we begin to accept with happiness whatever happens to us. This is known as *prasada buddhi* and is one of the important lessons which the Lord teaches us. Only then can we begin to participate in the great *yajna* of life, and realise that our actions are only a part of the great interchange between our life and the universal life. The mental giving up of the fruit of action coupled with the physical action of the body is the essence of *Karma Yoga*.

WHY ACT

It is our constant experience that the more we open ourselves to the Impersonal and Infinite, the less we are bound by our ego and the more we feel a sense of peace and happiness. The liberated person has nothing to gain either by action or inaction. She does not depend on man for anything. She seeks no profit; she has dependence on none, for she delights in the Self alone. So why should such a person act, is the next doubt. The answer given is that he or she will continue to perform desireless actions spontaneously for the welfare of the world. Lord Krishna gives two examples for this by giving the portraits of two great Karma Yogis. One is King Janaka and the other is himself. Janaka was the king of Videha and the father of Sita. He was a realised sage yet he continued to do his duty as a king for the sake of the welfare of his people. *Lokasamgraha* means the world maintenance and unity of all peoples.

The enlightened soul like Janaka works ceaselessly for if he remained silent, others would follow his example and the world would go to ruin. As an example to the world and for the sake of the welfare of the world, even a liberated soul should continue to work. Common people always emulate the example set by the elite. They blaze the path for others to follow.

The Lord is the greatest Karma Yogi of all. He took up the menial role of Arjuna's charioteer, and carried it out in his own inimitable fashion, thus setting an example to the world that all work is an act of worship, a *yajna* to the Cosmic Being. Every work, however menial, can be the means to spiritual progress if done with the correct mental attitude. It is said that at the end of each day's battle, he would rub down his horses and feed them before attending to his own needs. Thus, action cannot bind the truly enlightened one who has an insight into the true purpose of human existence, which is one with the purpose of cosmic existence. The life of Lord Krishna is thus the perfect example of how one can fulfil our part in the cosmic drama by the disinterested performance of one's *swadharma*.

SWABHAVA AND SWADHARMA

According to our nature must be the path, which each person takes up. Each one must seek his or her salvation by seeking the path as laid down by her nature and position in life. For a person to try to adopt another's way of life, however pleasant it may look, is to go against the laws of nature, and would thus bring harm to her and the society she lives in. This verse is very often misinterpreted. Should a person not try to better herself, is the question. By all means one can do this, but the best path for each of us would be to follow the path of disinterested action as dictated by one's own nature. For a tiger to file his claws and take up the *swadharma* of a lamb would be as foolish as it would be impracticable, and would result in death for himself and the end of all his spiritual aspirations. To one's own nature, *swabhava*, one has to be true, for therein lies the path to spiritual fulfilment. In this there is true justice. If all of us were expected to follow certain impossible standards, there would be no hope of salvation for most of us. But the *Gita* has decreed that each one can evolve according to his or her own nature and at her own pace. This is the most beautiful of the *Gita*'s teachings, that nobody is condemned or utterly cast out as being beyond the pale. Everything has a place and purpose in the evolution of life. The worship of the totem pole by the tribal is as much a necessity and a step in the ladder of evolution as the worship of the Supreme Brahman. Nothing is purposeless. God fulfils himself in all ways. Thus Krishna says that the enlightened soul should not unsettle the mind of those who are in a lower scale of devotion. Even those with crude views possess something in which they believe and thus are capable of taking them further up the scale of evolution. It is the faith or belief of the mind that makes the object important. We should not cast scorn on them. This is why Hinduism has tolerated and accepted belief in many idols even the tutelary gods of the villages. It has become an immense synthesis combining within its tolerant arms many varied elements, trying to harmonise and enfold every sincere conviction.

The next question which the *Gita* takes up is the power of *maya*. All works are actually done by the *gunas* or modes of *Prakriti* which are *sattva, rajas* and *tamas* but the ego-centred human being thinks of himself as the doer. Actually we are not free agents but totally under the sway of the three *gunas* which make us act differently depending on the type of *guna*, which is predominating at the moment. The empirical self is a product of its heredity, environment and the modes of nature as well as its own previous life's *karmas*. Yet we proudly consider ourselves to be the doer or actor. However, the man of knowledge should not unsettle the minds of such people. They will slowly have to evolve and come to an understanding of their own ignorance and the fact that they are really being manipulated by the *gunas* of nature. Freedom comes from the realisation that it is *Prakriti* which is the agent of action and the Self or *atman* is only the witness. At that point the personality melts into the role of the witnessing *atman*. Till that point is reached, the *jivatma* will have to go on acting in the same senseless bound fashion as it has always done. Duality is the basis of Nature by which the boundless Self thinks of itself as being bound by the body/mind equipment so Krishna tells Arjuna not to come under the sway of duality.

The next verse is often misunderstood. Krishna says it is better for a person to play the part which nature has best fitted him for rather than strive for some other part which may seem to be more important or bring more fame and name than one's own. In the spiritual path, quality is counted more than quantity. Evolution denotes perfection of quality. However small the part that we are asked to play in the drama of life, our intention and the fact that we are doing our best is what is important in the final count.

Arjuna immediately asks a question: "What is it that instigates a man to commit sin as if compelled by some inner compulsion?" The Lord says once again that desire is the only sin. Desire for personal, selfish gain, resulting in anger, will eventually destroy all knowledge.

> These two, desire and anger, act through the medium of the mind, and these are the enemies of even the wise,

he says.

Nature drags a person to a course of action only through the dualities of attachment and aversion. Even here there are three types of ignorance. The *sattvic* ignorance is like fire covered with smoke. It can easily be taken away by a gust of wind. The *rajasic* ignorance is like a mirror covered with dust. Some amount of effort is needed to take away the dust and uncover the self beneath. *Tamasic* ignorance is like the embryo inside the womb. Ten months have to pass before it can make an appearance. This means that the *tamasic* ignorance might take lifetimes to be cleared.

> Therefore O Arjuna! Kill these enemies within yourself. You think you are a mighty hero and have destroyed many enemies, but until you have destroyed these enemies within yourself you cannot be called a hero. Destroy them therefore, and only then can you be victorious in the battlefield of life.

The method advocated is through the gradual subjugation of the senses by the mind, the mind by the intellect and the intellect itself by union with the *atman*. Consciousness must be raised step by step. The higher we rise the freer we become. When we act under the sway of the senses naturally we are bound. If we allow the mind to take control of the senses then we become a little freer. When the mind is united with the *buddhi* or the reasoning power of the intellect, naturally we become more free. To become totally free this *buddhi* has to be suffused with the light of the *atman* or the Self within us.

ॐ *Hari Aum Tat Sat* ॐ

Thus, in the Upanishad of the *Bhagavad Gita* the knowledge of Supreme Brahman, the Scripture of *Yoga*, the dialogue between Sri Krishna and Arjuna, ends the second chapter entitled 'The *Yoga* of Action'.

4

JNANA KARMA SANNYASA YOGA

The Yoga of Knowledge, Action and Renunciation of Action

Aum Sri Krishnaya Paramaatmane' namaha!
Aum Sri Parthasarathaye' namaha.

In the last chapter Lord Krishna speaks of *Karma Yoga* as that *yoga* in which action is preceded by knowledge and both are offered to the Supreme *Purushottama*, who is the secret instigator of all action and master of the works of *Prakriti* or Nature to whom she makes all her offerings. This gives an impression that the Supreme is something, which is completely transcendental, something beyond our reach, far above us in some unattainable heaven! It was also told that the practice of *Karma*

Jnana Karma Sannyasa Yoga

Yoga is fraught with difficulty since desire is the enemy of even the wise and is ever lurking within the heart and mind of man and this enemy has to be conquered only by a gradual subjugation of the senses to the mind, the mind to the intellect and the intellect itself to the *atman* or Supreme Spirit within us. This does not seem to be such an easy method. Can anyone succeed in this practice? Our will is feeble and our desires all-powerful! Under these circumstances, is there any hope for anyone? Now comes the highly solacing message of the fourth chapter. Lord Krishna openly declares that he is the *avatara* or incarnation of the Supreme. The *avatara* or incarnation is the descent of the godhead into the form of the human in order to help and support us in our fight against our lower nature.

> This is the ancient *yoga* which I had first declared to the Sun God,

says Krishna.

This ancient tradition had become obscured due to the passage of time but it is a fact that the holy land of India has produced innumerable sages, saints and *avataras* who have come in every age to revive this unique teaching. Handed down from generation to generation it had been drowned in the river of time but now Krishna was reaffirming it for the sake of his friend and devotee, Arjuna. Nothing is new about this teaching. He is only reaffirming that eternal verity. God does not have any secrets and discloses his teachings to those whose hearts are filled with love and devotion and a desire to know. Not understanding the divine nature of his charioteer, Arjuna immediately asks how Krishna, whom he considered to be his cousin, friend and contemporary, could have revealed all this to the Sun God at the beginning of time! Lord Krishna takes this opportunity to reveal himself as the *avatara* of the Age.

THE AVATARA

The theory of the *avatara* is rather difficult for the modern mind to conceive. Even if we believe in the *advaitic* idea of the Supreme Brahman, the question arises as to how or why the unborn, impersonal and immutable Supreme should take on the form of a human being! According to the Vedantic view, everything is Brahman. Every particle in the universe is nothing but the divine. Far from the unborn being unable to assume birth, all beings are the one Unborn Spirit without beginning and without end. The assumption of imperfection on the part of the Perfect is the whole phenomenon of this mysterious universe. All existence is a working out, or an evolving of the one Eternal Spirit. Even what we know as inert matter is not really dead or devoid of consciousness, as even modern science is slowly coming to accept. Every atom and sub-atomic particle is imbued with the will and intelligence of the Spirit. This Universal Will develops its powers from form to form and in the human being it draws nearest to the fullest expression of its own divinity and is capable of becoming conscious of its divinity. This being the case, can we call every man an *avatara*? What is the difference between a Krishna and an Arjuna? The difference is that Arjuna is potentially divine while Krishna is consciously divine. The birth of an *avatara* is from knowledge to knowledge, with all divine powers and a full awareness and consciousness of his supreme state from birth itself. Human birth is a birth from ignorance, under the shroud of *maya* or the cosmic veil, in which all creatures are covered. Driven by their own *karma* they are born again and again. This veil of *maya* has to be removed before the person becomes aware of the divinity within it. The Lord, however, is the controller of *Prakriti* and takes on a birth of his own free will.

REASON FOR THE AVATARA

What is the reason for the birth of an *avatara*? The seventh and eighth verses give a clue. He comes in order to uplift the Eternal Dharma, which gets lost now and again and has to be re-established in the heart of the human from time to time. The Hindu religion is known as the Sanatana Dharma or the Eternal Dharma or cosmic law of righteousness, which has ever existed and will ever exist till the end of all existences. It gets obscured now and again and the *avatara* appears to uplift and revive it. The divine incarnation is an individual symbol of the universal purpose. The *avatara* comes so that human nature may, by moulding its thought feeling and action on 'Krishnahood' or 'Christhood', transfigure itself into the divine. The law of *dharma*, which the *avatara* re-establishes, is for this purpose and not for the mere upholding of an ethical ideal, which can be done through the agency of his *vibhutis* like the saints. Thus, we find that each *avatara* holds himself up as an example and declares his oneness with the Supreme. *Avatara* means descent and this descent is a direct manifestation in humanity by the Divine in order to aid the human soul in its ascent to the divine status. It is a manifestation from above of that which we have to develop from below. It is to give *dharma* or religion a new awareness, which will enable us to grow into the Divine that the *avatara* comes. But whereas the ordinary mortal has to evolve and ascend into Godhead, the *avatara* is a direct descent into any form of humanity. He is thus a dual phenomenon, for he appears human and is yet divine. This has to be, for the object of the *avatara* is to show that human birth with all its limitations can still be made the means for a divine resurrection! *Dharma* is the essential nature of a thing that determines its mode of behaviour. *Adharma* is acting against our nature and the cosmic law. As long as we are acting in conformity with both these, we are acting according to *dharma*.

If the *avatara* were to act in a superhuman way, all the time, his purpose would be nullified. Even human sorrow and suffering he might assume like Christ or Sri Rama in order to show that suffering itself might be the way to redemption. The theory of the *avatara* plays a great part in the teaching of the *Gita*, for the story is that of Krishna, the *avatara* of the Age, leading his *vibhuti*, Arjuna, into the divine birth through the path of divine action. The crisis in which an *avatara* appears is always a crisis in the consciousness of humanity when it has to undergo some new developments. When the crisis is only an intellectual or practical one, exceptional individuals or *vibhutis* are enough to tide over the crisis, but when the crisis has a spiritual basis, a complete manifestation is called for. This spiritual crisis has two aspects, an inner and an outer. In the inner, the enemies are desire, ignorance, and egoism. The outer is the struggle between *dharma* and *adharma*—righteousness and unrighteousness, the former, supported by man's god-like nature and the latter by his demonic side. In the Mahabharata war, this has been made the external symbol of a conflict both on the individual as well as on a universal plane. In such situations, the *avatara* appears in order to disclose the fact that the kingdom of heaven can be achieved on earth. The *avatara* shows that there is no opposition between spiritual life and life in the world. The divine nature is seen through the instrument of the human body and thus helps us to achieve our true potential.

As Krishna declares in the eleventh verse, it matters not in what form he comes, because in whatever way a person approaches him in that very way does he go to him. The catholic view of the *Gita* accepts many ways and many gates of approach to him. No one is condemned. All approaches are sanctioned, provided they are sincere. Men of lesser intellect may approach lesser gods for the gratification of their worldly desires, but even those are only stages on the path and must eventually lead to the Supreme One. The great consoling message of the *Gita* is that it accepts all humankind at whatever level of evolution it might be. It does not expect everyone to be at the topmost level before approaching him. A child cannot be expected to be able to grasp the theory of relativity however brilliant the teacher. So also we are all children on the spiritual path and all of us are at different stages of evolution. We stand at many different levels and can only evolve from the level in which we are placed. The *Gita* makes it clear that *yoga* is the establishment of harmony on all the different levels of our Being. There is nothing superior or inferior in the world, in the ultimate sense. Everything has been created for some purpose and has a value of its own. The level, in which we are now, however low it may seem, is equally valuable. Our action and conduct in this particular level has to be in harmony with that level. There is fitness and beauty in a child behaving like a child, however foolish it might look from the adult angle. To force the child to behave like an adult would be to detract from its intrinsic beauty. Hinduism realises that it is impossible for us to get a true picture of ultimate reality through logic and reason. Thus, Krishna does not speak of the forms of the various religions but of the impulse and desire to find the God which is inherent in them. The spiritually immature are reluctant to recognise gods other than their own. Their intense attachment to their own form makes then blind to the unity of the Supreme Godhead.

The four-fold order (*Varna*) was created by him in order to provide a secure basis for the unfolding of spirituality in all humanity. The basis is on aptitude and function and not on *jati* or birth. Our caste or *Varna* is determined by temperament and not by birth and heredity. According to the sages, conduct is the only determining feature of caste. The present morbid condition of castes and subcastes which exists in India is totally opposed to the unity taught by Krishna, which stands for an organic concept of society.

SECRET OF ACTION

After declaring himself as the *avatara*, the Lord continues to discuss the secrets of action. The Law of Karma or the way in which action binds us is one, which has confused the minds of even the sages according to the Lord, and in the remaining verses he outlines in a beautiful way the different aspects of action. There are three types of action—*karma*, *vikarma* and *akarma*—action, special action and non-action. The common view is that action binds us to the wheel of *karma* and forces us to take repeated births. But Lord Krishna has already declared that no one can remain inactive even for a moment. Does this mean that we are bound to this wheel, life after life with no hope of reprieve? This misconception of the Law of Karma has arisen from the fact that we think that only physical action is binding action and that so long as we remain physically inactive we will not come under the bondage of *karma*. Lord Krishna blasts this view when he declares that mental action is what actually binds us to the Wheel of Karma. A person can be physically inactive and still be continuously forging links in the chain of *karma* due to her selfish thoughts. Hence, in this chapter Arjuna is told of that special *karma* or *vikarma* which is the singular function of the mind, which can transmute the dross of physical action into the gold of non-action.

INACTION IN ACTION

Akarma refers to that work which is done without attachment and which does not lead to bondage. When there is detachment in our mind, our actions cease to be actions and become non-actions. This is called 'inaction in action'. That is to say, even if the body is active, the mind which is not attached to the rewards that might accrue from the action is not bound by the action and thus the action becomes a non-action. The action of the Karma Yogi can be called 'inaction in action.' The Karma Yogi's action is a *yajna* or offering to the Supreme Lord of all action. It is a movement of the universal force within him. The Divine alone is the Lord of all action and the individual is only a channel through which the divine action flows. By the flaming intensity of this knowledge, the Karma Yogi's actions are burnt up, as if in a fire and it is as if he remains inactive. This is the first sign of the Karma Yogi. The second, which is only a corollary to the first, is that he or she is without desire. Where there is no egoism of being the doer, where is the place for desire? Outwardly she or he may appear to undertake works of all kinds, perhaps on a larger scale and with more force and energy, for the powerful might of the divine will is working through her, but the thrust of personal desire is completely wiped out. The Karma Yogi has no personal hopes. She does not seize on things as her personal possessions. She receives what the divine will brings her and is jealous of none. She accepts whatever comes without revulsion and without attachment. What goes from her, she allows to go without grief. Her action is purely physical. She is totally un-involved mentally with the fruits of her actions. The result may be success, as the world understands it, or it may be utter failure. But to her it is always success because she does not seek for personal gain but only for the fulfilment of the cosmic purpose as decreed by the divine will using her as an instrument. This will works out its mysterious ends through apparent failure as well as, and often with greater force than through apparent victory. Arjuna is assured of victory but even if certain defeat were his lot, he must fight because that is the work assigned to him by the divine will. When a person who is thus filled with this knowledge and free from attachment, acts, it is only a *yajna* or offering to the Supreme and her actions become non-actions. Thus, we can call a Karma Yogi inactive even though he or she appears to be ceaselessly working.

When we act with personal desire, we expend a lot of energy in striving hard to achieve the fruits

Jnana Karma Sannyasa Yoga

of our desires. The Karma Yogi, on the other hand, though putting forth equal effort is not affected by the effort since the entire burden of the action—its method, its fruits etc., rests with God. Because of this attitude, the action is no longer a burden to her. A mother looks after a child, bathes it, cleans it, feeds it, etc. Does she ever complain of the difficulties of her labour? This is because it is a labour of love. As far as she is concerned, all these actions which she has to perform the whole day for the sake of her baby, though apparently arduous, seem to be nothing, for they do not produce any strain in her mentally. So also the actions of the Karma Yogi who performs actions for the sake of the Divine Beloved can no longer be called actions and will cause no bondage in her. If the waters of love do not moisten the outward action, even the performance of one's *swadharma* would be an arduous task. There is a lot of difference between a nurse looking after a patient and his wife looking after him. To the former it is an arduous task since she does it only for the sake of the salary. For the latter, it is a labour of love and no effort is grudged. So it is not the physical action which constitutes the bondage but the attitude of the mind which does it. Any action if done with mental purity becomes inaction. A mother beats a child and a stranger beats it. What a difference the same action produces. The former did it with love in order to improve the child and though the action was violent, it will not leave a residue of bondage. In fact, bondage might accrue if out of over-attachment and mis-placed love, she desisted from chastising the child even when it was absolutely necessary. The inaction of desisting from violence would itself forge a link for her in the chain of *karma* for having shirked her *swadharma*. Mysterious are the workings of the Law of Karma as the Lord says. Virtue and vice do not colour the outer deed. When a person is rid of desire and self will, he or she becomes a mirror reflecting the will of the divine. She becomes the pure channel of divine power. Action by itself does not bind. It is the selfish motivation due to ignorance of our part in the drama of life that binds us.

YAJNA

As we have seen in the third chapter, the idea of *yajna* or sacrifice is another great contribution of Hinduism to spiritual life. The English word sacrifice does not give the correct meaning of this beautiful word. Whenever the mind fixes itself on something other than its own selfish interest, that process can be termed a *yajna*. According to the famous Rig Veda hymn called the *Purusha Sukta*, the universe itself was created in the form of a *yajna* wherein the Supreme Being Himself was the first sacrificial offering. Lord Krishna says that the

Jnana Karma Sannyasa Yoga

Creator instilled the idea of *yajna* along with his creation and the whole universe acts and moves and has its being in this ideal. The human being alone goes against this universal principle and thus incurs bondage.

The twenty-fourth verse of this chapter is always chanted before we eat any food. This is because in this verse Krishna gives us a beautiful mystical interpretation of the ancient Vedic *yajna*. All of us may not be able to perform these great *yajnas*, which are elaborate rituals that incur a lot of money and priests who are well versed in the method of performing them. But there is one *yajna* in which all of us participate joyfully and with no additional expenditure and this takes place when we eat. All creatures know they have to eat to live but no creature knows what happens to that food when it reaches our stomach. In chapter fifteen, Krishna says that the Lord is the fire of digestion present in the bowels of every creature that 'cooks' the food so to speak and distributes the essence of it to all the organs that need it. No creature is aware of this internal mechanism of digestion and assimilation. The human being, however, can make a suggestion to himself every time he puts food in his mouth that he is indeed performing a *yajna*. The *yajna kund* or stove is the mouth and the fire inside is the Lord himself, the food which is being put is also Brahman, the agents of action like the hands, fingers, etc. are nothing but Brahman. Therefore, such a person who does all work, even that of eating with this attitude, will undoubtedly attain Brahman.

When the senses are withdrawn and fixed on the Higher Self, a *yajna* is performed. When the senses are concentrated on objects, which are regarded as helpful in the sublimation of desire, a *yajna* is performed. When the powers of the mind, intellect and senses are centred on the consciousness within, a *yajna* is performed. When the breathing is regulated by a technique known as *pranayama*, a *yajna* is performed. Whenever we share our joy with another, we perform a *yajna*. When we give charity without any selfish motive, a *yajna* is performed. Krishna says that a feeling of love and kindness is a greater form of charity than the actual parting of a few coins. Any action in which we surrender our egoistic enjoyment and our lower impulses is termed a *yajna* or a sacrifice.

It is the feeling that counts and when that is absent, the outward show of charity is a mockery and cannot be termed as a *yajna*! Therefore, the sacrifice of knowledge is the highest *yajna*. When the material offering is given with knowledge, it also can be termed as the highest. Going to a temple or church and mouthing prayers or offering sacrifices without the loving participation of the heart is a waste of time and can under no consideration be termed a *yajna*.

To understand the true meaning of *yajna*, the Lord asks us to go and sit at the feet of the sages whose whole life is a *yajna*. Ever united with the Divine within them, they tread the earth like emperors though clothed in rags! The lofty ideal of *yajna* can come alive only when we observe the life of a saint. Leaving our ego behind we must humbly make prostrations to him and they will destroy our ignorance and reveal the light of wisdom, which is ever burning within us. Hence the great insistence in India on *satsang* or the association with the good and the saintly, for their lives can teach us through precept and example, which a book or lecture cannot do. They need no words to teach. Their very existence is an imparting of knowledge. Thus, by association with saints who are ever living in that reality, we will find that the knowledge of the Real is revealed within us. As the qualities of desirelessness, equality and devotion grow in us, so we learn to act in the spirit of *yajna*. The *yogi* acts in such a way that even the involuntary acts like breathing or the mundane acts like eating, sleeping, etc. become a *yajna*—a grand offering to the Lord of Yajna. Whatever the *yogi* thinks or does is a mighty *yajna*. His entire life is an offering at the feet of that Godhead.

Ignorance alone is the source of bondage and with the dawn of wisdom our bonds will wither away. Krishna asserts very forcefully that even the vilest of sinners will be saved with the dawn of wisdom. Just as fire burns all fuel, even faecal matter and sandalwood in the same way and turns them into ashes so also the fire of knowledge burns all sins and makes everyone spotless. This is the faith which should nourish us so that our doubts are cleared and we can proceed on our march to freedom. The doubting heart however is constantly wavering and eventually perishes or rather goes into another cycle of birth and death.

Arjuna, the great warrior, is asked to wield his sword against the enemies of doubt and ignorance within him and do even the action of fighting as if it was a *yajna*. Only then will he be a true son of his motherland!

Hari Aum Tat Sat!

Thus, in the Upanishad of the *Bhagavad Gita* the knowledge of Supreme Brahman, the Scripture of *Yoga*, the dialogue between Sri Krishna and Arjuna, ends the fourth chapter entitled 'The *Yoga* of Knowledge and Renunciation of Action'.

> Free from attachments, fear and anger, with minds ever absorbed in Me, purified by the austerity of wisdom, many have attained to My Being.
>
> *Verse 24*

5

KARMA SANNYASA YOGA

The Yoga of Renunciation of Action

Aum Sri Krishnaya Paramaatmane' namaha!
Aum Sri Parthasarathaye' namaha.

In the previous chapter Lord Krishna has detailed the life of the Karma Yogi, who is not bound by action because of the knowledge she possesses. The difference between an ordinary doer of *karma* and a Karma Yogi lies in the attitude of the mind. It is the *vikarma*, which converts the action into a *yajna* and turns *karma* into *Karma Yoga*. The purifying power of knowledge will reduce the binding power of all action to ashes. Arjuna's doubts and fears about the sanctity of this dreadful action he has been called upon to do arise

Untouched by Materialism

Karma Sannyasa Yoga

from his ignorance of the workings of the Law of Karma!

At the beginning of the fifth chapter we find that Arjuna is still confused. The belief of the age was that asceticism and non-action are superior to action. The one liberates and the other binds. In fact, this belief persists to the present age so that the ascetic *sannyasi* wearing saffron coloured robes is considered far superior to the Karma Yogi. However, the *Gita* has been insisting all along that only action done with a selfish motive should be given up. Arjuna has been brought up in the old school so he asks the pertinent question as to who is the better of the two—the Karma Yogi or the Karma Sannyasi? Lord Krishna vehemently asserts that though the *yoga* of renunciation (Karma Sannyasa) and the *yoga* of action (*Karma Yoga*) both lead to the same goal, yet of the two the latter is to be preferred because *Karma Yoga* is easier to practice than Karma Sannyasa.

The Lord has already pointed out that no one can remain inactive in this world. Even for the maintenance of one's own body, one needs to act and we know the mind is never still. But it is said that the true Karma Sannyasi does not act nor does he need to act. Everything happens by his very presence. How is this possible? The concept of *sannyasa* is unique to Hinduism. It is pure spirituality. How can we imagine 'action in inaction?' What does it mean? How can a puny individual remain inactive and yet produce action. To remain silent and yet to make the world revolve! This is the ideal of *sannyasa*! What does this imply? The mind of a true *sannyasi* is a calm lake in which is mirrored the peace of the infinite. We are called upon to act only as long as we have requirements, which in turn produce dependence on someone or something. The only ones who do not have to act are those who have dependence on none but God! These people are called Karma Sannyasis. Such people are certainly not to be seen in the market-place of the world. They prefer to avoid crowds and move about in the high regions of the mountains. They have dependence on nothing, neither people nor society. They are totally self-sufficient. All their needs are met by God. They have no requirements and roam about the slopes of mountains or sit in caves and forests. They are pure beings of nature and incredible though it might sound, even their bodily needs are met by nature herself.

If *Karma Yoga* is 'inaction in action', Karma Sannyasa is 'action in inaction'! Though a Karma Yogi is ceaselessly acting, he does not act at all for he is not bound by the results of his action since he does it as a *yajna*. The sun is an example of the Karma Yogi, since it works ceaselessly for twenty-four hours of the day, is never tired and oblivious of the work it is doing. Lord Vishnu is the example of the Karma Sannyasi. He is pictured as lying in *yogic* trance on the cosmic waters, completely relaxed while lying on the coiled serpent of his mighty power. Though he is doing nothing, he makes the entire universe revolve and maintain its harmony and equilibrium!

'Inaction in action' is silence in speech and 'action in inaction' is speech in silence! The angry mother who refuses to talk with her naughty child is far more powerful than the one who spanks her. The effect on the child is devastating. She would far rather that she rants and raves and perhaps beat her than subject her to the torture of silence! The silence of the true Karma Sannyasi is capable of producing infinite action, and the action of a Karma Yogi, of infinite silence! Perhaps it would be impossible to find perfect examples of either in the world and that is why the Lord took many incarnations in order to enable us to have some idea. The *avatara* of Nara-Narayana is the example of the perfect Karma Sannyasi and that of Krishna, of the perfect Karma Yogi.

It has already been pointed out that total renunciation of action is impossible so a *sannyasi* who sits and meditates and thinks he is actionless, is mistaken, since according to the Lord it is mental action which is responsible for the bondage and not physical action. A *sannyasi* who has renounced

Equality of Vision

his hearth, home and possessions is not a true *sannyasi* until he renounces the mental craving for objects and desire for worldly possessions and power. Without this mental surrender, the external renunciation is mere hypocrisy. It is not our possessions that bind us, but our mind. A man might have renounced all his possessions and family and gone to a cave in the Himalayas to sit there immobile but if he is fiercely possessive of his one little water pot and his loin cloth, he is no *sannyasi* even though he may look like one. He has forsaken his home but clings to his cave and burns with jealousy at the fame, which comes to the man living in the cave nearby! So we see that possessiveness is a quality of the mind and does not depend on the number of possessions you have. By reducing possessions it does not necessarily follow that one has reduced possessiveness. *Sannyasa* without this inner renunciation is no *sannyasa* at all. This path is most difficult for the ordinary human being and that is why Lord Krishna advises against it. *Karma Yoga* is both the way and the end while Karma Sannyasa is only the goal. One cannot become a Karma Sannyasi without going through the path of *Karma Yoga*.

In the end, of course, both *yogas* lead to the same goal. A wheel in fast motion appears immobile and this is the state of the Karma Yogi, which is also the state of the Karma Sannyasi. But the practical value of *Karma Yoga* is more since it is easier to practice. The Karma Yogi, even though performing all action, thinks she is not the doer. Even while looking, hearing, touching, smelling, eating, sleeping, breathing, speaking, blinking or attending to the calls of nature, she knows that she does nothing at all and it is only the sense organs acting on the sense objects. Such a person is untouched by the binding effects of *karma* like the lotus leaf in the water. The lotus leaf lies in the water but the water can never wet the leaf. You can see many drops of water on the leaf but they simply roll away without affecting the leaf. Such is the *yogi* of the *Gita*. He or she lives in the world but is not affected by it. The lotus has always been the symbol of purity and of man's endeavour to reach the heights. It is born in the dirt and slime of the pond, and raises itself above the murky waters and opens its face to the dazzling brilliance of the sun above. So also the mind of man, though born from the seething passions of an animal heritage, can shake off these bestial origins and rise up to the sunshine of divinity. The Karma Yogi performs action through the medium of her body alone, for the sake of the Lord within and outside her and attains peace. She resides happily in the city of nine gates, says the Lord. This city is the human body, which has nine orifices. These are the two eyes, the two ears, the two nostrils,

Karma Sannyasa Yoga

the mouth and the two organs of excretion and generation. True renunciation gives us complete freedom of action in the world. It comes along with a perfect equality of vision to all things and persons. The *Gita* attaches immense importance to equality. This is because of its stress on action. The withdrawn sage sitting in the fastness of his mountain cave has no need to practice equality. Only when he comes to the work-a-day world of action can he test his superiority. The test of his greatness is the amount of equality he can show in his dealings with the world. True knowledge is the consciousness of the unity of all things. In relating with the different beings of this world, it must show itself as an equal oneness with all.

God does not create the sense of agency in people nor does he make us act or teach us to connect work and its results. It is nature or *Prakriti* that does all this. Again God does not create the sense of guilt or merit. It is *Prakriti* which envelops knowledge in her shroud of *maya* and produces ignorance which cloaks true knowledge. By continuously directing our mind to the divine, our ignorance will be destroyed and the Supreme Self in us will be revealed in all its glory like the sun lighting up the world when the clouds drift away.

> For the truly wise, a learned Brahmin, a cow, an elephant, a dog and an eater of dog flesh are the same

says the Lord.

This is a revolutionary statement to make in any age, even in this one, which proclaims to be classless, yet is most class conscious. But in that age, it was indeed only a God who could dare to declare that a *yogi* would make no differentiation between a Brahmin and an outcaste! The supreme effulgence is found in all creatures and is not affected by the difference of the bodies that it illumines. The characteristics of the Brahman—existence, consciousness and bliss—are present in all creatures. Differences are only in their bodies. This is God's view of the world and this is the view of the saint.

Such a person is truly liberated for he has conquered the limitations of this world of sense relationships and is a God-Man, for he lives ever in the faultless Brahman. True learning brings about true humility. The truly humble realises that all knowledge is supported by the Infinite Being and does not belong to him. In the nineteenth verse Krishna makes a revolutionary statement, which is not given by any other scripture. Krishna categorically states that if there be a heaven it must be found on this very earth. The *Gita* is not guilty of offering the doubtful bait of a glorious Heaven after death, to be given as a reward for those who have lived a meritorious life on this earth. It discards such type of childish prattle as being an unworthy gift for its master man! This earth with all its limitations and dualities shall be converted into a Heaven for one who abides in the Brahman. Such a person is yoked to the Supreme, which is a source of unalloyed bliss and he enjoys this bliss even while living in this vale of sorrows! This bliss has to be gained while inhabiting this body, filled though it is with deficiencies.

HEAVEN ON EARTH

Heaven is not some illusory state to be gained after death. One should not be misled into believing the claims of popular religions that liberation will come only after shedding the mortal coils. A perfect spiritual freedom can be won here on earth and enjoyed while inhabiting the human body. Such a *yogi* achieves the state known as Brahma Nirvana. This should not be confused with the Buddhist Nirvana, which is a negative state of the absence of sorrows. The Nirvana of the *Gita* is a positive state, conducive to action in the world and the sages who possess it will not shirk their duty to act for the sake of humanity. They have not renounced action but only divinised it. Action in the world is not inconsistent with living in Brahman but is an inevitable condition of it, because the Brahman in whom we find this Nirvana is not only within us but also within all these existences. Nirvana in Brahman is only a destruction of the limited ego and an entry into the Universal ego. Nirvana when we gain it is not only within us but also all around us. Brahman is not only the Supreme Self of the universe, but also the Self of all existences.

Once again Krishna tells Arjuna that the pleasure which comes from the contact of the senses with the objects of the world is only a source of sorrow since it has a beginning and an end. The one who is able to free her mind from the opposites of desire and anger while in the body is the true *yogi*. Peace can and must be attained in the midst of this turbulent human life. Joy and peace are to be found within us. Such a person is not an unfriendly recluse but one who rejoices in doing good to all creatures. The true *yogi* does not evade his social responsibilities. The *Gita* emphasises both sides of religion, personal and social. The *yogi* who has ascended to the world of the Spirit will also descend to the world of all creatures.

MEDITATIVE POSE

In the next two verses (27 & 28), there is a slight deviation from the main topic and a hint as to what is to come in the sixth chapter. The practical side of *yoga* is given. The *yogi* sits in meditation with his attention fixed on the *ajna chakra* between the eyebrows and practices *pranayama* or breath control. He regulates his breath and thus controls his mind and senses. This instruction is given as a special aid to overcome the outward-going tendency of the mind. The rate of breathing has a great deal to do with mental control. The *yogi's* breath is always calm and even. When our breath is even, we cannot remain angry. When the breath is agitated, the mind is also agitated. Conversely, when one wants to concentrate on something, one holds the breath. So the *yogi*, who is desirous of uniting himself with the Supreme, is asked to practice *pranayama* and meditate on the Supreme by fixing his inner gaze on the psychic centre between the brows.

In the last verse, once more the central idea of the *Gita* is postulated—that God is an Infinite Being who is not merely an impersonal witness but also the enjoyer of all actions done as *yajna*. He is the mighty Lord of the universe, yet the friend of all creatures. The Divine who is present in all existences and in all activities—Master of both the silence and the action—of both power and peace has incarnated now as the Divine Charioteer. He is both the Karma Yogi as well as the Karma Sannyasi. He is the enjoyer of all austerities and *yajnas*. Therefore, the *yogi* should do all action as a *yajna* to him. He is the Lord of all works, so the *yogi* should work for the correct upholding of *dharma* in the world. He is the sole friend of all creatures and therefore the *yogi* should be constantly engaged in work for the good of all creatures. Only the *yogi*, who has gained the Nirvana of bliss within him, is capable of divine love and service for humanity.

This is the superiority of the *Gita* over other *advaitic* texts. It brings the Supreme down from the imperturbable and impenetrable impersonality of the Brahman to the pulsating, intimate reality of the *Purushottama* seated within the heart of all—our only friend, relation and the beloved of all creatures, to whom all actions should be offered. We worship many gods in our life in order to gain money, power and security. For the sake of these gods we are willing to sacrifice many things. We sacrifice our sleep to make money, our money to gain power, and our power to gain comfort and security. So many countless actions are done from morn till night for the duration of a whole lifetime in order to propitiate these gods. All these actions only help to draw us further into the very rut we are trying to avoid. The root cause of all this vain activity is ignorance—ignorance of the purpose of human life, and of the nature of the Divine who alone is the instigator of all actions and the giver and enjoyer of all fruits. We are also ignorant of the fact that though he is the mighty Lord of the Universe, he is also the sole friend and benefactor of all creatures. Once this knowledge has been gained, all action will be automatically dedicated to him, all things will be done by him and for him and through him, this human body being merely an instrument. Thus, the culmination of both *Karma Yoga* and Karma Sannyasa will be achieved, for in essence they are both one and the same!

ॐ *Hari Aum Tat Sat* ॐ

Thus, in the Upanishad of the *Bhagavad Gita* the knowledge of the Supreme Brahman, the Scripture of *Yoga*, the dialogue between Sri Krishna and Arjuna, ends the fifth chapter entitled 'The *Yoga* of Renunciation of Action'.

> One who knows me as the great Lord of all the worlds, the enjoyer of all offerings and austerities and the sole friend of all creatures, attains peace.
>
> *Chapter 5, Verse 29.*

6

ATMA SAMYAMA YOGA

The Yoga of Self-Discipline

Aum Sri Krishnaya Paramaatmane' namaha!
Aum Sri Parthasarathaye' namaha.

Krishna begins the sixth chapter by reiterating the fact that *sannyasa* is an inward renunciation and has little to do with external acts. Renunciation means going through necessary actions without any striving for personal reward. This is also true *yoga*. Thus both *sannyasa* and *yoga* takes us to the same goal. By doing work without expectation of reward we achieve self control and when we have self control we attain peace.

> Know that the *sannyasi* and the *yogi* are the same for no one can become a *sannyasi* without controlling his mind and such a man of self-control is also a *yogi*.

Atma Samyama Yoga

Yoga is the step we take in the direction of impersonality, the direction towards the highest Person within us.

The seers of the Upanishads tell us that the Self or *atman* is in all creatures. This Self is not the psychophysical entity with which we identify ourselves but the divine spark existing in us and in all things. The urge of the senses towards external objects is itself the action of this Self. The mind is under the mistaken impression that objects produce happiness, but this is far from being the case. The object itself has no value. Satisfaction comes from the Self and not the object. When the mind is dejected even the most pleasant thing fails to give us pleasure. If pleasure existed in the object, it should be able to produce happiness whatever the state of the mind and it should produce pleasure to all regardless of whether they like it or not. However this is not true and we find pleasure in things only when we are in a good frame of mind.

It is only because of the presence of the Supreme Self in all objects that we find them pleasurable. If the Self were not there, love would be unthinkable. However, due to some sort of illusion we feel that it is the objects, which produce the happiness. The psychological reason for this illusion is because the possession of the object is followed by a cessation of desire for the time being.

The agitating thought waves of desire get stilled and we feel happiness. Of course this feeling is only a temporary phase, which lasts till the next object looms into view and the mind jumps after it! The metaphysical reason for this craving has already been stated.

DIVINE SELF IS THE OBJECT OF HAPPINESS

The divine Self is present in everything and is constantly beckoning to us, but we mistakenly believe that it is the material objects, which are pulling us. Ignorance of the source of attraction is what makes us dissatisfied even when we get the desired objects. All of us have experienced this. As Bertrand Russell put it, "There are two tragedies in life. One, not to get the thing you desire, and the other to get it!" The second tragedy is inexplicable until we realise that it is the Infinite Self, which is summoning the Infinite Self in us in every act of desire. In every act of desire, what we are unconsciously demanding is nothing short of that Infinite and the tragedy occurs when we find that the object is far from being able to give us the infinity we crave for! So it is the Higher Self, which is the attraction for the lower self in every object. Does this mean that there are two selves in us? If we use the word personality for the lower self and *atman* for the Higher Self, we will find it easier to understand.

Atma Samyama Yoga

What the personality subconsciously craves is for union with the Infinite Self within it, as well as outside it and when it tunes itself to the Higher it is in a state of *yoga*. As long as we are responding to the call of the Higher, we are on the path of *yoga*. In fact, this is the only way we can advance—step by step. There may or may not be a double promotion for exceptionally bright students but for the normal student the steps have to be attempted one after the other. Nature reveals her secrets by degrees. The one who thinks she knows it all, has no idea of what she is talking about.

SELF IS BOTH FRIEND AND ENEMY

Thus in the sixth chapter, the Lord makes us realise that we are our own friend and our own enemy. The only way to pull ourselves up is by having recourse to our own Higher Self. The moment we associate ourselves with our lower self, we start degrading ourselves. The Higher Self should be the object of meditation for the lower. To the extent that the lower is in tune with the Higher, to that extent we are successful in our endeavours. To the extent we are selfish and ignorant of even the existence of the Higher, we are bound to be failures. So the lower self is our friend when it strives to uplift itself to the level of the Higher and an enemy when it is not in tune with the purpose and motives of the Higher. He who has conquered his lower self exhibits that great equality which is stressed in the *Gita*, on all levels of his personality—bodily, mentally, and intellectually. The higher self and the lower are not antagonistic to each other. The higher can be both our friend and our foe depending on whether we have controlled ourselves. Everyone has the freedom to rise or fall.

EQUALITY TO ALL

Such a person is impervious to heat and cold, unperturbed in joy and sorrow and above honour and dishonour. One who is established in her higher Self is oblivious of the dualities, which trouble her personality—physical, mental or intellectual. This is the ascending order of self-control. We may find that many who are in perfect control of their bodies, who can bear great tortures of the body, will crumble when their mental equilibrium is disturbed. A patriot who can easily bear torture to his own body gives in when he knows that the life of his wife or child is being threatened. This is the mental or emotional personality. Another who may overcome the pull of these two levels breaks down when it is a question of his honour or the honour of his family. This is the intellectual personality. These three are only our different personality sheaths. The

Atma Samyama Yoga

yogi is one who has surmounted these sheaths and is established in his only reality, which is the *atman*. To him a lump of clay, a stone or a piece of gold is of equal value. This should not be taken to mean that the *yogi* himself is a clod who cannot differentiate between these objects. It only means that he does not place the same value on these as the world places on them. The value of gold lies in its rarity. It has no intrinsic value. If gold was as plentiful as rock, it would be quite valueless. So its value lies only in the mind of the person who possesses it. The *yogi* on the other hand has found the rarest thing of all—the Self within him— and therefore places no value on the baubles of the world. He or she does not differentiate between friend and foe, enemy and well-wisher. She does not even differentiate between saint and sinner, hateful or lovable. In the next few verses Krishna develops the technique of mental discipline on the lines of Patanjali's *Yoga Sutras*. He describes the steps of *dhyana yoga* or the *yoga* of meditation. Our minds are naturally outer-oriented and meditation, explores the inner world and helps to integrate both. When we read these verses on meditation we are struck by the extreme simplicity of the Lord's teachings. So much has been said and written about meditation that most of us get. But the Lord's teachings are simplicity itself.

MEDITATION

The person who wants to meditate should choose a lonely spot, since the mind is ever ready to be distracted and meditation in the market-place is quite unthinkable. For the time being at least she should rid her mind of desires and be without possessions and possessiveness. Without this preliminary requisite, no one should practice meditation because the mind of a person filled with desire can never become single-pointed. It would be a waste of time for her to sit down and try to meditate. This is why we find that many novices complain that they can never meditate. The mind of the meditator has to be filled with the all-consuming desire to achieve union with the Divine. If that desire is prevalent all other desires will vanish. The place for meditation should be quiet, clean and sequestered. The seat should be neither too high nor too low. In such a place one should spread a seat. The classic seat for the meditator consists of a mat of *kusa* grass, which is a certain type of grass with antiseptic properties. It keeps away ants and insects. On top of this she should spread a deer skin, which acts as an insulator and prevents vibrations from meditation from being lost and also gives protection from natural disturbances like lightening, etc. Over this she should spread a piece of cloth since the deer skin might prick her. It may be objected that these instructions are applicable only to those who sit

Atma Samyama Yoga

outside in the midst of nature and can have no meaning to us who meditate, often on top of multi-storied buildings. This is undoubtedly true and we should use our common sense in such matters. But it is important to keep some special cushion or mat or cloth or rug only for the purpose of meditation and not use it for anything else. These mats will absorb the positive vibrations of your meditation and if you use the same mats every time, it will ensure that there is no loss of energy, gained through meditation.

We should maintain a steady posture, keeping the head, trunk and neck in a straight and steady line. The inner gaze should be fixed at the point between the brows. Observe that the Lord does not specify any particular posture but only advises us to take a comfortable seat, keeping the head neck and trunk immobile, in a straight line. Psychic energy runs upward through the spine and a poor and twisted posture would prevent this and thus retard the process. The *ajna chakra* or the spot between the eyebrows is supposed to be the seat of psychic wisdom, the resting place of the mind and so the inward gaze should be fixed on that. The mind should be calm, self-controlled and free from fear and the vow of *brahmacharya* or continence should be followed mentally. The whole direction of the lower self should be turned to the Higher, which is within us. So the purpose of meditation is simply to clear the mind from cluttering thoughts, which automatically allows the divine light to shine. Thus, with regular meditation on the Cosmic Beloved, the Supreme object of love, one will surely attain him.

VIA MEDIA IN YOGA

Does this all mean that the meditator should shun all pleasures of life and go to the other extreme of shutting herself in a cave without food and sleep!

To disabuse us of this notion the Lord says, "This *yoga* is not for him who sleeps too much or too little, who eats too much or too little."

It is for one who is regulated in all the activities of daily life. This is an easier method of controlling the mind than the enforcement of too many strict rules. Like a naughty child, the mind will inevitably tend to stray into forbidden paths! The *yogi* is moderate in all activities and is not given to excessive indulgence. By using the word *yukta*, which means united, the Lord reiterates the central idea of the *Gita*—that the *yogi* is one who is constantly united with the Divine! So the meditation of the *Gita* is not a mere five or fifteen minute affair but a constant communion with the Divine. The *yogi* is one who is united with the Divine in all the daily activities of her life, however insignificant. In fact, the *yogi* of the *Gita* carries on a twenty-four hour meditation. There is no difficulty for the lover to think of his beloved; in fact, the difficulty would be in not thinking of her. Even when busy, the thought of his sweetheart is always hovering at the back of his mind. So the *yogi* who has placed her entire heart and mind on the Divine Beloved will find no difficulty in meditating on him.

"He abides in Me and I in him," says the Lord.

The love of the world is spiritualised and changed from a sense experience to a soul experience and in this there is no place for fear. Fear exists only where there is experience of duality. When we are established in unity there is no room for fear. To see all as divine is to hate nothing and fear nothing. The *yogi's* mind is like a lamp in a windless place, never flickering, always absorbed in the Self and rejoicing only in that. Once established in that, he never falls away from it.

Thus established in a constant awareness of the beloved even the greatest sorrows of the world will not shake her. This is truly the final separation of our mind from sorrow. The mind of man is ever a prey to sorrow. It seeks happiness yet it always finds sorrow. With the achievement of this state, the mind makes its final break from its constant companion, 'sorrow'! So let the mind practice this *yoga* with resolution, undismayed by the many pitfalls, which might accrue on the path. Such a person sees the Self in all things and all things in the Self. He sees all with equal vision.

This tranquillity of the mind is gained slowly. The wavering mind should be brought back again and again and fixed on the Self alone until the final union is reached. In that experience God is no longer a vague aspiration but a vivid reality with which we are in actual contact.

After listening to this, Arjuna has a serious doubt: "Will I ever be able to control this fickle mind which runs hither and thither like the wind?"

Krishna calmly says that though the mind is indeed difficult to curb yet it can be accomplished through *vairagya* and *abhyasa*—detachment and practice. These are the negative and positive sides of meditation. One has to clear the field of weeds before the seeds can be planted. The method of *vairagya* or detachment has already been described but without continuous practice, this detachment would be quite impossible. So the person who is striving to achieve perfection should resort to *dhyana* or meditation as described above.

NO FALL FOR THE YOGI

Arjuna's next question is about the status of a *yogi* who, for some reason, is not able to achieve the goal of *yoga* in this life.

> Having given up the normal pleasures of life and yet unable to reach the goal of *yoga* perhaps through death or perhaps some other deterrent, will he not perish like a torn cloud? is Arjuna's question.

Atma Samyama Yoga

The Lord gives a very beautiful and consoling answer to this.

O beloved Arjuna,

he says,

there is no fall for one who has started on the path of *yoga* with sincerity. Such a person can never meet with misfortune either in this life or another.

After death he or she may attain the world of virtuous souls and then be reborn in the household of pious and spiritual-minded people, where she will get the opportunity to pick up the threads of that *yoga* which were broken off in a previous birth and continue on her path to liberation. Due to the impressions of her previous birth, she will be drawn to a life of *yoga*. Thus purifying herself through the effort of many lives, she will reach the supreme state. Whoever strives for perfection even in the least measure cannot go to ruin.

That is the beautiful side of the Law of Karma or the law of action and reaction. We are always apprehensive of this law. We believe it to be a binding chain but we forget that it has a positive side to it. Every effort at practicing *yoga* will be given credit. God knows our weaknesses and the efforts we make to overcome them. On this path no effort is a waste. He is not concerned with outward success or failure. What he expects is the sincerity and honesty of purpose, which instigates us. Even though the memory of our previous lives may not be a conscious operation of our mind yet many of us feel an urge towards certain things and this propulsion is due to our previous practice. So the *yogi* who is reborn in this manner is irresistibly impelled to move in the direction of the same practice, which she was unable to complete in her previous life and this very Law of Karma will provide everything that is necessary for the continuation of her practice! When there is sincere movement towards God, even though it might be without a proper conception of the divinity, it will be rewarded in a most miraculous manner. Whatever your conception of God, the sincerity that you exercise in your endeavour to attain him shall be your saviour in your future life. Even in this life you will be taken care of. The goal of human life will not be accomplished until every human being is redeemed and enlightened even though it may take millions of births.

At the end of the chapter, the Lord extols the state of a *yogi* as being superior to all other *sadhanas* like *tapas*, *jnana* and *karma* for the *yogi* seeks for just one thing and that is union with God whatever the path she or he might follow. These three words have slightly different connotations in this chapter. *Tapas* is a retreat to the forest for performing arduous practices, *jnana* abstains from all action

Atma Samyama Yoga

and depends only on knowledge and *karma* is the performance of Vedic rites for attaining some object. But even amongst *yogis*, those who worship him exclusively with the *yoga* of devotion is the best of all. This is the concluding idea of the *Gita*, which is taken up in the next chapter.

ॐ *Hari Aum Tat Sat* ॐ

Thus, in the Upanishad of the *Bhagavad Gita* the Knowledge of the Supreme Brahman, the Scripture of *Yoga*, the dialogue between Sri Krishna and Arjuna, ends the sixth chapter entitled 'The *Yoga* of Self-Discipline'.

> When the mind is withdrawn from all sides and focused on the Self alone, the yogi becomes free from all desire for the objects of the world and can be called a 'yukta' (one established in *yoga*).
>
> *Verse – 18*

7

JNANA VIJNANA YOGA

The Yoga of Knowledge and Discernment

Aum Sri Krishnaya Paramaatmane' namaha!
Aum Sri Parthasarathaye' namaha.

From the seventh chapter onwards there is a distinct change in the tone of the teaching. The first six chapters give us the relation between knowledge and action and the next six chapters give us the relationship between knowledge and devotion. The seventh chapter throws open the door of the beautiful mansion of Bhakti *Yoga* or the *yoga* of devotion. The *bhakti* of the *Gita* is not blind belief but is based on an understanding of that to which devotion is to be offered. In fact, the flower of devotion can blossom only when the garden of the mind has been tilled with the action of *Karma Yoga* and watered with the knowledge of Jnana *Yoga*. That is why the foundation of action based on knowledge has been firmly planted in us before proceeding to the most misinterpreted *yoga*, of *bhakti* or devotion. It is to be hoped that by the time we come to the end of the sixth chapter, the individual will have become an integrated personality, ready to take the leap into the sea of *bhakti* and comprehend the nature of devotion. From this chapter onwards, Krishna gives Arjuna the integral knowledge of the divine not merely as the Brahman but also as its manifestation in the world. To make our knowledge complete, we must have knowledge of the relationless Absolute as well as its varied manifestations.

BHAKTI OR DEVOTION

Normally devotion to God is equated with visiting places of worship, be it temple, mosque or church. Of course this might be the beginning of devotion but it is far from being the end. Very often we find that devotees of certain sects and religions are fanatics who consider their own beliefs alone to be true. They are taught not to question anything that the priesthood says. In fact, a true devotee is supposed to be so full of faith in the written word that she just cannot think for herself.

The Infinite Truth is brought down and caged within the narrow limits of sectarian belief. The door of the cage is locked and the key thrown away so that there is no possibility for the light of reason to creep in unnoticed. The devotee is also caged in with her deity and both of them have to suffer together. The unfortunate part of this type of devotion is that the devotee thinks she is superior to everyone else. Of course there is only one God and that is her God. This is a very limited concept of the Supreme, and *bhakti,* which is based on this false concept, has every opportunity of turning into fundamentalism. The very concept of the deity as being a Supreme, all-encompassing Being is totally beyond the ken of such people. The sectarian One is a mathematical one—an exclusive God, exclusive to the ones who believe in him. The Vedantic One, however, is a metaphysical truth—an all-inclusive transcendental Being existing at all places, at all times and available to anyone. The Hindu religion, even though apparently crawling with gods, insists that all gods are just reflections of the One Absolute. As long as this idea is understood, we can worship God in any form. In other words *bhakti* or devotion has to be based on *jnana* or knowledge. *Bhakti* without *jnana* degenerates to fanaticism while, *jnana* without *bhakti* becomes arid and joyless. Hence, the preceptor of the *Gita* teaches the esoteric

Jnana Vijnana Yoga

knowledge of the formless divine as well as the secret of action at the very beginning of his discourse so that it can serve as a foundation for *bhakti*.

THE SUPREME PERSON

From the beginning of this chapter Lord Krishna completely identifies himself with the Supreme *Purushottama* or the Supreme Person. This he does to ensure that Arjuna is not misled into believing that he is starting a new sect or cult. He is not a separate person but is one with that Supreme who is one with everything. Till now he had only hinted at this identity and stressed the role of individual effort. Now he starts this chapter without an instigating question on Arjuna's part in order to instil in him the knowledge of both the transcendental as well as the external world. The Divine is inclusive of everything. If he is known fully, the world of Nature will also be known. But we flit from one department of knowledge to another, never seeking for the unity behind. Barely one in a thousand strives to realise God and even amongst those who strive, very few come to know him in truth! The quest for God is not the aim of the ordinary person and even amongst those who attempt this quest, only a few succeed. The path of the Spirit is hard in the beginning, especially for the individual filled with egoistic impulses who may well give up the quest before the end is reached. The world is filled with so many wonderful things and man's ingenuity has produced even more. The mind is led from one delight to another and sees no necessity to look for anything beyond the senses. Very often it is only at the stroke of misfortune that the person thinks of searching for a truth beyond the senses. Even Arjuna thinks of turning to Krishna only when he is faced with a serious dilemma for which his own reason can find no solution. The thirst for God is indeed a very rare thing. Most of us go through life without knowing this thirst for God. Even amongst those who strive for truth, only a few succeed.

TWO NATURES

In order to instil in Arjuna the integral knowledge, which he had promised to do at the beginning of the chapter, the *Gita* makes its great distinction between the two types of Natures—the phenomenal and the spiritual. The five elements along with the ego, mind and intellect are what constitute the phenomenal eight-fold nature of lower *Prakriti*. These elements were later elaborated into twenty-four. Using only the seven basic colours of the spectrum and utilising the same canvas and brush, the artist proceeds to paint many pictures, which are totally different from each other. With the seven basic notes the musician produces the most enticing symphonies and

Jnana Vijnana Yoga

melodies. Using just a few letters of the alphabet, the writer expresses an endless variety of thoughts, which can either exalt us or depress us! So also the Creator has made this external creation using the eight-fold divisions of lower *Prakriti*—earth, air, water, fire, ether, mind, intellect and ego. Beyond this gross nature is the subtle nature on which the universe is sustained. In other words, the whole of this creation both internal and external is made of the two Natures—the Spirit within and the Spirit outside. The love of the lover, the agony of the sufferer, the laziness of the idler, the activity of the worker are all apparent manifestations stemming from the same source and supported by that One single Consciousness.

By *Para Prakriti* is meant the original power or *Shakti* of the Supreme and this is the womb of all creation. In other words, the *Purushottama* himself is *Para Prakriti*. The Supreme Being is infinite consciousness. *Para Prakriti* is his will, which projects itself as energy. Birth and evolution are the movements of this conscious energy of *Para Prakriti* out of the Pure Consciousness into the activity of the mutable universe. Dissolution is the withdrawal of that energy back into the immutable existence of that Pure Consciousness. The *jiva* or *jivatma* is the individual spiritual existence of the Supreme *Purushottama*, found in all human beings. This spiritual entity is to be found in all things.

Therefore, all existences are instinct with the nature of the One Spirit. It is because of this unity that the cosmos is a whole, which is sustained and maintained by this unseen force. The *jiva* is the Supreme Soul seen in manifold coverings. "All this is strung on me like pearls on a string," says the Lord. This should not be misunderstood to mean that there is a multiplicity of *jivas* even though we are apt to use the plural in ordinary parlance. The necklace retains its form only because of the thread on which it is strung. The manifold *jivas* have reality only because of the One Reality which upholds them. In fact, all things are initially, ultimately and in the interim nothing but the one Supreme Spirit. The world with all its becomings comes from the Supreme and at the time of dissolution it is withdrawn into Him.

THE ESSENCE OF ALL THINGS.

In order to make this message clear, Krishna gives a list of things in the physical world and points out that in each substance it is his presence which gives reality and utility to the thing.

> I am taste in the waters, light in the sun and moon, the sound Aum in the Vedas, manliness in men, fragrance in earth, effulgence in fire and life in all living beings.

All the sounds come from the sound *Aum*. It is the one universal foundation of the energy of sound and speech, which contains and releases all the potential spiritual powers in all sounds. The Lord also says that he is the eternal seed in all beings from which all other things have emerged. This eternal seed is the power of the Divine, which is cast into the womb of lower *Prakriti*, composed of its eight-fold nature, from which all are born into the phenomenal existence. This seed is what constitutes the *swabhava* or essential quality of all existences.

> But the whole world, deluded by the three *gunas* (qualities of lower *Prakriti*) does not know me, the Supreme Spirit lodged within these perishable form,

says the Lord.

> Veiled by my *yogamaya* I am not perceivable by all!

The different forms and qualities of his eightfold nature which makes up his lower *Prakriti* is what is known as *maya* and that is what deludes the whole world! The *yogi* alone understands that he alone is the source from which all this arises and is not deluded.

A musician can raise us to the heights of ecstasy or drown us in the depths of melancholy by the masterly skill with which he plays his instrument. A poem can bring tears to our eyes or exalt us. A sunset can entrance us and thunderstorms terrify us. The face of our child can fill us with joy and that of a villain with horror. All this is nothing but the power of his *maya*!

> The ignorant world does not recognise me as the Unborn and Imperishable Spirit. All creatures are shrouded in this veil of *maya*!" says the Lord. "Difficult, nay almost impossible is it to overcome my *maya*!

Caught in the web of *maya* we see only the changing forms and not the Eternal Being of which the forms are only manifestations.

Maya does not mean illusion as is popularly supposed. *Maya* is that which bewilders our knowledge and creates false values and conceals from us the supreme truth of our existence. But this *maya* is nothing but his power, his art, his skill and though this veil of illusion is difficult to pierce yet, "he who has recourse to me can easily rent it!" says the Lord.

HOW TO OVERCOME MAYA

Is there no hope for us? Are we condemned to revolve everlastingly in the wheel of *maya*, now laughing, now crying—at the mercy of the relentless drummer who makes us dance incessantly to his tune! There is only one way out for poor humanity, caught in the grip of *maya* and that is to catch hold of the drummer himself, the master magician who has waved his wand and cast this spell on us. He is the one who has wrought this magic. He is the one who has hypnotised us so that we believe the unreal to be the real. Some of us are willing and some unwilling participants in this cosmic magic show. Those unwilling ones who desire to pierce the veil have only one recourse and that is through the path of *bhakti* or devotion. If we have *bhakti* we will be able to appreciate the skill of the Great Magician. We will be able to enjoy the show without being hypnotised by it. We can see the show and return home without weeping for the lady who was sawed in half or exulting with the child who was flying in the air! How can the meaning of this mysterious universe be comprehended by the five senses alone? They are poor narrators at best and deluders at worst. It is only when his grace flows through us by the power of our devotion that the veil is rent from our eyes and he stands revealed in all his glory before us!

The doers of evil are foolish and cannot attain the Supreme for their minds have been made into tools of their own ego. They have to go through the process of purification of the mind, which has been detailed in the sixth chapter before they can attain the highest. Krishna then proceeds to give us the nature of different types of devotees.

TYPES OF DEVOTION

To help us understand the nature of *bhakti*, the Lord gives us pen portraits of the four types of *bhaktas* or devotees. Devotion can stem from many sources, and our love for God can have many motivations! The more perfect the love, the less the motivation, and the greater the chances of realisation. People are born at various levels of evolution and thus their devotion will also be of different levels. The horizon remains at a level with our eyes, however high we might climb so also our idea of God will always depend on our level of consciousness.

> Four kinds of men worship Me, O Arjuna,

says the Lord,

> They are the sufferer, the seeker of worldly objects, the seeker of knowledge and the man of wisdom.

These devotees can be classified psychologically as those having an emotional nature, a practical nature, an intellectual nature and an intuitive nature—*artha, artharthi, jijnasu* and *jnani*. The Lord accepts all and does not scorn those who approach him with baser motives, for in his infinite compassion he knows that they are totally bewildered by his *maya* and find it difficult to recognise him in and through these infinite forms. As long as we are seekers, we have to remain in the world of duality. However, duality does not exist in one who has attained the Supreme.

The first type of devotee described by Krishna is the sufferer. When the whole world is happy, when youth, health and wealth are in their possession, most people do not find it necessary

Jnana Vijnana Yoga

to approach him. But when everything turns against them, when friends and family desert them, when disease and hardships overtake them, they turn to him. This is the first type of devotee described by the Lord, the devotee of the emotional order. They beat their breasts and cry and weep for they have lost everything and have come to him empty-handed for help and comfort!

The second type is the devotee with practical nature, who turns to him for some material prosperity, success in examinations, success in love or in getting a job, etc. The third are the intellectual seekers, who approach him for knowledge to satisfy their insatiable curiosity for Truth. Finally, there are the men of intuition who ask nothing from him, not knowledge, not freedom from suffering, nay, not even enlightenment. They approach him because they love him. They seek him because their soul thirsts for him. They run after him, uncaring of what the world thinks, uncaring of the consequences, blind to the demands of their body and senses, prepared to sacrifice everything the world holds dear for his sake!

The Lord approves of all four categories but the last is undoubtedly supreme. The first three may be taken as preparatory steps. The Lord does not question our motive and simply accepts all those who enter the portals of *bhakti*. Though you may enter with a motive, eventually with his grace, you will become pure. There is nothing wrong in approaching God for the cessation of our pain, or in order to procure something from him. Who else should a child go to, but to her father or mother if she wants something? In fact, it is rare to find someone who depends entirely on God for her requirements! The Supreme does not reject any of the devotees who approach him, whatever be the path they choose. According to the nature of their approach, he blesses them and grants them their desires, if their faith is strong enough. These paths are but the different manifestations through which the imperfect human intelligence can approach him. The desire for the cessation of suffering, the desire for worldly benefits, for knowledge, etc., is the means by which people turn to him. Only one ingredient is common to all—faith. By the force of that faith they get their desire and the type of spiritual experience for which they are best fitted at the moment. In the course of time, through the habit of seeking for all their goods from the Divine, they would come to the state of seeking from the Divine all their 'good'! Thus, with the development of spirituality, devotion becomes one with knowledge. The soul comes to delight in the One God as the Self as also that which exceeds the Self. When we make prayer a part of our life, slowly it turns into the feeling of the presence of God at all times. The first three types attempt to bend God

Jnana Vijnana Yoga

into following their will whereas the *jnani* belongs to God, to be used by him according to his will.

QUALITIES OF THE SUPREME DEVOTEE

The *bhakta* is ever in union with God. In him is centred all her devotion. This becomes her law of life and she goes beyond all creeds, religions and rules. She has no grief or desire for she possesses all! She has no doubts or misconceptions for all knowledge streams into her. She loves the Divine with a perfect love and is loved in return perfectly. Such a devotee is known as the *jnana bhakta*, the seer saint, the devotee with knowledge and devotion. Only at the end of many existences is such a one born! Rare indeed is it to see a person who perceives everything and everyone as the Supreme! The knowledge of the Divine as all things is difficult to attain and rare to discover. God lets the flower to unfold at its own pace. It takes nine months for a foetus to become a baby and it takes a much longer time for the spiritual foetus to be born as a *mahatma*.

> *Bhaunam janmanam ante, jnanavan mam prapadyate.*
> *Vaasudeva sarvamiti, sa mahatma, sa dhurlabha!*

The distance between the human being and God gets progressively bridged as one rises on the spiritual scale and finally the distance gets abolished altogether. The Supreme object of our search is found to be the Supreme subject within us. At such a time we will come to see nothing but God and then we, as individuals, will cease to exist!

"Such a devotee is my very Self!" says Lord Krishna.

While others seize only on certain aspects of his nature, the *mahatma* or noble soul catches hold of his entire aspect and is in constant communion with him. The *jiva's* physical existence is fulfilled in such a person. When we attain unity with him, it is not that we lose ourselves but that we discover our true nature in him. This is done by a conscious giving of ourselves to him. To him who is the source of all that we are, we offer all that we are! We have come to the world as paupers and we will leave with empty hands so what can we offer him but what he has given us!

"But those whose minds have been distorted by desires resort to other gods," says Krishna.

Whatever form the devotee has faith in, is confirmed by the Supreme since he alone is the one source and foundation of all. God stoops to meet the devotee, who is struggling to reach him by whatever path he or she chooses. As long as our reverence for some god or ideal is serious, God helps us. This is because all forms are forms of the One Supreme. Thus, it stands to reason that answers to prayers to any god can come only from the Supreme. God is patient with our imperfect vision. He accepts our prayers and answers them at the level in which we approach him. Devotion of any type can never be regarded as worthless. The forms we impose on the formless are due to our limitations. He is the immutable centre of endless mobility.

"Veiled by my *yogamaya*, I am not revealed to all," says Krishna.

Sin is not a violation of a law but the source of ignorance, the assertion of independence by the limited ego, which seeks its own private gain at the expense of others. Thus, Krishna says that those who have abandoned this sin of ignorance attain that perfect knowledge which sees the same Supreme in everything.

Knowledge is the first condition of this self-surrender. The *Gita* insists that the knowledge of the *Purushottama* or the Supreme embodiment is also the perfect knowledge of the Brahman. In case Arjuna makes any mistake about this, in the last verse Lord Krishna reiterates.

> Those who have recourse to me as their sole refuge, those who turn to me in their spiritual efforts, also come to know Brahman and the whole of Nature as well as the nature of *karma*. And because they know me to be the Supreme Spirit with an all-pervading influence over the field of matter, they will also come to know me at the moment of their death!

The expressions *adibhuta*, *adiyajna*, *adidaiva* give the essential truths of the manifestations of the Supreme in the cosmos. The chapter ends with the Lord's assurance to a doubtful Arjuna that those who follow his *yoga* will reach the same Brahman which the *Upanishadic* seekers gain, by following the razor's edge of the path of knowledge!

ॐ *Hari Aum Tat Sat* ॐ

Thus, in the Upanishad of the *Bhagavad Gita*, the knowledge of the Supreme Brahman, the Scripture of *Yoga*, the dialogue between Sri Krishna and Arjuna, ends the seventh chapter entitled 'The *Yoga* of Knowledge and Discernment'.

> After an evolutionary growth of many life times is such a wise man born who worships me constantly with the knowledge that 'All is God alone'. Rare indeed is such a great Soul.

8

AKSHARA BRAHMA YOGA

The Yoga of the Imperishable Brahman

Aum Sri Krishnaya Paramaatmane' namaha!
Aum Sri Parthasarathaye' namaha.

The technical terms used at the end of the last chapter are quite confusing and Arjuna immediately asks Krishna to explain them. Krishna answers very briefly. Nowhere in the *Gita* do we find any lingering over purely metaphysical explanations. Krishna always makes us try and fit all transcendental realities into our physical actuality and thus bridge the gap between physics and metaphysics! As the Buddhist philosopher said,

> The mystic knows the root of Tao and the scientist knows the branches. The mystic does not need the scientist

and the scientist does not recognise the mystic but man needs them both!

Krishna fully realises man's need for both so he briefly explains these terms to Arjuna.

ADHYATMA

By Brahman is meant the immutable, unmanifest, formless, self-existent Being on which all the rest of creation that moves and evolves is founded. By *adhyatma* is meant the *atman*, which is of the *swabhava* or nature of the Brahman. Though confined within the body, it is not affected by the pains and pleasures of the body and does not die at the death of the body. It is the highest Self in us and is inseparable from the Brahman. As every ripple and wave in the ocean is nothing but the ocean, the secret Self or *atman* which remains constant and hidden in the recesses of every individual, is that which is known as the *adhyatma*. It is incapable of further reduction. It is because of this 'person' within us that our personalities can act and have their being. It is the immovable stage on which the individual struts and prances and plays out the drama of his mortal life. Without that stage there would be no drama and no actor.

KARMA

The word *karma* is used here in a very special sense. That action that causes the emanation of all things

Akshara Brahma Yoga

on to the stage of life is said to be *karma*. It is the kinetic power of the Lord, which ejects all types of objects for the sake of the great universal purpose. The whole of cosmic evolution is known as *karma*. All the little individual *karmas* that we perform are a reverberation or refraction of this cosmic impulse to action. This is the secret of *karma* as has been said before. In the end, all action is universal action. It is not my action or your action. Every ripple on the crest of the wave is nothing but the work of the ocean though the wave may claim it to be its own particular handiwork. Every breath that we breathe is nothing but the cosmic breath. Every exhalation is our contribution to that cosmic breath. Our intelligence is a faint reflection of cosmic intelligence. Our existence is part and parcel of the universal existence. This is the great secret behind the Law of Karma. Only by thoroughly assimilating this knowledge can we become Karma Yogis. Only when we consciously and willingly accept the fact that we are but mere instruments in the movement of the great universal *karma* can we give up our egos and our personal desires and thus become fit to be called Karma Yogis. As long as we consider ourselves to be the doers and actors, we will we be bound by the results of our actions. This is because we have consciously accepted the action as our own and hence we cannot avoid the consequences.

Normally, we are more than willing to accept the results if they are what we wanted and quite unhappy about accepting them if they go against our wishes. The Karma Yogi, on the other hand, who knows himself to be a mere instrument in the hands of the Lord, does not weep at negative results or exult at positive ones. Both come from the Lord and the *yogi* accepts both with joy. This is *prasada buddhi* as has been discussed before.

ADIBHUTA

Adibhuta is the world of physical nature, the world of our gross physical experience, the world of elements. Everything that we experience with our five senses comes under this category. *Adibhuta* is composed of the five elements or *pancha mahabhutas* and keeps changing its appearance. It is impermanent even though there is an illusion of permanency. It is just a combination and recombination of the elements.

ADIDAIVA

Adidaiva is the *Purusha* or Cosmic Person, the soul in nature, the secret Being who observes and enjoys the *adibhuta* or the world of 'becomings' as worked out by the force of the cosmic *karma* and the individual's own *karma*. How does this *adidaiva* affect us? Any experience of the world of nature by the individual *jiva* is not possible without a transcendental element being involved in it. That element is the *adidaiva*, the divinity which shapes all ends, which controls our destinies and is the deciding factor in everything. As has been mentioned before, the fruits of any action are not in our hands but are decided by some outside factor. This factor is the *adidaiva*. All these are not independent but the manifestations of the Brahman, which however is above the distinction of subject and object by which the cosmos operates.

ADIYAJNA

Adiyajna is nothing but the *Purushottama*, who is the supreme enjoyer of all action and to whom all fruits have to be offered without any expectation of personal gain. The whole of Nature is constantly offering all her fruits to him—the *adiyajna* without any ulterior motive. The enlightened being does the same and offers the fruit of all his or her actions to him without expectation of reward. It is only then that she becomes a participant in the universal *yajna* in which Nature offers all her goods to him— the secret self within her. This can be done only when she has the knowledge of the workings of the Spirit within, which is the sole witness of all action and the sole enjoyer. When we sacrifice our desire into the fire of knowledge, we perform a *yajna* and the results are to be offered to the Yajna

Purusha or the *adiyajna*. In other words, it is the Lord Himself who is present as the *adhyatma*, *adiyajna* and *adidaiva* in the body and the *adibhuta* outside and it is his *Prakriti*, which is responsible for the cosmic *karma*.

THE HIERARCHY

To sum up, first there is Brahman, the highest, immutable self-existent beyond the play of cosmic nature, beyond time, space and causality. Because of it, all things proceed but by itself it does nothing and determines nothing. It is impartial and equal and though supporting, does not select or originate. What then originates and determines? It is the *swabhava* or self-existent nature of this Supreme which gives the divine impulse to unroll the canvas of cosmic becoming into the field of time and space. This is called *karma*. The *swabhava* or self-existent nature of the Supreme is also the nature of the *jiva* or embodied soul. It is the inherent principle of divine manifestation in each *jiva*, which gives the impetus to action in every creature. Hence the insistence in the *Gita* that action which is done as one's *swadharma* should be according to the dictates of our *swabhava* or inherent nature. At each level of our existence, if left to it, this *swabhava* will propel us to our target. All this activity is known as

Akshara Brahma Yoga

karma, the action or energy of *Prakriti*, which is the kinetic power of the Supreme.

All these multifarious forms and changes of nature constitute the *adibhuta*, which is the object of the *jiva's* quest in the world. The *adhyatma* within the *jiva* revels and delights in the multifarious creation—the *adibhuta* of its own making. The divine power of the mind, will and intellect, which enable it to enjoy, is the *adidaiva*. It is the secret witness and enjoyer of the *adibhuta*.

Possessing at once the calm of the immutable existence of Brahman as well as the enjoyment of the mutable action of *Prakriti*, there dwells in the human, the *Purushottama*. In his Supreme status he is remote from us but he is also here in the body of every being, in our hearts and in the heart of Nature. Here he receives the works of Nature as a *yajna* and waits for the conscious self-giving of the human soul or *jiva*. The distinction between Brahman and Iswara, the Absolute and the personal God is clearly brought out in the *Gita*. Brahman is the immutable divine and the *Purushottama* or Iswara is the personal God, the object of our devotion.

The *jiva* revolves from world to world in the action of *Prakriti*. All that it had been and consciously desired determines its present birth. All that it thinks and does in this life up to the moment of its death determines what it will become in the worlds beyond and in the lives to come. If birth is a becoming, death is only a birth into a new becoming. It is certainly not the end. The remaining portion of the chapter answers Arjuna's last question as to the fate of the *jiva* after death and the way in which a man has to conduct himself at the point of death in order to attain union with the Divine.

DEATH

The importance of the state of mind at the moment of death is emphasised both here and in the Upanishads. The phenomenon of death is something that has terrified us from the beginning of our existence on earth. We can never understand it and what we cannot understand, we fear. The phenomenon of birth is equally inexplicable to us. From where did the little baby come? Where was it before it took up residence in the mother's womb? These are questions to which we can find no satisfactory answer, but at least after birth the creature is visible to our eyes, so its previous invisible state does not bother us, but after death the whole body on which we set such store, disintegrates and this we cannot bear, because we do not know the reason for it. Thus, we find that in all languages the very word 'death' is considered most inauspicious and some other word is used

Akshara Brahma Yoga

to denote it. We say instead, "he has passed away", or "is no more", etc.

Arjuna's question was, "How are you to be realised by the self-controlled man at the time of death?"

Arjuna accepts that there is a method in dying as there is in living. In fact, the method of our dying depends entirely on the method of our living, is Krishna's answer. He who leaves the body remembering the Lord attains him. Of that there is no doubt. At the time of death, the body is abandoned by the *jivatma*, which proceeds on its way to its future destination. Whatever we think of deeply in our hearts at the time of our departure from this world shall fructify into the form, which we will experience in our next birth. This is the psychology of rebirth. The final thought at the critical time of departure from the body, is that to which the *jiva* must go since it is *Prakriti*'s business to work out the *jiva*'s desires through her action or *karma*. So the *jiva*, which desires to attain the state of the *Purushottama*, has to think of him at the time of death. Death is not a punishment meted out by the Creator but it is part of a natural law. Transmigration is a necessity for the *jiva* allowing it to proceed in the direction of the Supreme. By falling and getting up several times a child learns to walk, so also by living and dying many times the *jiva* learns the types of action, which will take it towards God! Once we attain true knowledge, the process comes to an abrupt end. Spiritual evolution begins when the *jiva* consciously accepts the fact that there is something called God or the Supreme. Then there is a deliberate orientation by the *jiva* of all its actions, both mental and physical, towards this Supreme Reality. Nature insists that we shall attain whatever we entertain in our hearts as the dearest of our objectives. Every desire has to be fulfilled because it is connected finally with the fulfiller of all desires! Whatever we ask for shall be given, so think how careful we have to be in our asking, for there are very few of us who really know what we should ask for! And if we ask for God himself at the time of death, to him we shall go. Of that there is no doubt! This sounds an easy method but it is not as easy as it sounds! We cannot live a dissolute and evil life and expect to remember God at the end of it. It is not the casual fancy of the last moment but the persistent endeavour of the whole life that determines the future birth.

SAMSKARAS

Life is full of the play of *samskaras* or tendencies, which are imbedded into the subconscious by repeated action. Every action and every thought leaves a faint trace in us and builds up tendencies of the mind known as *samskaras*. When water starts to run down in a special path, every time more

Akshara Brahma Yoga

water is thrown, it will have a tendency to run down the same path. Similar is the case with our actions both mental and physical. We may not remember every one of our actions in the past but *samskaras* or familiar patterns of behaviour are stored up in our memory and tend to reappear when similar situations occur and force us to react in the same way. If we were to keep a diary, only a few of the major events of each day would be jotted down. At the end of the day, it would be impossible to write down every single thing we thought or did. At the end of the month, if we were to write down the events of the month, most of the details of the daily diary would be skipped over and only the outstanding events would be noted. Important actions and events leave an impression and others fade away. Though innumerable actions are performed and endless knowledge is acquired, the mind retains very little of it. Out of all these, only a few *samskaras* remain and those are our true earnings for this life.

THE LAST THOUGHT

The businessman keeps his daily and monthly accounts of income and expenditure and at the end of the year, the accountant checks this and arrives at a single figure, which might be either profit or loss. This is also the case with our lives. At the end of our life a single, firm, clear, figure remains in the column. This final figure depends entirely on our daily balance sheet. Thus, the target on which the mind wishes to fix itself at the time of death should perforce be the one towards which it was growing at every moment of its daily life. At the moment of death we can never expect to think of something which we have not trained the mind to think of during the major portion of our life! The fruit of the tree is nothing but the essence of the whole tree and if our last fruit has to be sweet, the whole of our life must also have been lived in sweetness. Our last thought is the cumulative force with which the whole personality is ejected like a rocket out of this physical system towards that which it has consciously directed its thoughts during the major portion of its temporal life. At the end of our lives, it would be impossible to think of some casual occurrence. The mind would automatically rotate towards the major passion of its earthly existence.

Just as butter comes out of milk as its very essence, so also our last thought is the cream of our life. The idea that *yoga* is only for the old and that there is time enough to think of God at the end of our lives when we have nothing better to do and thus gain liberation, is a notion of those who do not know the law of cosmic living. First of all, none can say when our last moment will occur. It may come today, it may come tomorrow,

Akshara Brahma Yoga

and it may come fifty years hence. What guarantee is there that we will be able to think of him at that time when we have frittered away all the days of our earthly sojourn! For an actor to remember his lines when he goes on to the stage, he has to practice them for quite a while before. So also the nature of our final exit would depend on the amount of practice we have put in previously.

Thus the Lord tells Arjuna, "Think of me at all times and fight. Thus thinking you will undoubtedly come to me."

This applies to all of us. We are all warriors on the battlefield of life and no one can say when we might be hit by a passing car or have a heart attack. No astrologer can give us a guarantee of the exact date of departure from this life, so the wise warrior is one who thinks of God constantly and fights. Thus, it will not matter to him at what moment the fatal blow is struck. Therefore, *yoga* has to be continuously practiced as the teacher has been reiterating in every chapter. The *Gita* is not satisfied with a religion, which is reserved for certain days, or certain times. It demands nothing less than the total dedication of our entire life to him at every moment—*nitya yoga*. The thought of God has to be enshrined in one's heart throughout life if one wishes to go to God at the end of it. The Law of Karma though strict is also just. It knows no friends or foes. There is no hope of bribing your way to a marvellous future. Hence, it is incumbent on us to act in tune with this law, which is the will of God. If we regard all actions as our own personal effort, which is directed towards to the attainment of some personal and selfish aim, the reaction will surely come and we will have to experience the consequences, either good or bad. If however we take our stand on the knowledge that all action is divine action, then we become instruments in the hands of the universal power. Like the flute in the hands of Lord Krishna, we become mere instruments through which the Divine plays his music. We are no longer agents of the action but mere instruments. The thought of God who is the sole agent will ever be present in our minds and we will no longer accumulate positive and negative consequences from the action.

At the critical moment of death, the importance of our state of consciousness becomes evident. It is not the deathbed remembrance of our usual mode of thinking which is meant here. This is not the usual religious indulgence, which makes the deathbed confession and absolution, a passport to Heaven, even after having lived a profane and uncharitable life. What is meant here is an undeviating *yoga* of constant communion by which alone one achieves union with the Supreme *Purushottama* at the end of our life. Thus, the *yoga* of the *Gita* can well be called *nitya yoga* or the *yoga* of constant communion.

THE PURUSHOTTAMA

The *Purushottama* of the *Gita* can be equated with the Brahman but there is a slight difference. He is not a relationless Absolute standing aloof from our life, but an ever present participant in the game of life, ready and willing to give help at all times if called upon. He can be compared to a perfect charioteer of a vehicle who if left alone can and will carry the passenger to her right destination. Hence Krishna's role as the charioteer! However, it is to be noted that if the owner of the chariot demands that the charioteer follows his orders, the charioteer will no doubt accede to her wishes but in that case, the owner has to take total responsibility for the outcome of the action. Though the *Purushottama* is at once the seer, the creator and ruler of all these worlds, he gives us freedom to exercise our own will and direct our own chariot if we wish to do so. It is only when we understand the truths of life, which have been explained so far, that we come to realise that our safest course of action would be to allow the *Purushottama* within us to take over the reins of our chariot. This is the whole allegory of the *Bhagavad Gita* and Arjuna's request to Krishna to become his charioteer. Even after having taken up the reins, the Lord does not advise him until Arjuna makes the final surrender of his ego and begs Krishna, the *Purushottama* to tell him how he should act. From then on to the end of the battle you find that it is Krishna who decides the mode of action. The *Purushottama* like the Brahman is the self-existent Being of whom the Vedas speak. He is the supreme goal of the *jiva's* journey through this space/time continuum, which is not a movement at all, but only a return to its original status. It is only by knowing him and loving him as 'Vaasudeva Sarvamiti'—God is all—that we will get absolute release.

POINT OF DEPARTURE

The *Gita* now describes the state of the mind of the *yogi* at the time of his departure from this life. A motionless mind, a soul armed with the strength of *yoga*, united with the *Purushottama* through *bhakti*, the life-force drawn up and fixed between the brows in the seat of mystic vision, the intelligence concentrated on the utterance of the sacred syllable *Aum* and the constant remembrance of the Supreme. This is the perfect *yogic* way of departure from life. The final offering is of our entire being, to the *Purushottama* who has been our constant companion in the battle of life. But this is only the goal. The essential condition is the constant, undeviating memory of him even when engaged in battle! The state to which the *jiva* arrives when it departs

Akshara Brahma Yoga

thus, is supracosmic. The highest heavens of the cosmic plan are subject to rebirth. But there is no rebirth for the *yogi* who departs in this fashion. This practice is only possible for those who can choose the moment of their death by the power of *yoga*. The highest heavens about which Krishna speaks of here is called 'Vishnor paramam Padam' in the *Bhagavad Purana*.

In another chapter the body has been described at the city of the nine gates. At the moment of death, the devotee should close all these gates, fix the mind in the heart *chakra* and the *prana* in the *sahasrara chakra*, and chant the *mantra Aum*, remember God constantly and thus departing, he or she attains the highest state.

Maybe Krishna saw Arjuna's perplexed look so he says comfortingly,

> I am easily reached by one who constantly meditates on me and leads a disciplined life. Having reached my state, these great souls do not return to the impermanent world of sorrow for they have reached the highest.

COSMIC CYCLES

In order to make the cycle of births and deaths clear in the mind, Lord Krishna describes the ancient theory of cosmic cycles. There is an eternal cycle of alternating periods of cosmic manifestation and non-manifestation called the night and day of Brahma—the Creator. Day is the period of cosmic manifestation and night of non-manifestation. These are of equal length of time and keep alternating. At the coming of Brahma's day the whole manifest world emerges and at the coming of his night, this manifestation will vanish. Our own days and nights are reflections of this. When we sleep the world does not exist for us and when we wake up, the world comes into being. This periodic emergence and dissolution does not affect the Brahman—the Lord of all existences. Krishna says that this supracosmic condition can be achieved through *bhakti* by a conscious giving of our entire being to that *Purushottama*. The Brahmic state is also the supreme abode of the *Purushottama* or the personal God.

Next is given another curious thought of early Vedanta. The paths, which have to be taken by *yogis* who want to return to a mortal existence and the paths of those who do not want to return, are given here. These are called the dark and bright paths. Fire, daytime, the bright fortnight, and the six months of the year when the sun goes towards the north is known as the bright path. Proceeding by this the *yogi* will not return. Smoke, night, the dark fortnight and the six months of the sun's movement towards the south are the dark path of constant return. The year is divided into two parts of six months each. The six months of the northward movement of the sun are known as

Uttarayanam and the six months of its southward movement – *Dakshinayanam*.

The psychological idea behind this description comes from the age of the mystics who saw in every physical phenomenon an effective symbol of the psychological and who traced every action of the inner mind with the outer forms of nature. Fire and light have ever been symbols of spiritual energy. The path of light implies a gradually ascending movement of the consciousness in the direction of the Divine and the path of darkness, the opposite. Life is a conflict between light and darkness. The former implies release and the latter rebirth. *Yogic* experiences show that in the struggle between the godly and demonic forces in the mind, the former tend to have a natural prevalence in the bright periods of time and the latter in the dark. Most crimes are committed at night and so on. The main point which is made here is that those who live in the night of ignorance are subject to re-birth and those who live in the day of knowledge will be liberated.

Krishna reiterates that the states which result from the study of the Vedas, sacrifices, austerities and gifts are all lower stages and cannot be compared with the bliss of the *yogi* of the *Gita* who is in constant communion with the *Purushottama*.

Thus, the main point of the chapter is that one should make our whole being one with the Divine so that naturally and spontaneously our minds will turn to him at the time of death. For this, the whole of life should be a meditation. The remembrance of God should not be just an occasional affair of the mind but the natural condition of our life and the very substance of our consciousness. Then the *jiva* is one with the *Purushottama* in this life itself and the transition from life to death will no longer be a terrifying shock but a beautiful melting into the arms of him who has been enshrined in our hearts at every moment of our waking state and figuring in every one of our dreams during the hours of sleep and to whom we have perforce to return joyfully and with full consciousness.

ॐ *Hari Aum Tat Sat* ॐ

Thus, in the Upanishad of the *Bhagavad Gita*, the knowledge of the Supreme Brahman, the Scripture of *Yoga*, the dialogue between Sri Krishna and Arjuna, ends the eighth chapter entitled 'The *Yoga* of the Imperishable Brahman'.

9

RAJA VIDYA RAJA GUHYA YOGA

The Yoga of the Sovereign Knowledge and Sovereign Secret

Aum Sri Krishnaya Paramaatmane' namaha!
Aum Sri Parthasarathaye' namaha.

Each verse of the ninth chapter is saturated with devotion and drenched with love for God and as we begin to read it, we become aware of the fact that we are indeed proceeding on the royal road leading to the *Purushottama*. It is as if Krishna decides to stop beating about the bush and reveal the whole truth of what it means to be in love with the cosmic beloved and to be loved in return by him. This is a truth, which has been revealing itself slowly in all the chapters but now Krishna makes an open declaration of his love for humanity.

Hence, this chapter is placed in the middle of the *Gita*, just as the *Gita* itself is placed in the middle of the *Mahabharata*. Krishna takes care to draw Arjuna's attention to the importance of what he has to say by declaring this to be Raja Vidya and Raja *Yoga*—the sovereign knowledge and sovereign secret—the highest and purest knowledge which has to be experienced directly. No amount of talking about it can really explain the ecstatic feeling which the beloved of God experiences. What is meant here by *jnana* is metaphysical knowledge and by *vijnana*, scientific knowledge. We have two methods of obtaining the truth—intuitive as well as intellectual. *Jnana* is that knowledge which is beyond words but which can be tested on the touchstone of direct experience. Now the doubt may arise whether such knowledge would not be too difficult to practice. In order to dispel this doubt, the Lord says that it is very easy to practice when one understands it and faithfully tries to live up to it. Faith in this *dharma* is an essential ingredient, without which one will not be able to follow it. The *jiva* that fails to get faith in this higher mode of life must perforce return to mortal life again and again until this faith is generated. For this is a faith born of experience and not something to be argued about by the intellect. One has to grow into it, to become it. That is the only way to verify it. One cannot grow into something, which one denies mentally. It is only by going beyond the lower self and the inexhaustible arguments of the un-evolved intellect, which goes by outward facts, that we can understand the love of the divine. It is not a matter for argument but one which can be verified by direct experience.

GOD IS IN THE PRESENT

When we read these verses we feel as if Krishna is making a desperate attempt to make his dear friend Arjuna, and through him an unthinking humanity, understand how close God is to us. His presence permeates and enlivens every single thing. Our mind is prone to maintain an unbridgeable gap between the Divine and us. It converts God into a future possibility and not a present existence. We are prone to think that God can perhaps be contacted tomorrow or the day after or perhaps only after death and after many births but never now and at this moment.

This is a psychological error based on the notion that the *jiva* is a separate entity from him and exists in a different time-space continuum, totally different from the continuum in which God exists. In the next few verses the *Gita* emphatically asserts that God is inclusive of everything and enfolds into himself all beings, all individuals, everything that exists. There is nothing on earth or heaven, which has a separate identity and existence apart from him, so that nothing can ever be, if God was not to be! Therefore, we cannot exist as a present phenomenon and cast God into a future existence. If we are sure that we have a present existence, we can be equally certain that God is also a present existence. In fact, God lives in a state which is beyond time and space. Time unfolds before him like a canvas—the past melting in the present and flowing into the future. Nothing is unknown to him. If we could but make him the director of the drama of our life, he would accomplish everything for us.

The sovereign knowledge which Krishna gives in the ninth chapter is that the incarnation is indeed nothing but the Brahman. Illumination of the highest order will come to us if we worship Krishna, the incarnation, with this knowledge. Direct contemplation of the Absolute is much more difficult. Because Arjuna believes in Krishna, this knowledge is given to him. But those who do not have faith in him must perforce return to the world of re-birth.

EVERYTHING IS DIVINE

> Everything is permeated by me. I sustain all beings. As the all-pervading air eternally dwells in space so also all things eternally abide in me.

Whatever was whatever is and whatever shall be, is engulfed in his infinitude. He is the cause of all causes, as well as the effect. He is both creator as well as creation. Those who know him thus, adore him, worship him, and sing his praises in many ways. The One Absolute is the manifold creation, and is revealed in each and every single thing. All faces are his face, all forms his form. Every speck of space, every atom of matter can be regarded as a mirror, which reflects his face. Even to think of him is to drown our little self in an indescribable ecstasy of joy in which the ego would melt like mist before the glory of the rising sun.

Now Krishna makes a strange pronouncement: "Everything exists in me but I am not in them!" How is this to be understood? Though the Supreme is all manifestation, he is also beyond it. What we see in the world is only an illusory self-created form or *roopa* and not his actual form or *swarupa*. In fact, he has no form. Formlessness is his form! All this mass of becomings and existences cannot contain him either in their sum total or in their separate existences. Though everything exists in him and because of him, he does not exist in them or because of them. All things are his becomings. He, however, is their Being! He is at once one with all this, yet he exceeds everything immeasurably! Their non-existence would not affect him or change him. Though fish live in water, water cannot be said to live in the fish! The mystery of his being is that he is supracosmic and not extra cosmic.

That infinite being lives in a timeless and spaceless continuum out of which this mutable and finite universe has been projected by only one ray of his infinite powers. Totally uninvolved though he might be, the fact is that he has a constant and intimate relationship with this world of becomings. His presence alone is enough to set the mighty machinery of the world process into existence. But this cosmos cannot be a complete expression of his greatness even though it is indeed his manifestation.

This esoteric truth cannot be understood till we attain another state of consciousness, so for the time being he makes use of the terminology of space and time and asserts that everything exists in him as air exists in space. Space is the background on which all phenomena take place. Air exists in space but does not consist of space and has nothing which is essentially in common with it.

CREATION

Unmanifest *Prakriti* when enlivened by the Unmanifest Brahman produces the objective universe. Creation is described as a pressing down by him through his *Prakriti*, which lets loose the whole phenomena of existences in a cyclical order of creation and dissolution. The *jiva* follows the cycle of its own becoming in ignorance, circumscribed by its own *karmic* nature. In ignorance it is subject to *Prakriti*'s wheel of *karma* and is dominated by her. Only by a return to its own divine consciousness can the *jiva* realise its destiny and attain freedom. The Supreme that supports and pervades these workings of *Prakriti* is not affected by her changes because he does not participate in them. He is only the witness. It is something like a wise mother who watches her child playing in the mud and does not reprimand. Even if the child falls, she does not rush to his aid unless he asks for help. In this way she helps him to develop faster and become self-reliant.

The Supreme precedes and exceeds all the workings of *Prakriti* and is the same before, during and after, all these processes that take place in the vast cycles of time! Even though the Supreme controls creation and dissolution, he is not involved in them and is above the procession of cosmic events. Yet, since *Prakriti* is his nature, he is immanent in everything she creates. Even though this is not the whole truth of his existence, yet it is an important truth and those who ignore his presence in creation and despise the divinity clothed in human form, whether manifest as in the *avatara* or veiled as in the world of living beings, becomes prey to the nature of the *rakshasas* or demons who see everything as separate and are prepared to sacrifice everything for the insatiable satisfaction of their own separate egos. However high such people may appear to be in mortal life, yet all their knowledge, their actions and their hopes are in vain, says the Lord, for their knowledge is a false knowledge which sees the many but misses the one, a blind hope which chases after the transitory and misses the eternal and a useless action whose fruit is a failure from the spiritual angle since it is something which brings satisfaction only to themselves. But those who know the truth of his being, worship him in all ways. They value nothing for its own sake but for the sake of the all-blissful divine within.

CONSTANT YOGA

Life is a constant *yoga* for the devotees. Their knowledge is an inevitable part of their life and it turns to adoration and action, for to know him is to love him and to love him is to act for him. In fact, *Karma Yoga* is love in action. All our activities are then offered as a *yajna* to him. Though the ancient Vedic sacrifice is a powerful ritual, yet the real *yajna* is the inner oblation in which the one who conducts the *yajna* experiences the truth that the Divine Himself is the ritual, the sacrifice, the fire and the offering. All that is received from him is given back to him in an act of worship. He himself is the Veda as well as that which is made known by the Veda. He is both knowledge as well as the object of knowledge. He is the father who creates as well as the mother who sustains and lavishes on us the sweetness of her love and fills this universe with her manifold forms of beauty. He is master and ordainer, the path and the goal—a path in which there is no fear of getting lost and a goal which he himself leads! He is husband, home, country, refuge and friend—the imperishable seed and the origin of all. It is he that burns in the heat of the sun and the flame and he who gives rain and withholds it. Death is his mask and immortality his self-revelation. He is both existence and non-existence. To see nothing but the Divine, to be at every moment in union with him, to love him in all creatures and delight only in him, is the enviable state of the beloved of God. Human perfection is a combination of knowledge, devotion and action. The Vedic ritualists who worship him with sacrifices find their way to heaven and enjoy heavenly delights. They return to the mortal world when they exhaust their stock of merit. If heaven is our goal, we will indeed get it but we will have to return to this mortal existence as long as we do not attain the *summum bonum* of life. Human life is very precious since it gives us an opportunity to attain our divine nature. In the twenty-second verse, Krishna makes a solemn promise that those who worship him constantly without any recourse to anyone or anything else will be protected by him in all ways. If we surrender totally to him, giving up all other loves, he will take up our burdens and lead us to eternal bliss.

Even those who worship other gods actually worship him for he is the sole enjoyer of all acts of worship. But people do not realise this and so they are likely to fall. Those who worship the *devas* or the shining ones, the ancestors and other spirits will all receive limited results since their devotion is not of the highest quality. Only those who worship him with knowledge will get the highest state of unity.

Does this mean that such a person misses out on the joys of life and that his physical life will be a failure? In order to disabuse the mind of the devotee on this point, the Lord gives a solemn promise in the twenty-second verse that he himself will cater to all the needs of such a person. Both his acquisitions and their safekeeping will be taken care of, by no less a personage than the Lord Almighty Himself. The needs of a devotee who worships him with the *yoga* of constant communion will be completely looked after. He will take care of everything that belongs to the devotee and also lead her to liberation. Even a thousand fathers and mothers cannot equal God in his compassion and concern, in his love and care! The love that God has for us is a million-fold greater than the love that we think we have for God. His overall care is infallible because he is present everywhere, at all times. Whenever we are in need, whatever the time of night or day, whichever the place, he is immediately present to cater to our needs, to rescue us and succour us, to help us and to comfort us, so long as we are united with him mentally. The joys of heaven and earth are mere shadows compared to the ecstasy, which engulfs such a devotee. As the devotee grows into him, the Divine also flows into the devotee with all the light, power and joy of his infinite existence. This is the highest knowledge, according to the Lord, as well as the highest secret. This is an esoteric truth, which can only dawn in the heart of one who has totally obliterated her ego. That is why he calls it a secret. Only one who has experienced it can believe it. Thus, it is not to be shouted from the treetops for nobody who has not experienced it will believe it.

RELIGION

Ordinary religion is actually a sacrifice to the partial godheads and not to the integral divinity. Men consecrate their lives to these partial powers of the divine existence as they see them. But even this, if they do with faith, will be justified because the Divine accepts whatever symbol of himself is present in the mind of the votary and rewards her according to the faith that is in her. With its usual generosity, the *Gita* accepts all sincere religious belief to be a seeking after the One Supreme and Universal Godhead, for after all he, the Supreme, by whatever name you call him, is the only one to whom we can offer all our actions or rituals or whatever else you want to offer. He is the only enjoyer, experiencing through various forms and bodies. However low or misguided the form of worship, however limited the idea of the Supreme, however restricted the offering, still the faith and effort to go beyond the veil of one's small ego is always rewarded and there is an immediate response. But naturally the worshipper has to attain the form or idea worshipped by her. Until her ideas change and all her offerings and actions are to the highest, she will have to go from form to form until she attains the Supreme Form, which is beyond all forms. Absolute self-giving and a single-pointed surrender of the mind to the Divine is the crux of the *Gita*'s message. It is not important what you give, but how you give. Even if it were a leaf, flower, fruit or water, he will delightfully accept it, if it is offered with love. But even this special offering of a material object is not necessary.

Lord Krishna says,

> Whatever you do, whatever you eat, whatever you offer as a sacrifice, whatever you give, whatever austerity you perform, offer it to me!

The slightest circumstance of life, the most insignificant gift of what one has, the smallest action assumes a divine significance and becomes the most precious offering to God, who makes it a means for raising the devotee to the pinnacle of his own status.

GOD IS IMPARTIAL

The Divine is equally present in all existences, therefore he is equally a friend to all and enemy to none. None has he cast out or eternally condemned. In the end all have to go to him alone. Single-pointed love for him and a total submerging of the mind in him is the swiftest way. If this self-surrender has been made with faith and sincerity, anyone can have access to him, anyone can enter the temple of divinity. All worldly considerations disappear in the presence of the Supreme. There is no demarcation between the sinner and the saint.

"Even if a man of evil conduct were to turn to me with sincerity and an offering of his entire love, he should be considered a saint," is what the Lord tells us.

"He will become the soul of spirituality very soon and obtain eternal peace."

This verse does not mean that there is an easy escape from the Law of Karma. We cannot prevent the cause from producing an effect. Arbitrary interference with the Law of Karma is not tolerated. When the sinner turns to God with total surrender, a new cause is introduced. His redemption is conditional on his repentance. When the *jivatma* surrenders his heart and mind to God, the divine takes up the burden of his life and lifts him up to a spiritual plane. The piece of coal becomes golden when it enters into the fire.

In other words, this pure self-giving brings an immediate response from the Divine. To her who surrenders her all, the Lord gives himself. To others may be given the petty objects of their desires but to her who asks for nothing and yet gives her everything, the Lord also gives the highest prize of all, the gift of himself! By the force of her love, the devotee tears apart the veil between herself and God! Such love annuls every error, which might have been committed previously, and thrusts aside every obstacle. To the ignorant he gives knowledge, to the feeble he gives power and to the sinner, a divine purity. Their weaknesses are swept away in the might of is strength.

"This is my promise," says the divine charioteer to Arjuna, "My devotee shall never perish!"

NO DISCRIMINATION

This is the royal path which is reserved not for the elite but for all devotees. There is no class or sex discrimination. God does not judge by the external show but he looks into our hearts and when he finds it filled with love, we are allowed to go on this regal road. On this road, paved with the love of the human heart, man and woman find their equal rights. The Divine is no respecter of social or sexual distinctions! All can approach him without fear or trembling. Down this supreme path, the Brahmin leading a pure life and the outcaste, born of the womb of sin, travel with ease! No doubt the purity of the wise Brahmin and the saintly king has their value but this value lies only in as much as it makes it easier for them to achieve self-surrender since they have the knowledge. But even without these benefits those who take refuge in him, find the gates of God opening for them. It matters not whether it is the tradesman (*vaishya*) preoccupied with the getting and spending of wealth, the servant (*shudra*), hampered by a thousand restrictions or women who in the past were shut in and stunted by the will of man, or outcastes on whom their past *karmas* have imposed the very lowest of births. In this glorious *yoga* of love, all external distinctions cease. This was indeed a revolutionary statement for Krishna to make. In the Vedas, liberation was reserved for the upper castes alone and women of whatever caste could gain it only through the service of their husbands. But the Lord in his extreme compassion brings the God of the Vedas into the arms of the afflicted and the outcaste, and demands nothing but a total self-surrender of the ego. Neither austerity nor charity, neither knowledge nor birth can be compared to this constant outflow of love towards him. This is the famous doctrine of *prapti* advocated by the Vaishnava saints, many of whom belonged to the lower castes. The ignorant human being is bound to a wheel, which turns through endless cycles of births and deaths. Man suffers only so long as he attaches himself to this narrow wheel of sense objects. The way to liberation is to turn from the outward to the inward, from the appearance to the reality. Love for the world, which is only his mask, should give way to love for God—the face behind the mask! By the mysterious power of a divine *yoga*, the *jiva* has come into this world of dualities and by a reverse movement of the same *yoga*, it can transcend the limits of its phenomenal nature and retrace its steps to the divinity from which it came! No amount of intellectual arguments can convince us of the existence of God. Only by establishing a direct contact with him through the process of *nitya yoga*, which is the process of emptying oneself of one's limited ego, can we come to realise him. Once this

Raja Vidya Raja Guhya Yoga

inner God is known and embraced, the whole of life undergoes a sure and swift uplift.

> Fix your mind on me, be devoted to me, worship and revere me. Taking me to be the goal and disciplining yourself, you will surely come to me.

To make the mind one with the divine consciousness, to make the whole of our emotional nature turn towards him, to do every action as a *yajna* to him and all our thoughts into adoration of him, the Divine Beloved, to direct the whole self towards him is the sure way to rise above the trammels of this mundane existence. It is the synthesis of the three *yogas* of *jnana*, *karma* and *bhakti* wherein all the aspects of our personality are directed for that one purpose for which they were given to us. The *jivatma* realising its true nature, divorces itself from the clamouring demands of its phenomenal existence and turns to God for its entire support. No longer does it depend on friend, lover, husband or adviser. God plays all roles for this devotee. Hence, this is called the royal road, "the Supreme secret and the Sovereign science"!

ॐ *Hari Aum Tat Sat* ॐ

"Thus, in the Upanishad of the *Bhagavad Gita*, the Knowledge of the Supreme Brahman, the Scripture of *Yoga*, the dialogue between Sri Krishna and

Arjuna, ends the ninth chapter entitled 'The *Yoga* of the Sovereign Knowledge and Sovereign Secret.'

> However for those who think of me alone, making me the sole object of their worship, who are in constant communion with me, I myself will provide for their every need and safeguard their possessions.
>
> *Chapter 9, Verse 22.*

10

VIBHUTI YOGA

The Yoga of the Divine Manifestations

Aum Sri Krishnaya Paramaatmane' namaha!
Aum Sri Parthasarathaye' namaha.

The message of the *Gita* is not merely a detached turning away of the mind from the world to God. It is a technique by which the mind is made to recognize and become aware of the divine within us and outside us, through the methods of *yoga* as described by Lord Krishna. A sure sign of this increasing union is the lessening of the individual ego. By degrees the person becomes aware that there is a force within her which is capable of directing all her actions if she allows it to work without interference of the personal ego. This realization is what reduces her ego. Knowledge is what makes the normal self-centred and selfish person into an impersonal being, who is directly acting according to God's commands. We become one with God through knowledge and a conscious will directed towards him, culminating in a supreme self surrender and love.

This love is not restricted to God alone. It sees all beings as manifestations of the One Being and thus love extends to all creation. Such a *yogi* does not retire from the world but continues to act in the world for the sake of the Divine in it and not for the fulfilment of her egoistic desires. She does not even work for the sake of a social ideal! Even though she is ever ready to help all people and may even be involved in some noble enterprise, which will benefit the society, yet her purpose is not social but spiritual. She is not interested in creating an ideal socio-economic society but a society which acts with the awareness of the divine within it. It is of course a fact that such a society will be an ideal society but this is a side benefit. The *Gita*'s purpose is to call Arjuna and through him, all humanity, to this type of action, to make a person aware of the power that is in him or her, which is acting through her. It was for this end that the *avatara* became his charioteer.

All religion is a seeking for the Divine and all *yoga* is a striving for union with him. According to the extent of our knowledge will depend the

Vibhuti Yoga

way of our search and the goal that is reached. But the human is a mental being and can approach the Infinite only by making use of our finite mind. Therefore, it would be good for us to have some finite conceptions that our mind can cling to. We need some form or at least some ideas, which our mind can seize upon. We cannot think of the formless as has been said and we long to have some concrete shape through which we can arrive through direct experience to the reality, which the form signifies. The saint and the *yogi* might be able to experience the truth of 'Vaasudeva Sarvamiti' or 'God is all' and have the vision of all things as God but for the rest of humanity, this is not a direct experience. We may mouth this formula a thousand times, yet remain unconvinced, and even though we may say we are intellectually convinced, our actions prove otherwise. It is our ignorance that makes us think that the Divine is shrouded in an impenetrable mystery, which our minds can never fathom. In one way it is true that our small intellect can hardly comprehend the cosmic mystery but on the other hand we find that the whole of nature is an open book through which we can discover him if we had the eyes to see! In this chapter, a part of the mystery of the world existence is revealed, for who can exhaust its infinite depths? Which is the religion, which can claim to have shut up in its brief system the entire significance of the world mystery and the cosmic existence?

METHODS OF SEEING HIM

In order to help us in this, Lord Krishna lovingly declares to Arjuna in the tenth chapter that he will give him some important hints that will enable him to control his mind in an easier fashion and to discover Reality in and through the manifest world. Arjuna is beloved by him and delights in his words and this is why he gives the discourse to him. He alone can reveal himself for as he says not even the gods or the sages know his origin for even they have come after him! He dispels the ignorance of those who have surrendered their egos to him and fixed their hearts on him and confers on them the light of wisdom.

"They, who know me as the unborn and the mighty Lord of the worlds, are undeluded and free from sin."

All emotions and dualities emanate from him in accordance with the *karma* of all beings. He is indirectly responsible for the pain and suffering of the world even though he is unaffected by its oppositions.

> Understanding, knowledge, freedom from illusion, patience, truth, self-control, calmness, pleasure and pain, existence and non-existence, fear and fearlessness, non-

> violence, equality of mind, contentment, austerity, charity, fame and calumny are all proceeding from me alone.

The seven sages and the Manus, who are progenitors of the human race, proceed from him. One who knows this truth about him will be always united with him. The devotee will begin to participate in the work of the world, understanding it to be his manifestation. Then Krishna goes on to say that God or Iswara is both the material and efficient cause of the world. The true devotee is not deluded by the changing forms because she knows that the Supreme is the source of all forms. To those who are thus constantly devoted to him, he grants the divine understanding or *buddhi* by which they will attain him. He destroys the darkness of ignorance by the shining lamp of wisdom, is what Krishna says. In fact, as has been mentioned before, *bhakti* becomes a means to *jnana*.

Arjuna then asks him to name those aspects of Nature in which the Lord's presence is more clearly manifest so that they will be an aid to meditation.

As has been mentioned before, the *Gita* does not set up an opposition between the Brahman and the world, between the Transcendent Reality and its inadequate expression. It is easier to approach the Supreme through its relation with the world since he is also the personal God who controls the action of nature and dwells in the heart of every creature. The *Parabrahman* (Supreme Infinite) is also the *Parameshwara* (the supreme incarnation and controller of the world).

> O Arjuna I will declare to you my divine forms, which are most prominent since there is no end to my glories.
>
> I am the Self seated in the hearts of all creatures. I am the beginning, middle and end of everything.

This comprehensive statement makes it very clear that he is everything that can be conceived of by the human mind and senses. The world is a living whole—a cosmic poem written and sustained by him. However, there is an ascending order in the world. The divine is revealed more in those things with life than in matter, in consciousness than in life and in saints than in ordinary mortals.

The sun and moon are his eyes and the air his breath, is what the Vedas declare for the Vedic *rishis* looked around and saw nothing but God. Unfortunately, we have lost that innocence of outlook. We pride ourselves on being able to see things with the clarity of the sophisticated vision. But this very sophistication is what hides him from our gaze. The great intellectuals try to arrive at this Reality through the tortuous process of an abstract negative knowledge. They negate the visible in order to discover the invisible, negate life in order to find its source. In the end, knowledge itself is negated in the unknowable. But this abstract method of self-negation is not for everyone because not only our intellect, but also our hearts, will and senses yearn to know and experience that Supreme and thus find a justification for their existence. The greatness of the *Gita* lies in its holistic approach to the discovery of that Reality.

RELATIONSHIPS ARE IMPORTANT

The divine is the source of all relationships so he can be approached by us by enfolding all relationships. There are a thousand ways in which God is secretly in contact with us so the approach to him is many-sided. God does not deliberately make himself difficult of approach by us. Only one thing is needed the indomitable will to break through the veil of our ignorance and a persistent seeking by the mind and heart for that which is really all the time closest to us. Once the sight has been fixed, the way chartered and the wheel turned towards the goal, the Master Himself will send a favourable wind to take us to the goal. This Godhead is not just our *ishta* or favourite form like Krishna, Christ or Rama for such names and forms are only the faces of that one Supreme, who is the universal Lord and goal of all religions. All creation is a manifestation of this one Infinite. The world of space and time is his phenomenal self-extension. Therefore, we have to see and adore him in all things animate and inanimate, to worship him in sun and star and flower—in man and mouse and mountain. This Godhead is the fulfilment of all relations—father, mother, lover, friend and refuge. Thus, he is ever before our eyes, ever present. It is we who cannot recognize him in his humble, ordinary form. If he came in an extraordinary form, we might recognize him but in these ordinary forms we do not have the eyes to see.

EXTRAORDINARY MANIFESTATIONS

Lord Krishna understands Arjuna's problem, which is the human problem—we cannot think of him as wearing an ordinary garb. Therefore in the tenth chapter is given the theory of the *vibhutis*, which will enable us to see him in all things. *Vibhutis* are the majestic manifestations of God. They are the extraordinary manifestations of might and glory, which we see in the world. This is an easy way to learn to see him. There are two methods, which are generally used in teaching in the nursery class. One is to introduce the letters by writing them in capitals and once the children have learnt to read and recognize these, their size is reduced. The other method is to teach the easy letters like 'A', 'I', 'T' and 'L', which have just straight lines, and then go to the difficult letters which have curves, like 'C' and 'S' and lastly to the combination letters of lines and curves. We are also in the nursery class of spirituality.

Vibhuti Yoga

So this is the method which Krishna uses to teach Arjuna in this chapter. Though we have been told countless times that God is in all things, we just can not perceive him in everything. So first we should try and see his presence clearly in the grand things—in the magnificent and the mighty, like the oceans and the mountains. Once we have learnt to recognize him in these, we shall recognize that every drop of water and every grain of sand, which makes up the ocean and the mountains, are filled with the same divinity. There is no difference in meaning between capital 'A' and a small 'a', between the large and the small. The grossness is only apparent and actually comes from the subtle.

COMPLICATED FORMS

The first step is to recognize the Supreme in forms that are easily seen and from there we can go on to the more complicated types. For instance, the divinity manifest in Krishna or Arjuna can easily be seen but not so in Duryodhana and Dusshasana. The divinity in a Christ can easily be seen but not in a Judas. In Rama it is evident but what about Ravana? The second of each team is a combination letter, which the child has to learn the hard way. We have to see him in the good before we can go on to the villainous. The Lord who is in Rama is also in Ravana. What is found in the simple is also found in the complex.

The Vedas say, "Salutations to the Prince of robbers! Salutations to the cruel ones, to the doers of harm, the thieves, the thugs and the robbers. Salutations to them all!"

The book of creation is the Lord's picture album filled with self-portraits but we do not recognize him in these strange roles. The divine is the unborn, eternal, and has no origin. Nothing existed before him from which he could have been born and nothing can exist if he ceased to exist, which in any case is an impossibility. The person who knows him in reality as the Unborn is lifted beyond the limitations of mortality. God is not a negation, empty of all relations. He is the Supreme Positive, soul of all souls, mind of all minds. All cosmic relations proceed from him. He does not create from a void but out of himself. But even though it is true to say that all are in him, we should not misunderstand that he is limited by their becomings. Though assuming multifarious forms, he continues to remain formless and infinite. The *Gita* stresses the distinction between Being and becoming but does not turn them into opposites. All becomings are but a temporary expression of the Absolute. In him lies the positive key to their mystery, the reconciling secret of their existence. The mind and intellect as well as all the various feelings of all creatures emanate from him alone. Therefore, this knowledge on the emotional plane becomes an ecstatic love and adoration of God. The heart delights in the greatness, beauty and perfection of this Being, now seen everywhere. The whole consciousness becomes full of grace and replete with his fullness. All speech and thought become an utterance of his glory.

Arjuna accepts the knowledge that has been given. His mind is delivered from its doubts and from the baffling appearance of the world, to its Supreme basis. He has recognized his charioteer's real identity as the Supreme *Purushottama*, the Supreme Person. He has accepted the truth and is prepared to act with self-surrender but he desires a deeper understanding. He accepts the revelation that 'God is all' but feels the need for other supports like the rest of us. So he asks for a complete enumeration of the sovereign powers of the Lord's becoming.

O Lord of *yogis*,

he says,

How can I know you through meditation? In what manner arte you to be contemplated upon? Tell me more and more of it. It is the nectar of immortality and however much I hear, I am not satiated.

GLORIES OF GOD ARE INEXHAUSTIBLE

The divine teacher accedes to his request but with the reminder that a full tabulation of his glories is not possible, for God is infinite and so his manifestations are also infinite. Every form is the symbol of some divine power. To the seer, each finite thing carries within it, its own revelation of the Infinite. The objective facts of nature are only expressions of the subjective and always go back to the spiritual cause of their appearance. In lower nature, the expressive power of God gets disfigured through ignorance. Thus, everything originates from him, not merely the good and the beautiful but also their opposites like, ignoble, grief, destruction, fear and ugliness. Such things vibrate painfully on our sensitive ears. We are ever ready to see him in the sublime aspects but the mind balks at seeing him in the bad for it is opposed to the sublimity of our concept. In order to avoid this problem, the Semitic religions created a devil on whose poor head all evil could be cast so that we can still believe in our fairy tale God who can only do good. Hinduism never played this game of make-believe. We cannot deny the fact that good and evil exist side by side in the world. We have to accept the fact that both come from God alone. Otherwise, we will have to accept the fact that our God is far from being omnipotent. In fact, he appears to be impotent for it appears that the devil can bring down everything that God creates. Thus, the *Gita* teaches us to see him equally in man and beast, in noble and ignoble, in sinner, criminal and saint! This is a difficult task and some indications are needed, some supports called for, in this effort at oneness and this is what Krishna gives in the remaining verses.

ASCENDING POWER OF THE INFINITE

This chapter has been called the *vibhuti yoga* because though we must impartially identify ourselves with the divine in all its manifestations both good and evil, we must at the same time realize that there is an ascending and evolutionary power in Nature, a secret something that carries us upwards from the first concealing appearance through higher and higher forms towards the ideal nature of the universal Godhead. The list begins with the statement of the first principle that underlies all existence—the fact that God lies concealed in the mind and heart of everything and every creature. He is the beginning, end and middle of all that has been and will be. This divine consciousness develops its powers from plant life to animal, human and superhuman life. Seen from this angle we will realize that all things are in fact *vibhutis* of this universal spirit, all is a *yoga* of this Master Yogi, a self-creation of this marvellous creator. But the fact is that he reveals himself only through the power of his becoming. To our limited human eyes, he is especially apparent in what is of prominent value. So in each classification of species we can perceive him most easily in those in whom the power of his nature has reached the highest. We must remember that respect for the divinity in everyone is not diminished but given a deeper significance by lifting our eyes to the highest in each species.

CLASSIFICATION OF CATEGORIES

The chief among all living beings, cosmic godheads, superhuman and subhuman creatures, can be considered as a special power or *vibhuti*. Krishna declares that amongst luminaries, he is the sun, the mind amongst the senses, Himalayas amongst mountains, the lion amongst animals, the Ganga amongst rivers and so on.

> I am the glory of the glorious, the victory of the victorious. The resolution of the resolute, the purity of the pure and gambling amongst the fraudulent! I am the divine seed of all existences!
>
> There is no end to the list of my divine glories O Arjuna! What I have told you is only a brief description of my unlimited splendour!

Time is the most evident power of his becoming, and the essence of the whole universal movement. Therefore, he declares that he is imperishable, endless time. He is also the universal Spirit of destruction, who seems to create only to undo his creation. Rebirth and re-creation keeps

Vibhuti Yoga

pace with death and destruction. The divine is the sustaining Spirit of the present, the withdrawing Spirit of the past, the creative Spirit of the future—Brahma, Vishnu and Maheswara—the trinity of Hinduism.

The finite alphabet can never enumerate the list of infinite glories so after having given a few examples, he sums up the whole discourse with the following verses:

> All the beautiful and glorious creatures you see in the world, all the mighty and forceful humans, sub-human and super-human, are but a spark of my splendour. But what need is there for further details O Arjuna! Take it from me that I am in all and I constitute all. There is nothing other than me. I support this entire universe with a single ray of my illimitable power and infinitesimal portion of my fathomless spirit. All these worlds are but sparks coming out of me, who am eternal and immeasurable.

THE LESSON

The lesson of this chapter is first to train our eyes to see him in the large and simple letters and then proceed to the small and complex until at last one achieves the spiritual vision to see the whole world of matter as nothing but the divine Spirit! Thus, the partial human consciousness expands and becomes more and more aware of God underlying everything. Yet, it has to be understood that the highest power is only a very partial revelation of his infinite power. Even the whole universe is only one small portion of his greatness, illuminated by one ray of his splendour, fascinating us with only one tinge of his beauty.

The liberated person does not see nature as we see it. In everything she sees the divine *Prakriti* secretly awaiting the opportunity to evolve. She sees the action of both the godly and the demonic as the actions of the Divine wearing these masks. It is the play of the divine Shakti that is in the meekness of the lamb as well as in the ferocity of the lion. Arjuna himself is a *vibhuti*, the chosen instrument of the divine will. The historical cycles of humanity are a progressive movement towards the unveiling of the Godhead in the soul and life of humanity. Each great movement is a divine manifestation. Arjuna is the key figure in this great work, terrible in appearance but essential for a long leap forward in the march of the race. Therefore, he must become the divine man capable of doing the work consciously as an instrument of the Divine. For this he must be able to see the aspect of the Godhead as Time not merely in its creative aspect but also in its destructive aspect. Thus, in the next chapter this figure of God in his mighty and terrible aspect of Time is to be revealed to

Arjuna the *vibhuti*, the chosen representative of the age.

ॐ *Hari Aum Tat Sat* ॐ

Thus, in the Upanishad of the *Bhagavad Gita*, the knowledge of Supreme Brahman, the Scripture of *Yoga*, the dialogue between Sri Krishna and Arjuna, ends the tenth chapter entitled 'The *Yoga* of the Divine Manifestations.'

> I am the origin of all creation. From me everything proceeds. Knowing this, the wise, filled with devotion, worship me.
>
> *Chapter 10, Verse 8.*

11

VISWAROOPA DARSHANA YOGA

The Yoga of the Vision of the Cosmic Form

Aum Sri Krishnaya Paramaatmane' namaha!
Aum Sri Parthasarathaye' namaha.

The description of the Universal *Purusha* as given in the eleventh chapter is one of the most poetic and powerful passages in the *Gita*. It is invoked by Arjuna's desire to see the living image, the visible greatness of the unseen Divine. The illusion that all things exist separately from God has been dispelled from his mind. The tenth chapter showed him that God resides in all things, good and bad. There is nothing apart from him. The whole cosmos is but a revelation of that Godhead. Now

Arjuna begged to be granted a graphic portrayal of that One in which is contained all these myriad manifestations! This was indeed a startling request but the Lord, because of the love he bore him, was willing to grant even this. It is one thing to know that the Eternal Spirit dwells in all things but to have a vision of that form in which all these things live, is a totally different thing. Arjuna has been shown how the many live and have their being only in the One and now he yearns to see with his own eyes an all-comprehensive vision of that One!

INFINITY AND ETERNITY

We use words like infinity and eternity regarding space and time without the least idea of what they mean. This world is but a small part of the universe and even this small part we cannot see, in its entirety. When we look up at the night sky, we see innumerable stars and planets. If we had strong telescopes we would see still further stars. With more powerful instruments we might see even more. What we see is just a tiny portion of infinity. The world on which we stand is itself only a speck in space and we ourselves are not even specks and yet we glibly talk of infinite space as if we knew all about it.

What about eternity? Our knowledge of past history goes back to almost ten thousand years. It is equally impossible to conceive of the time that is yet to come. Just as our earth is only a mote in the infinity of space so also our human span of perhaps hundred years or even ten thousand years is a speck in the eternity of Time! The river of time is ever flowing forward. We neither know its source nor its end. We see only a few drops of the flow in the middle. The Supreme is above both space and time, so the cosmic vision has to be a timeless, spaceless experience, which by our very nature is impossible for us to see. But since Arjuna was very dear to him, the Lord could not refuse. This mighty warrior, whose pride had been totally humbled, had become a child before him and thus Krishna could not refuse even this seemingly impossible vision. The tenth chapter showed the various different manifestations of the divine. The eleventh chapter is the very opposite. It unifies all the differences and presents to Arjuna a unified whole in the one body of the divine.

> You shall see my divine forms by the hundreds and thousands, various in kind and shape and colour. You shall see today many wonders that none have beheld. You shall see the whole world related and unified in my body and whatever else you wish to see, is what the divine charioteer declared.

It is the vision of the many in the One, the vision of beginningless, infinite space and endless, eternal Time that Krishna showed Arjuna. How can the human eye behold this? The cosmic vision is the vision that God himself has in respect of the whole of creation and thus it can be seen only through the eyes of God and not through human eyes and so the Lord tells Arjuna that he would give him divine eyesight.

In the following verses, the poet tries to capture and enclose this infinite, eternal vision into the cage of ordinary language. Words have to be employed as vehicles in the description of this glory since we have no other instruments. Even the highest poetic genius has to employ images, which belong to the world of language. Hence, usually we find that the one who has actually had a divine experience is silent. Through his silence he speaks volumes. If he spoke at all it would be blasphemy. So here we find that Arjuna is struck dumb, by this dazzling vision and the poet describes it through the mouth of Sanjaya, since Sanjaya was seeing it on a television screen as it were, while to Arjuna it was a real life experience.

THE COSMIC VISION

The Supreme form which was made visible to Arjuna was that of the unbounded Godhead whose faces and feet and arms were spreading to infinity, in whom were seen all the wonders of existence, watching with innumerable eyes, speaking with innumerable mouths, armed for battle with numberless, divine uplifted weapons, bedecked with divine ornaments, robed in heavenly garments, adorned with garlands of divine flowers, fragrant with divine perfumes. If one were to look at the noonday sun in the tropics one would go blind, and here was a light, which was as brilliant as if a thousand such suns had risen all at once on the firmament. Arjuna saw this dazzling vision of the Godhead, which was at once supremely beautiful as well as terrifying, the vision of the One who had manifested this wild and wondrous world, and he was struckdumb! Arjuna looked up and saw this mighty vision stretching far above him and below him and all around him. He himself was enfolded within this vision so that he could not see where it began and where it ended. This is something which we might feel when we look up at the sky and see space stretching far beyond our vision.

The description of the Universal Being in the *Purusha Sukta* of the Veda is very similar to this.

> If the light of a thousand suns were to blaze forth all at once in the sky, that might resemble the splendour of that exalted Being.

Apparently, Oppenheimer, the maker of the atomic bomb, repeated this verse from the *Gita* when he watched the blast.

Arjuna gave one look at that form which was enfolding him with its splendour. He was terrified

Viswaroopa Darshana Yoga

and his hair stood on end. He could not bear to look at it for more than a few seconds and threw himself down before that mighty form. For a long time he lay thus, trembling with fear. At last he raised himself up and began to hymn the fearsome form with words, which were an outpouring of his entire soul.

"O Lord of Lords!" he said,

> I see in Thy body all the gods, Brahma seated on the lotus seat, sages and other divine beings. I see numberless arms and feet and eyes and faces. I see Thy infinite forms stretching on every side but I do not see either Thy end or middle or beginning.

> I see Thee with mace and discus and many uplifted weapons, yet I can hardly bear to look at Thee for Thou art a mass of blazing energy on all sides. Thou art the supreme immutable. Thou art the foundation and abode of the universe. Thou art the imperishable guardian of the eternal laws, the soul of all existence.

The form filled all the regions and occupied the whole space between heaven and earth. It had a terrifying aspect—the image of the destroyer embracing the world with its numberless, uplifted arms all carrying weapons of destruction. The sun and moon blazed from its enormous, fiery eyes. The blazing furnace of its face was burning up the whole universe with its energy. Its mouth was agape to devour, and it had terrible tusks on which some of the heroes and generals of both armies were pierced, while others were bleeding and crushed between the mighty canines. Like moths into fire, all the nations seemed to be rushing with helpless speed into its mouths of flame. All regions were being baked in the fierce heat emanating from this strange Being. The world was shaking with terror and so was Arjuna.

"Declare to me O mighty Lord, who Thou art for I am ignorant of Thy workings," was his pitiful cry.

In a thunderous voice the mighty figure replied,

> I am the Lord's power as Time O Arjuna! I am the great destroyer. Everything that happens is due to my power as Time. In my form as Time these people have already been killed. Arise and slay those who have already been slain by me. Be thou my instrument alone O Arjuna!

Kala or time is the prime mover of the universe. It is that which is perpetually creating and destroying. The Supreme of the *Gita* takes responsibility for both creation and destruction. He has control over time because he is above it. He knows how events come to pass due to causes, which have been at work for years and which are now moving towards their natural effects. We cannot prevent these effects from fructifying by doing anything now. The destruction of the

Viswaroopa Darshana Yoga

Kauravas has been decided irrevocably by their acts committed long ago. The Law of Karma is an impersonal law and will pursue its own ends. No one can gainsay it.

This law has already decided all things which are to come and Arjuna's part is to be an instrument alone. If he refuses to fight, he will be guilty of presumption for no individual can encroach on the inevitable workings of the Law of Karma. This is the greatest teaching of this chapter and of the *Gita*—that we have to act with the attitude that we are mere instruments in the hands of the divine. All action whether bitter or sweet has to be performed by the human being with the attitude that we are only instruments of the Supreme. Thus acting we will incur no sin. The dictates of this law have to be worked out through human beings. The role of the instrument is most befitting for the devotee for then there would be no ego involved. In another chapter, the Lord had already stated that all action is performed by his *Prakriti*. The confused human being thinks herself to be the sole doer of the action. As long as she considers herself to be the doer, she has to face the consequences of her action, which she has claimed as her own. The moment she realizes that God alone is the actor, she is no longer chained by her actions whether good or bad. She learns to accept them for what they are worth and thus frees herself from the clinging bondage of the Law of Karma. This is the intellectual understanding. But the devotee's approach is slightly different. To Arjuna, the devotee, the Lord's advice was to play the role of the instrument. The instrument is not responsible for the good or bad music, which is played by the musician. It needs only to keep itself in a state of surrender to the whims of the musician. So Arjuna, like the flute in the hands of Lord Krishna, needs fear nothing, neither success nor failure, or life or death for he has surrendered everything into the hands of his divine charioteer.

BEYOND TIME AND SPACE

This vision is supposed to widen our horizon and allow us to soar into solar space. We come to a realisation that God's creation is not limited to our tiny planet, which is only an insignificant speck in the cosmos. Our visualisation of the world is within the framework of time and space. We cannot see the past, present and future at the same time. The cosmic vision however is a timeless piece of eternity, where everything is a here and a now. Human beings are occupied with one object after another. We think consecutively but the divine mind knows everything at one fell stroke. The experience that Arjuna had was that of a total grasp of the whole cosmos as extending endlessly in space and existing constantly in time. In the cosmic

Viswaroopa Darshana Yoga

vision there is no difference between past, present and future, as we know it. Everything is a magnificent here and now. So Arjuna was told that in this timeless comprehension of God, everything has always existed. All action has already been accomplished in the firmament of infinity and eternity. The war has been fought and won and the only thing left for the mortal hero is to carry out the will of God without egoism, merely as an instrument, without personal enmity, hatred, desire or ego. Hearing the resonant, thunderous voice of the mighty figure of God as *Kalaswaroopa*, (the Spirit of Time), Arjuna trembled and quaked and in a voice choked with emotion, hymned the vision. His words proved that behind, the mask of this awe-inspiring figure he recognized the reassuring reality of his beloved friend who had come to him in the form of his charioteer.

> O Lord of Lords, abode of the universe! Thou art the Imperishable! Thou art the primeval one, the ancient person, and the supreme abode of the universe. Thou art both the knower and the knowable. Thou art all the gods, Yama, Vayu, Agni, and Varuna. Salutations to Thee a thousand times over and over again, from the front, from the back and from every side, for Thou art each and all that is. Infinite in might and immeasurable in strength, Thou pervades all. Thou art everything. Thou art the father of all this world of moving and unmoving things. Thou art the one to be worshipped and the most solemn

object of veneration. None is equal to Thee in all the three worlds.

Having said this, Arjuna was overwhelmed with the feeling of shame at not having recognized this mighty figure in the humble guise of his friend and cousin, Krishna. So far he had seen the humanity alone and had treated Krishna as a mere human creature. He had not pierced through the mask, to the God of which the humanity was only a symbol. He was appalled by his stupidity and begged for forgiveness.

> Not knowing Thy greatness and taking Thee to be my friend I have addressed Thee familiarly as, O Krishna! O Yadava! O friend! Through negligence, fondness, or force of habit I might have slighted Thee while sitting, walking, eating or lying, either alone or in the company of others. O Krishna! For this I beg Thy pardon, offering myself at Thy feet. I appeal to Thee, O adorable Lord, pray pardon me, as a father would forgive the faults of his son, a friend of his friend and a lover of his beloved. I have seen that which was never seen before and I rejoice, but my heart is troubled and filled with fear. Therefore O gracious One, show me Thy other and pleasing form once again.

The Supreme is not a transcendent mystery but as close to us as any of our relations—a father, a friend or a lover. Of course, the fact is that he is even closer—he is our very Self.

REASON FOR THE VISION

However, this vision is not the final goal of our search. If that were so, the discourse would have ended here. Even *Samadhi* is not the end of the religious life. The vision as shown to Arjuna served two purposes. The first was to make Arjuna and through him all humankind realise that all aspects of nature arise from God alone. He is Brahma, the creator as well as Vishnu, the preserver and guardian of the eternal law. He is also Rudra, the performer of the dance of destruction, Kali his consort with her garland of skulls, trampling over the world amidst the din and destruction of battle. He is the gentle breeze as well as the powerful typhoon, the life-giving rain as well as the destroying tidal wave, the flood, the famine, and the fire, the earthquake, revolution and ruin! This is the aspect from which Arjuna's mind as well as ours turns away in terror since we find it hard to understand and harder still to accept. Like the ostrich we hide our face from this aspect in the hope that we may escape seeing it and in so doing, escape also from being seen by it! The cowardly human heart wants only comforting truths or in their stead, pleasant fables. It balks at facing the complete truth. Most religions pander to this human weakness. Hinduism does not play this universal game of hide and seek. It places squarely before the mind of man both the terrifying as well as the fascinating aspects of the Divine. Arjuna, the mighty Aryan hero, has to be taught to look truth courageously in the face and see that God and God alone made the world as it is. We have to face the challenge of Nature devouring her children—Time eating up the lives of all creatures. We have to accept the fact that the bed of pain and the touch of bliss are both his. We have to recognize that behind the grim visage of Kali is the sweet face of the divine mother ready to suckle her young. In the midst of destruction, we find the protecting arms of the friend of all creatures.

The *asuras* or ego-filled ones who are ignorant of this, flee in terror but the *siddhas* or the perfect, all-knowing ones, bow before him in adoration. Nothing has need for fear except that which has to be destroyed, and that is only ignorance.

GOD IS OUR FRIEND

This vision is only outwardly the figure of the destroyer, Time, who destroys all finite forms. The inner truth of the vision is that all these finite forms are really found within God. It is a dual appearance of all that is and all that is not, of all that appears and all that disappears. It is also the vision of the Supreme, which holds all things together in the single eternity of an ever-present Now. This is his final truth in which all opposites are reconciled.

Viswaroopa Darshana Yoga

He is the inner preceptor who develops in man the truth about himself. All our knowledge is only a partial unfolding of his infinitude. This is the important lesson to be learnt from this vision.

The next is the idea that this great Godhead is also to be found in man. Like a stunning blow this thought hit Arjuna—that in the body of his friend who was sitting beside him, who had sat by his side, lay beside him on the same cot, ate with him from the same plate, in this ordinary figure of a mortal was all the time concealed, the *avatara*. Having seen this universal reality in the individual frame, the Divine clothed in humanity, he was aghast at the enormity of his crime in having insulted this divinity. We also should be aghast when we think of how we too are prone to miss this divinity lurking within everything. Our minds can barely see the 'humanity' in man, let alone the divinity. Thus, the cosmic vision was shown to Arjuna so that he would be able to go beyond the humanity and discover the divinity in everything and everyone. Arjuna was able to see it because he was given divine sight but such a vision would be too much for us, as it was even for Arjuna. The gulf between the cosmic form and the individual soul is too much, so a bridge is necessary for us. This bridge was created by the *avatara*, Lord Krishna is the universal godhead clothed in humanity, who can help us to raise ourselves through an intimate relationship with him. This relationship between God and the human is closer than the closest bond between man and man. The awe and adoration with which the finite creature bows down before the awe-inspiring Absolute deepens into the most intimate love, which thrives on the enchanting qualities of the cosmic lover. We begin to understand that he is the sum total of all relationships—mother, father, brother and beloved. The intense love between man and God is sweeter and deeper than any human love. The Hindu philosophy accepts that this gap can be bridged by any of the *avataras*—Krishna, Rama, Christ, Mohammed or any other. To Arjuna, however, this bridge between him and the transcendent lay in the beloved figure of his friend and charioteer. So he begs Krishna to appear before him in that same enchanting form. Responding to Arjuna's request, the Lord once again appeared before him in his original form of sweetness and beauty. But once again he pointed out to Arjuna the importance of the cosmic vision.

> In this mortal world O Arjuna! I cannot be seen in this form by anyone else. It is not to be seen through the study of the Vedas nor through rituals, charity or penance.

Why is it that this form cannot be seen through all the ordinary endeavours of human beings? By various means a person can come to know many of the exclusive aspects of the divinity. But that in which at one and the same time and in one and the same place, all is manifested and revealed, is impossible to achieve except though constant communion. Only through a perfect adoration or *bhakti* can the intimate union of God and man be achieved. This is the crown of both action and knowledge. To know, to see, to enter into and become one with that Supreme Consciousness is the goal, which the *Gita* proposes for its master *yogi*. Until and unless the little self melts away into the 'All-self', this vision is not going to materialize. Any austerity or charity, even in the name of religion or spirituality, which retains even a trace of the ego, is against the requirements of this great realisation. Thus we come to the last verse of this chapter, which according to Adi Shankara, the great exponent of the Advaita Vedanta philosophy, contains the quintessence of the *Gita* as well as of all religions.

> O Arjuna, he who bears enmity towards none, who stands impartial and free from attachment and serves me selflessly, who dedicates all his actions to me, who is filled with devotion and is free from passion and desire, who is free from malice to all beings, such a devotee will attain me!

This is the quintessence of *bhakti*. The devotee who considers God as her only goal in life, who thinks of him alone and who loves all equally since she sees her beloved, clothed in every human form, only to such a person will the cosmic vision become a continuous state. Absolute love for the Supreme, who is found equally in all, is the way to that spiritual fulfilment which is the *summum bonum* of human life.

ॐ *Hari Aum Tat Sat* ॐ

Thus, in the Upanishad of the *Bhagavad Gita*, the knowledge of Ssupreme Brahman, the Scripture of *Yoga*, the dialogue between Sri Krishna and Arjuna, ends the eleventh chapter entitled 'The *Yoga* of the Vision of the Cosmic Form'.

> There within the body of that God of gods, Arjuna saw the whole universe with its manifold divisions unified into one whole.
>
> *Chapter II, Verse 13.*

12

BHAKTI YOGA

The Yoga of Devotion

Aum Sri Krishnaya Paramaatmane' namaha!
Aum Sri Parthasarathaye' namaha.

The *yoga* of devotion has already been touched upon in all the chapters starting from the 7th. In all these chapters, the devotion which has been described is both to the transcendental Supreme and the *Purushottama*. In this chapter, the question asked by Arjuna is about devotion to the personal God. It is to be noted that Lord Krishna embarks on the confusing doctrine of *bhakti* only after having driven into Arjuna's mind and therefore into our minds that devotion to be really true has to come only after having understood the nature of that Supreme to which devotion is to be given. After this knowledge has been instilled, the seeker has to start on unselfish action done for the sake of the divine alone. He or she has to act as a selfless instrument of the divine and not for any personal reason. Only such a person is fit to be given the esoteric teaching of *bhakti*. Devotion which is devoid of knowledge will definitely lead to fundamentalism, which is what we are witnessing in the world today. Of course, it is also true to say that knowledge alone without the spark of devotion will be a dry and arid thing. Arjuna has understood all this but he is still perplexed about the relationship between the Brahman and the *Purushottama*. Devotion he feels can be given only to the *avatara*—to the form of his beloved friend and charioteer but where does the picture of the impersonal Brahman fit into this? Which is better, worship of the impersonal Brahman or the personal Iswara, this is Arjuna's question. This doubt of his will be cleared in this chapter since it is a doubt which has troubled all devotees.

LOVE DEMANDS RECIPROCATION

Bhakti comes from the Sanskrit word *bhaj*, which means to serve and therefore *bhakti* is service of God and intense attachment to him. It is love which demands nothing in return and in which all works are dedicated to him. Devotees are not even interested in liberation and have absolute subjugation to the will of God. The *bhakta* is *sarvarambaparityagi* or one who instigates nothing. She waits patiently for god to make the first move in everything and prompt her to act. In the *Bhagavad Purana*, the great devotee Prahlada defines the nine attitudes of *bhakti*: *Sravanam, keertanam, Vishnor smaranam, padasevanam, archanam, vandanam, dasyam, sakhyam*, and *atmanivedanam*. Hearing the tales of the Lord, singing his praises, constant remembrance and service to all since they are all forms of the Lord, constantly offering everything to him, bowing to him in all things, through the attitude of the servant or the friend and finally complete surrender of oneself. These are the nine attitudes of *bhakti*. Adoration is the essence of *bhakti*. The greatest *bhakta* is one who sees the Lord in everything and the lowest is the one who sees the Lord only in the idol. However, the duality between creature and creator is basic to *bhakti*. Even though non-duality is the truth of his Being, duality is the truth of his becoming. If one does not know this fact, duality alone will be misleading and can lead us into strange paths and cults but when our understanding has been enlightened, we perceive that duality is equally beautiful and is essential for the sake of worship.

Arjuna is very familiar with the current Vedantic view of the transcendent Brahman, aloof and intangible, above all personal relationships.

In the second chapter at the very first discourse, Krishna mentioned the attainment of this Being as being the initial step in the spiritual path, and thus emphasized its great importance. Up to the first six chapters, knowledge has been emphasized since it is the basis of all understanding and the foundation of spirituality. But from the seventh chapter onwards the Lord seems to be increasingly insistent on the adoration and love, which has to be offered to the Supreme. But such an adoration of the Supreme Brahman seems impossible, for love demands some sort of reciprocation, an intimate personal closeness, which the impersonal Brahman seems to be incapable of giving. From the seventh chapter onwards, Lord Krishna has been hinting about an all-consuming love, which is prepared to give everything, and demands nothing, which holds within it the highest power of release from the stranglehold of the ego. Love without the sacrifice of the personal ego is not love at all. The true lover is prepared to renounce everything for the sake of the beloved. The mother is prepared to sacrifice her very life if necessary for the sake of her child. But can such a love be given to the impersonal Brahman, is the question. The Impersonal wants nothing. It is merely the witness of our joys and sorrows and does not participate in the world process. But we feel from the depths of our being that there is something else which

Bhakti Yoga

actively participates and remains with us always, helping and guiding us throughout our lives. Krishna has been hinting at such a Being, which has both the impersonality of the Brahman as well as the adorability and accessibility of a personal deity. This is the *Purushottama*, the Supreme who embodies itself and projects that part of its own being, which is filled with *ananda* or bliss. Though the impersonal Brahman has the three aspects of existence, consciousness and bliss—*sat, chit* and *ananda*—the bliss aspect is always hidden from our eyes. It is only when it projects itself as the *Purushottama*, who is capable of taking on the form of the *avatara*, that the aspect of bliss comes to the forefront. When Krishna refers to himself in the first person singular, it is not only to the transcendent Brahman but also to that which is both transcendent as well as immanent. He is *Purushottama*, Parameshwara and Paramatma— Supreme Person, Supreme Lord and Supreme Soul, all at once. It is to this Godhead in the unity of all his aspects that our work and knowledge and adoration have to be directed in a constant *yajna*. The liberation promised by the *Gita* is not just an absorption into the Vedantic Supreme, but it is all kinds of union at once, for the divine is capable of many roles and all roles at the same time. He can be many things and all things simultaneously and separately to all mankind, such is the glory of this

Parameshwara. To limit him just to one or another of the roles which ordinary religion thrusts upon him, is to do him an injustice and betrays our total ignorance of his mighty powers. In the various chapters of the *Gita*, you find described many types of union—a complete absorption, an ecstatic dwelling, and an identity of the liberated nature with the divine nature—an eternal nearness as well as a oneness of power and glory. All these are suggested in the *Gita*. It must be remembered that till this time this difference between the Impersonal Brahman and the *Purushottama* had not been clearly defined though constantly referred to. Here Krishna makes some differentiation but the final definition will be made only in the fifteenth chapter.

The current Vedantic view which Arjuna knew and recognized was the *yoga* of pure knowledge, of the Supreme Brahman, intangible and above all relationships, but now he was confronted with the vision of the Godhead whom he has been told to adore with all aspects of his being, so he asks this pertinent question at the very beginning of the chapter.

WORSHIP OF THE FORM

Which of the two types of yogis is better—they who worship you as the *Purushottama* with form or those who worship the formless, unmanifest, incomprehensible Supreme?

Bhakti Yoga

The Lord replies with great emphasis:

> Those who fix their mind on me through constant communion and who are possessed of supreme faith, I hold to be the most perfect of *yogis*. However, even those who worship the immutable, transcendent will reach me provided they are lovers of humanity.

Once before, in the fifth chapter, Arjuna had questioned him on the respective merits of the Karma Yogi and the Karma Sannyasi to which Krishna had emphatically stated that both were equally good yet of the two, *Karma Yoga* was better since if had more utilitarian value. Here also the Lord's preference for the worship of God with form as against the formless Brahman is based on practical considerations. In the *Gita*, metaphysical truths are not expressed solely for their own sake. The highest truth has the highest practical value. Spiritual verities are not to be studied for mere intellectual satisfaction or even for spiritual satisfaction. These truths are to be known because they lead us from our present mortal imperfection to our actual, immortal perfection. The *Gita* is, above all, a text on the practical application of spiritual truths in our daily life. Time and time again the lord has insisted that knowledge which has no utilitarian value is of no use to the spiritual seeker. A religion, which emphasizes a heaven after death, finds no place in the *Gita*. If there is a heaven, it should be found here and now is what the teacher of the *Gita* insists. Worship of the Impersonal is not as practical as worship of the *Purushottama*. This is why the *Gita* says that worship of the Supreme with form is better. Krishna does not say that it is the only way but that it is more practical. We are all creatures with forms and our minds are so made that we can only think of forms so how can such a mind be made to concentrate on the formless? As the Puranas say, the mind can only think in terms of *nama* and *roopa*—name and form. This is why there is always an insistence in the *Gita* that the lover of God should also be lover of humanity. Those who profess to love him without recognising him in all creation are not considered to be true devotees.

In the *Avadutha Gita*, the sage Dattatreya asks,

> How can I bow to him who is formless, undifferentiated, blissful and indestructible, who has through himself and by himself and in himself filled everything?

Both *Karma Yoga* and Karma Sannyasa lead to the same goal but the former is both the way and the goal while the latter is the end alone. Here also the Lord says that while both these types of devotees attain the same goal, the fact remains that the path of the devotee of the *Purushottama* or God with form is much easier for the embodied human

Bhakti Yoga

to follow. He does not denounce the former but only points out the greater utility of the latter. A thousand-rupee note is equal in value to a thousand one-rupee notes! But the latter has more utilitarian value since the one rupee notes can be used in any small tea stall while the thousand rupee note will only be taken in a big shop. Actually a comparison between the *saguna* and *nirguna bhaktas* or the devotees of God with and without form is as unfair as that between the Karma Sannyasi and the Karma Yogi. The comparison can only be made from a practical point of view and not on a spiritual one.

If a mother were forced to choose between her infant son, who depends entirely on her, and her elder son, who is a system analyst, whom would she choose? Naturally she would have to give preference to the infant, not because she loves the elder any the less but because the former needs her more. Similarly, the devotee who has no other recourse but the Lord and clings to him as her sole and only support in all aspects of her life—spiritual, material, mental and intellectual has perforce to be helped by him in all aspects. This type of complete surrender is the easier path since the entire responsibility of our lives will then be in the capable hands of the Divine. But according to all current notions, worship of the Unmanifest through the path of knowledge or *jnana* is the superior path. Arjuna's question voices the doubt of all intellectuals.

THE SUPREME YOGA

The supreme *yoga* is that which sees God in everything and to its eye the manifestation and non-manifestation are one and the same. The perfect union is that which encounters the Divine at every moment, in every person and in everything. But those who seek by a hard ascent to reach the unmanifest immutable, also arrive to him provided they are equal minded to all and well-wishers of all, says the lord, for they are not mistaken but they follow a more difficult path. The feeble instrument of the human individuality lodged in this body cannot comprehend the loftiness of God's impersonality. We are persons and no stretch of imagination can tell us the meaning of utter impersonality, so the devotees of the impersonal Brahman impose on themselves a painful struggle against their own nature. They deny themselves all types of satisfactions and by constant suffering and repression they strive to reach their goal. The Supreme Impersonal neither accepts nor rejects all who clamber up to it nor does it offer any assistance. Everything has to be done by severe austerity and individual effort. The Lord has already mentioned that howsoever a man approaches him, in that same manner would he go to him. So if the devotee chooses this austere path, the Lord will remain impersonal and remote, waiting for him to approach by his own unaided effort. But just because this path is more difficult, it must not be assumed that it is the higher or more effective path. Even those who find unity with the Supreme still have to work for the welfare of the world—*sarvabhutahite rathaha.* The liberated ones rejoice in the doing good to all creatures. Krishna always stresses that service to humanity is an essential part of *yoga.*

TOTAL SURRENDER

Actually this *yoga* is not as easy as it appears on the surface for Krishna demands nothing less than a complete submerging of our ego into the Divine through a constant communion and we as egoistic individuals will find this most difficult. This total surrender is known as *prapti.* In this we simply place ourselves in the hands of God leaving him to deal with us as he chooses. We have absolute faith that he knows what is best for us as the small child has faith that its mother knows best. When we empty ourselves of the ego, God takes possession of us. To fit into the divine pattern, all our personal claims have to be surrendered. The obstacles to union with God are not only our vices but our virtues our knowledge, demands, pride and prejudices. So we see that this path is not as easy as we think it to be. The only reason it is called easier is because on this path we are never alone and can continuously ask for help and every time we fall, we can cry and stretch our hands out to him and he will come running. He will pick us up and put us on the right path. The devotee of the Impersonal, however, has to hobble along, however painfully, a path in which no hold is offered and no help given, since none is asked for! One child learns to walk the hard way, running and falling many times, the other constantly clutches its mother for support and both reach the same goal. The option is left to us to choose our path. When the devotee casts on the divine all the responsibility of her life, the Supreme comes swiftly and lifts her out of this ocean of transmigratory existence. This then is the easiest and swiftest way. The Puranas describe these two paths as the *Markada Marga* and the *Marjara Marga*—the monkey path and the kitten path. The baby monkey has to cling on to his mother's belly while she jumps from branch to branch. If he releases his hold, he will fall to the ground. Only his own effort can save him. The kitten on the other hand just has to mew pitifully and the mother cat will come running and pick him up by the scruff of his neck and take him carefully to all places.

"On me repose all thy mind and understanding and doubt not that you will dwell in Me," says the Lord to Arjuna. God is our deliverer. When we set our hearts and minds on him, he will lift us from the sea of *samsara* and take us to the eternal abode.

This is easier said than experienced. At some moments we feel that we are indeed living in him and we experience bliss but there is great difficulty in keeping up this state of consciousness. There are days and nights of loneliness when we feel that he has deserted us. There are moments of revolt when the ego demands its rights—moments of doubt when we start wondering what it is all about and why we are striving at all; moments when we are sure we are utter failures, both on the spiritual as well as on the material level, and moments when we think we are fools to waste our lives in this senseless endeavour. Krishna tells Arjuna that we should never allow our minds to sink into such depths of despondency. Hinduism does not believe in the Christian doctrine of grace, which is that of special selection. Krishna has mentioned many times that he is the same to all beings and partial to none. It is only through constant practice that the mind can become totally engrossed in the divine. We have to make ourselves worthy of being elected by him. A certain amount of effort is needed to attain this attitude of total surrender. It cannot be totally unintentional or effortless. If concentration and meditation is found to be too difficult, then we should train ourselves to dedicate the fruits of all action to him. All fruits have to be renounced to the power that directs the work and the work itself has to be done perfectly by us, the chosen instruments. The Lord declares the *Karma Yoga* or the *yoga* of action done without desire to be the best way to train the mind. If this cannot be done then we should work without desire for the fruits. Devotion, meditation and concentration are more difficult than renunciation of the fruits—*karmaphalatyaga*. The latter immediately brings about peace. Worry over the results of the action is what produces the greatest anxiety in the mind so when we renounce the fruit and direct our mind in a continuous stream of love towards him, it is as if a great load is shaken off from our minds. This continuous thought-flow directed towards the divine is called *bhakti*.

PROCESS OF TRAINING THE MIND

In chapter ten on Vibhuti *Yoga*, the Lord says that amongst *yajnas*, he is Japa Yajna. *Japa* is the constant repetition of the *mantra* or the name of God mentally. One can use a rosary to help us in this. After practicing this for some time, the mind will become accustomed to repeating the name continually even when there is no rosary. Name and form are totally connected with each other even in ordinary language. The moment we mention the name 'cat', the form of a cat flashes on to the canvas of the mind. In the Sanskrit language, the sound of every word has the power to produce the form. So the repetition of the name of God ensures that there is a constant communion with him. Even a purely mechanical repetition has the power to wipe off the dross of material negativity from our minds and allow the form to shine clearer and clearer in our hearts. The *mantras* are spiritually charged words and when we fix our mind on the *mantra*, we receive the divine current directly from the Lord even without our knowledge. If this is the case, think of the powerful effect it will have on one who uses it consciously and lovingly, repeating it all the time, whatever task he or she is engaged in. No extra effort or expenditure of time or material is needed for this particular *yajna*—*japa yajna* or the chanting of the Lord's name. This constant practice of turning the mind away from other objects and fixing it again and again on him is a powerful *sadhana*. When it is done with the knowledge that all things are in him and he is indeed in all things, it is even better.

BHAKTI

In Sanskrit, many words are used to denote love, depending on the object towards which our love is directed. *Bhakti* is love directed to God. But this love is a little different from the devotion which is normally considered acceptable in religious parlance. *Bhakti* without knowledge or *jnana* can degenerate into fanaticism just as *jnana* or knowledge, which is not sweetened with love, can freeze into intolerance and rigidity. This is why the *Gita* does not mention *bhakti* till the seventh chapter when the mind is already steadfast in knowledge. The elaboration takes place in this chapter when the neophyte has been drenched in the ocean of wisdom and entranced with the glories of the Beloved. The foundation of the *Gita's* teaching is *jnana* and its walls are *karma*. It is only the super structure, which is *bhakti*. Love is the cream on the top of the cake but the cream alone might give us indigestion while the cake by itself would be dull and uninteresting. It is love alone which oils the wheels of both *karma* and *jnana*.

THE BHAKTA

In the second chapter, the pen-picture of the *sthitaprajna* or the man of wisdom was given. In the fifth chapter, the picture of the Karma Sannyasi was presented and here we are shown a portrait of the *bhakta* or devotee. Most of the qualities are the same. The insistent demand is on equality, desirelessness and constant communion. This foundation has to be there always. Equality implies absence of egoism. The *bhakta* of the *Purushottama* is one who has a heart overflowing with love for the whole of creation. Her love is not reserved for humanity alone but overflows into the animal and vegetable kingdoms, nay even into inanimate creation! The mosquito, which stings her, and the snake, which bites her, are both seen as the energy of the Beloved. Therefore she is patient, forgiving and enduring. She is ever content, equal in pleasure and pain due to the steadfast control of the lower self and a love, which gives up the whole of her mind to God. She is one who is untroubled by the world and who does not trouble the world. This is a difficult task indeed. Sometimes even though we may not trouble the world, yet we are troubled by it. So it is only the perfect *bhakta* who will not be troubled by the world or rather we might say that she is not bothered even if the world troubles her, for she is ever engrossed in activity for the sake of her Beloved. Even when the mosquito of the world bites her, she is oblivious, for her mind is immersed in the bliss of the Divine and through this perfect knowledge she realizes that the mosquito is also divine.

QUALITIES OF THE BHAKTA

The *bhakta* is one, who allows the divine will and knowledge to flow through her without deflection by the ego, yet because of this, she is swift and skilful. The unity with the Supreme will and mind is conducive to the greatest skill in action. She who allows the divine will to act through her finds that every action becomes perfect. Combinations and calculations, which are far too complicated for the human mind, are foreseen and catered for by the divine will, so no hitch occurs in the plan of the devotee and even if a so-called hitch does occur it will later be seen that it was the best possible solution. Every detail is looked into and no effort is spared in order to cater to the slightest needs and temperament of the devotee. Such is the tenderness and care with which the Divine Beloved looks after her. It is impossible to describe this state of affairs to one who has not actually experienced it. No detail is overlooked and no action omitted, which might bring pleasure to the devotee. The Divine is the perfect lover, the perfect mother and perfect father all rolled into one. If we only have the courage to take the leap unhesitatingly and unreservedly into his ever-outstretched arms we will be cradled and carried without difficulty through the crocodile-infested waters of the world. The lover of God therefore neither rejoices at the pleasant nor desires it, not does she hate the unpleasant or feel sorrow at its presence. She has abolished the distinction between fortunate and unfortunate experiences, for in her eyes her Beloved can do no wrong just as in the eyes of the faithful wife, her husband can do no wrong. She has no attachment to persons or things or places or homes. She is content and satisfied with whatever surroundings she is placed in. Today it might be a five-star hotel with all modern conveniences and tomorrow it might be a rat-ridden hut or a cave or an open field. Whatever attitude men adopt towards her, whatever life or fortune brings to her, she will be unperturbed, for her mind is constantly fixed of the one divine object of her love and adoration. What others think about her or say about her is of no consequence for she is secure in the love of the Divine. The world can offer no security as great as this. The multimillionaire with multiple bank accounts in many countries cannot dream of the security which the beloved of God enjoys, living in the open air, having nothing to call her own but the Lord of the Universe! Another hallmark of the perfect person of the *Gita* is that she initiates nothing and expects nothing. These two qualities have been reiterated in almost every chapter. The words used in the *Gita* are *sarvarambha parityagi* and *sarvasamkalpa sannyasi*. The literal meanings are "one who no longer initiates or instigates anything" and "one who has given up all expectations". These two are amazing words. Only the one who is perfectly devoid of ego, who has given up her entire life into the hands of the divine, can relax without taking the initiative or work without worry over the results of the action (without expectation). The latter is what produces the greatest anxiety in the mind so when we renounce the fruit and direct our mind in a continuous stream of love towards him, it is as if a great load is shaken off from our minds. Of all the teachings of the *Gita*, these two instructions are the most difficult to follow yet they form the very crux of Krishna's teachings. Why initiate any action when all decisions are taken by him? All we have to do is to follow orders. Why have expectations when all our expectations are being fulfilled? Only a person who has actually experienced the truth of these two statements will be able to understand the meaning of the two words.

OMNIPRESENCE OF GOD

Such a person has a feeling of utter security because the divine Beloved is not living apart from her but is always seated within her heart. Neither time nor space separates her from her Beloved. He is ever present, loving and considerate, never boring, ever fascinating, always exciting. In fact, he is the perfect lover. And what is more amazing is that she meets her Divine beloved in every other form in the world. She sees him in every face, and he looks at her from every eye and speaks to her from every mouth. Even on the physical level when one is in love, we love the whole world and everything in it is bathed in a golden mist. Nothing can affect us, nothing trouble us. If such is the state of the ordinary lover, who can describe the blissful state of the God-intoxicated person!

"Such bhaktas are exceedingly dear to me," says the Lord.

The lover of God sees only the Divine Beloved reflected everywhere—twinkling in the stars, shining from the sun, reflected in the moon, gurgling in the waters and majestic in the ocean. She even sees him in the leper, the lame and the lustful! For these are all the many forms of her lover. Having chosen to worship him with form, she has perforce to see him and only him in every form, whether pleasant or unpleasant, ugly or beautiful. In fact, in her eyes these differentiation and discriminations do not exist. The beloved of God is the lover of the world. The world reflects in a million ways the multifarious forms of that infinite Being so how can she love one and hate the other. As a mother sees only beauty in her child, which others consider ugly, so the beloved of God sees only beauty even in the ugliest face since that is also a face of her divine lover. Protected and cherished by him and madly in love with him, the state of bliss of such a *bhakta* is indescribable in any human language.

ॐ *Hari Aum Tat Sat* ॐ

Thus, in the Upanishad of the *Bhagavad Gita*, the knowledge of Supreme Brahman, the Scripture of *Yoga*, the dialogue between Sri Krishna and Arjuna, ends the twelfth chapter entitled 'The *Yoga* of the Devotion'.

13

KSHETRA KSHETRAJNA VIBHAGA YOGA

The Yoga of the Distinction between the Field and the Knower of the Field

Aum Sri Krishnaya Paramaatmane' namaha!
Aum Sri Parthasarathaye' namaha.

The twelfth chapter ended with the Lord's assertion that one who follows this *dharma* faithfully and who thinks of him always was the best of all devotees. This chapter starts with Arjuna's question as to the nature of *Purusha* and *Prakriti*, the field and the knower of the field, the nature of knowledge and the object of knowledge.

The object of spiritual life is to rise from the lower to the higher nature through the process of *yoga* as the Lord has described throughout the previous chapters. All human *karma* or action is a transaction between us and Nature with the Supreme Spirit acting as the witness alone but what is the nature of the original transaction and what is the relationship between the two seemingly opposite things—Spirit and Nature—*Purusha* and *Prakriti*? How can the opposition between consciousness and matter, subject and object, seer and seen, be unified in a spiritual whole? The mystery of life is to discover as to why the all-encompassing and all-knowing Spirit incarcerates itself into the small space-time capsule of the body? All *yoga* is an attempt by the physical body to re-unite with that Spirit. In this chapter, the Lord gives a unique and most modern explanation to describe the relationship between *Purusha* and *Prakriti* or Spirit and Matter.

The Lord says,

> O Arjuna know this body to be the *kshetra* or field and know me to be the *kshetrajna* or the knower of the field. Know also that I am the sole knower of all fields, and all bodies. This alone is true knowledge.

The word *kshetra* or field is used to signify the body and *kshetrajna*, the soul or *atman*. The Lord goes on to say that the whole of physical existence is his body—it is the *kshetra* or field of the Spirit's operation. The *Purusha Sukta* hymn of the Vedas also defines the whole of material nature to be the body of the Supreme *Purusha*. The field or *kshetra* is composed of objects in which the Supreme Consciousness or Spirit operates. All of us think we know everything about our bodies but actually we know only a part of the surface and nothing else. The Lord alone is the proprietor of all the bodies in the universe for he alone pervades all bodies and has profound knowledge of them. So truly he is the sole knower of all bodies. The word *kshetra* has another meaning. It means a temple. From this we can understand that this body is the temple of God and this universe is also his temple. So we have a responsibility to take care of this body as well as the whole of Nature for it is his house and place of worship. We can use this body as an instrument to attain the purpose of life. The infinite fields or bodies which we find in the world belong to only one farmer, who is the Lord. There is nothing which is not known by this divine farmer since he is the *kshetrajna* or the knower of all fields both on the individual level and the universal level. One who knows that he is the *atman,* realises that there is no difference between his body and the universal form of the Lord. The same *atman* that dwells in him, also dwells in the whole universe. As Krishna says, only one who can understand the true nature of the field and its knower can be said to have perfect knowledge.

Kshetra Kshetrajna Vibhaga Yoga

This word 'field' is surely a strange word for Krishna to use. It is only recently that quantum physics has described everything as 'The Field'. Ten thousand years ago, Lord Krishna declared that the whole of physical existence was 'the field' of the Spirit's construction.

When we consider how modern Physics has evolved in the past five hundred years, it appears as if their understanding of the world seems to be heading towards the description of the universe as propounded in the *Bhagavad Gita*. In fact, Einstein says, "When I read the *Bhagavad-Gita* and reflect about how God created this universe everything else seems so superfluous." He has also said at some other place, "the Field is the only Reality".

On the quantum level, all living beings including human beings are packets of quantum energy constantly exchanging information with this inexhaustible field of energy called the Zero Point Field. Information about all aspects of life, all of which are found in the field, is relayed through the interchange of information on the quantum level. Even our minds—thinking, feeling, etc.—get information from the quantum field pulsating simultaneously through our body and brain. In fact, we resonate with the universe.

These fields are found both on the individual level and the universal level. What Quantum Physics calls 'The Field' is only their physical manifestations and not their subtle emanations. In Hinduism, all manifestation is from the subtle to the gross and not vice versa as we imagine. Where the *Gita* scores over physics is in its spiritual angle. The fields are many but the knower of all these fields is one and the same. This witnessing consciousness is the same whether it lights up a blue sky or a mound of dirt. Though the fields which are lit up may be different, the light which illumines them is one. Physically all of us are microcosms within the macrocosm and this macrocosm is the universal field, inhabited by the divine knower, the *kshetrajna*. The totality of the lower *Prakriti* or Nature as we behold it is the field of action of the consciousness or Spirit. In more poetic words, we might say that *Prakriti* is the playground of the *Purusha*. In each embodied creature there is only one and the same knower, one and the same consciousness. Knowledge of the world differs in different bodies because of the differences in the reflecting media on which the consciousness is projected. Sunshine reflected in different types of liquid like muck, muddy water and crystal clear water, differs, even though the sun is one and the same and does not change. In the human being however this seemingly small consciousness, which is really the all-consciousness, can enlarge itself into the super consciousness.

One of the great things that modern physics has proved for us is that at this fundamental level of the Field, all of us are connected with each other and with everything else. Through scientific experiments they proved that there may be something called a life-current flowing through the universe, which some religions have called divine consciousness or the Holy Ghost or Brahman or whatever. They have provided solid evidence for what mankind has had faith in but no proof from the dawn of time. Whereas Newtonian science had totally divorced man from the universe, Quantum Physics has demonstrated that there is a purpose and unity in life and we are an important part of it. What we do and think is critical in creating our world. Those of us who have read the *Gita* will realise that this is because the fields both on the individual level and the universal level have only one knower and that is the *kshetrajna,* which is none other than the *Purushottama*.

Now let us see what Lord Krishna has to say about the Field of lower *Prakriti*. The relationship of the body with the *atman* is the same as the relationship between *Prakriti* and *Purusha*. The universe is produced by the union of these two fundamental principles, *Purusha* (consciousness) and *Prakriti* (primordial matter). *Prakriti* is unconscious activity and *Purusha* is inactive consciousness. From this union, all the animate and inanimate forms of the world are created, maintained and destroyed. *Prakriti* is made up of the five *mahabhutas* (primary elements), which are *akasa* (space), *vayu* (air), *agni* (fire), *apas* (water) and *prithvi* (earth). In the human body these *mahabhutas* have their corresponding agents, which are the sense organs comprising of the ears, skin, eyes, tongue and nose which in turn have their abilities to hear, touch, see, taste and smell. The organs of action are also five—hands, feet, mouth, organs of procreation and excretion. We also have the mind, intellect and *chitta*, which he refers to as the *avyakta* or unmanifest. All these aspects which we think of as subjects are actually the objects of knowledge of the subject, which is only one, which is called the *kshetrajna*, which he later calls the *Purushottama*. The knower or witness of the world of objects is not the individual embodied mind but that cosmic consciousness for which the whole cosmos is an object. That consciousness is eternal and does not need the use of the senses and mind for its witnessing.

Armed with this equipment, how we get knowledge of the world is what we want to know. Krishna touches briefly on this. Our minds come into contact with the universal structure of the *kshetra* and *kshetrajna* through the experience of duality like *iccha*, *dwesha* (like and dislike), *sukha*, *dukha* (joy and sorrow). We live in a world of duality and it is this which enables the *jivatma* or embodied soul to enjoy

Kshetra Kshetrajna Vibhaga Yoga

the universe. All dualities like the qualities of pain, pleasure, desire, aversion, etc. are the methods employed by lower *Prakriti* in order to enable the ego to experience and enjoy the world. Without duality we would not be able to do this. We feel that the world would be a wonderful place if there were nothing bad or negative in it. But the fact is that the only way we can appreciate the beautiful is because we have seen the ugly. If only beauty existed, we would not be able to appreciate it. For any sort of appreciation we must have had some experience of its opposite. A person who lives in the sun would never know the meaning of light since he has never experienced darkness! Experience and appreciation of duality constitute the nature of our first transaction with the field of Nature but this is not the limit of our possibilities, as the true spiritual experience goes beyond both these negative and positive reactions. The human being is a union of the universal infinite and the universal particular. In his subjective aspect, he is not a part of a whole but is a potential whole. To actualise universality is the aim of Hinduism. The ideal personality is unique and unrepeatable.

We are so ignorant of the workings of the cosmic law that we just take everything for granted as it appears to the sense organs. We think that we are here, totally independent, and the world is there, totally independent and that we have practically no connection with the world. On the contrary, the microcosm is part and parcel of the macrocosm and can never stand aloof from it. Every breath we draw is a part of the universal breath and every exhalation is something we give back to the universal life. So we are active participants in the cosmic order and not impartial witnesses. We do not realise that a connection is established every minute by the consciousness through the mind and sense organs.

We can see how the trained human intellect is capable of finer and finer discriminations in all the objects of the senses. For instance, the musician can discern nuances, which the untrained ear cannot even hear; the gourmet can appreciate subtle flavours, which ordinary people do not taste. So the senses are capable of finer and finer degrees of refinement. How can we refine our minds as we refine our senses in order to enable us to know the Knower? For this we have to realise that nothing in the objective world is an authentic reality. We can realise the subject in us only by overcoming the enslaving power of the objective world. After having a surfeit of all the possibilities of the field, the *jiva* or *jivatma* at last turns its attention to the knower of the field, which is none other than the *atman*, the inmost reality within itself! The object of its knowledge is finally cognized as the Supreme Subject or the knower, which the Lord calls the *kshetrajna*. This *kshetrajna* is that which is to be really known and this new orientation of the *jiva* is the beginning of the dawn of wisdom or *jnana*. We can realise our true self only by overcoming the enslaving power of the objective world.

In this chapter the Lord details a series of qualities, which the seeker should cultivate in order to understand the details of this relationship and contact the knower.

"According to me, the real understanding of the field and the knower of the field is true knowledge," says the Lord. All other knowledge is only knowledge of the *kshetra* or field and cannot contact the *kshetrajna* or the Lord, who is the actual knower of the field. All knowledge of the material universe, however extraordinary, is only knowledge of lower *Prakriti* and misses out on the true and vital knowledge of the Spirit or *Purusha*. Both are, in truth, consciousness itself but this truth can only be discovered by one who has discovered the truth about himself. Therefore, he gives a list of values by cultivating which the truth of our divinity will become clear to us. In this aspect, this is one of the most important chapters of the *Gita* in as much as it gives us clear cut clues as to the type of values we should cultivate in order to attain liberation. This is the only chapter which gives such concrete instructions.

TWENTY VALUES

In the next few verses, Krishna enumerates twenty values or collection of qualities of the mind in the presence of which alone the knowledge of the unity of Spirit and matter can take place. Krishna calls these qualities *jnana,* which is a word normally used for the knowledge of the Self, but here it is used for a collection of the qualities of the mind in the presence of which knowledge of the Self can dawn. Without these basic qualities, this knowledge can never be realised however competent the teacher and however authentic the teaching. A child of five can have the best teacher and the teaching itself can be of the highest type but with all this he can never be made to understand the quantum theory. The same is the case here. There are certain fundamental qualities of character, which are prime requisites for the dawning of spiritual knowledge. These are the qualities which are enumerated here. The list is not meant for mere superficial reading. Each quality is a value in itself and has to be assimilated into the structure of our character before it can open the doors of the Spirit for us. The list seems rather long but the values are inter-related and they define that harmonious frame of mind in which knowledge of the Self can occur. Each of these values has to be painstakingly cultivated by us so that they become second nature to us and form the foundation of all our thinking and acting. This is one of the most important teachings of the *Gita*. Unless we cultivate these qualities, no amount of talking about the *Gita* and giving discourses on it will enable us to contact that Kshetrajna within us. In the sixteenth chapter, he gives a list of twenty-seven qualities which are described as the *daivi sampat* or the qualities of the *deva*. Many of the qualities have been reiterated.

The list starts with the absence of pride—*amanitwam, adambitwam*. He gives two words to describe two different types of pride. A *maani* is one who takes pride in the fact that he is born in a noble family, has a long list of degrees after his name and has won the acclaim of society and so on. He has some basis for his pride even though from a spiritual angle he has no right to it since none of these were of his own making. The *damba*, on the other hand, has only false pride. He has nothing to be proud of yet goes round boasting about his various activities and achievements. There is a subtle difference between the two but neither are acceptable in the true devotee. The Lord keeps humility or absence of pride in the vanguard of the list for a very special reason. Even if we possess all the other eighteen qualities listed herein, if we do not have humility, the entire edifice would crumble. Then we have non-violence, forbearance and rectitude. Next we have service to the teacher, purity of mind and body, self-control, indifference to the objects of the senses, self-effacement, and no clinging attachment to home and family. We should have a keen perception of the illusory nature of the life of the ordinary man with its aimless absorption in worldly matters, starting with birth and ending with death. Our mind should naturally turn away from the bustle and din of cities to lonely places and more than anything else we should burn with a desire to know that Supreme Reality. Above all, we should have an unswerving devotion to God.

These are the list of qualities which have to be cultivated before the mind can understand deep spiritual truths. This constant turning of the mind to the eternal is a most important aspect of *yoga*. For the mind to be fixed on the impermanent world is to accept mortality. When the *jiva* allows itself to be mesmerised by the illusory appearance of lower *Prakriti*, it misses the true meaning of life, and goes about whirling in the cycle of births and deaths. To feel an aspiration for God is a movement towards the true goal of life and is the birth of wisdom. Every other type of knowledge, however greatly acclaimed by the world, is tantamount to ignorance for it misses out on the true purpose of life. The nineteenth value is *adhyatma jnana nityatwam* and it means "constantly pondering on the nature of the Self" by which alone the twentieth value *tatwa jnanarthadarshanam,* or 'the knowledge of Reality' can be experienced.

PROGRESS OF SPIRITUAL EVOLUTION

At the beginning of its evolutionary cycle, the *jivatma* or the embodied being is apparently subject through ignorance to the manipulations of *Prakriti* or Nature. It seems to be a puppet in her hands, for its every thought and action is dictated by her will. Even though the *jiva* considers itself to be totally liberated and independent, it is in fact totally bound and dependent since it does not know its true Self and equates itself with the individualised ego. The ego itself is only a myth based on ignorance of the nature of this universe and ignorance of its own relationship to the universe as well as ignorance of its own true nature. Thus, a triple ignorance is the womb of the ego. Even when the *jiva* thinks itself to be acting as a free agent, we can see that it is actually acting within the framework of its own nature-born qualities as well as the environment, into which it has been ejected. Both of these are totally beyond its control. The mythical freedom, which the *jiva* thinks it enjoys, is only the freedom of the chained dog. It is chained by its own nature and bound by the environment into which it was born, the education it receives and the types of knowledge it is exposed to. The length of the chain is the length of its freedom. When this *jivatma* evolves, it discovers its own higher reality to be an eternal and impersonal Self—an immutable Spirit that apparently has no share in the action and movement, other than supporting it by its presence. It is the eternal and impersonal witness to all the cavorting and manipulations of the ego, above the dualities of existence and non-existence. The one who experiences this will realise that birth and death are only outward events, which do not affect the Self.

These two—the embodied *jivatma* and the Supreme *Paramatma* seem to be irreconcilable opposites but the *Gita* has always been moving towards a reality, which is both these, as well as something which transcends them. This is the *Purushottama*, who is not only the Master of all Nature but also the origin, support and scene of the workings of his own energy in the cosmos. He is also the spiritual inhabitant in all these forces. The *Gita* refers to this force by many names. In the fifteenth chapter, it is called the *Purushottama* and in this chapter as the *kshetrajna*. Whenever Krishna refers to himself in the first person singular, he is identifying himself with this *Purushottama*. This *Purushottama* or the Supreme Person is at once the field, and the knower of the field. No wonder the Puranas declared all life to be a *Lila* or game of the

Supreme Lord. It is indeed a marvellous game in which he himself is the playground, the ball and the players! Every whirling proton, electron or positron, in fact the whole dervish dance of energy, which creates the illusion of matter, is he and he alone. The dance known as the *thandava nritta* of Lord Shiva as Nataraja is supposed to depict this cosmic dance of energy. This is what is known as the Lord's *maya*, this fantastic illusion of a solid universe, which is actually nothing but the energy of consciousness, which baffles the gaze of even the keenest eye. Even the master intellect of an Einstein could only penetrate it in theory but could not actually discern it in operation. This is because the Lord himself is the sole knower of the field, and only the one who has attained union with this *kshetrajna* or divine knower can shatter the illusion, overcome his *maya* and see the truth in all its startling, blazing glory.

THE BRAHMAN

This *kshetrajna* as we have seen is the *Purushottama*, which is none other than the Brahman, which is both transcendent and universal. In its supracosmic state it is transcendent but when we look at the world after having gained this knowledge we see that the world is other than what it appears to the mind and senses. Then we see this universe not just as a solid block of matter but also as the eternal

Brahman. So this Brahman is the supreme knowable. It is a bodiless, yet million-bodied Spirit with hands of strength and feet of swiftness on all sides, whose heads and eyes and faces we see wherever we turn, whose ear is listening to the throb of the universe and the silence of eternity. This is the universal Being in whose embrace we all live. It sees all but not with the physical eye, hears all but has no ears of its own. It is without attachment and without attributes yet is the enjoyer and sustainer of all attributes. It is attached to nothing yet supports in its immortal freedom, all the action and movement of its universal *Prakriti*. It is at once the inner and the outer, the far and the near, the moving and the unmoving. It is the subtlest of all subtleties beyond the grasp of our minds. It is the density of force and substance, which we can see and touch and smell and hear! Through indivisible, it seems to divide itself into innumerable forms. All is eternally born from it as Brahma, sustained by it as Vishnu and taken back into it as Shiva! It is the light of all lights and luminous beyond all the darkness of ignorance—*jyotishamapi tat jyoti, tamasa paramuchyate*. It is both knowledge as well as the object of knowledge. What is most important is that one need not go to universities or *ashrams* to seek for this Being for it is seated within the hearts of all! When the devotee sees the internal divine indweller, he acquires the divine nature of freedom, love and equality. Many of these ideas are found in the Upanishads.

The Lord then goes on to describe the nature of the two selves—*Purusha* and *Prakriti*. Spirit and Nature—*Purusha* and *Prakriti*—are both aspects of the eternal Brahman and they are both eternal. What are the means used by lower *Prakriti* to bind the immortal Spirit to her mortal nature? She does this by using her *gunas* or modes, which are known as *sattva*, *rajas*, and *tamas*. These three strands are used to bind the *jiva* and give it a false sense of being a free agent. The three modes create the illusion of change and impermanency in the world. The *Purusha* described here is not the multiple souls of the *Samkhya* but the *kshetrajna* who is one in all the fields. The bifurcation is only an apparent one. Actually, there is only one Self. The body and mind are products of *Prakriti* but the experience of pleasure and pain is by the *Purusha*. The blissful nature of the Self is stained by joy and sorrow due to its identification with the body. It enjoys the *gunas* of *Prakriti* and gets attached to them, which in turn are the cause of its birth in good and bad wombs.

ASCENDING ORDER OF UNDERSTANDING

The spiritual knowledge, which sometimes floods the mind of the seeker, is this Spirit manifesting itself in the obscurity of our ignorance. It is seated within our hearts and directing us, as and when the time comes. Seated within the chariot of the human body, it plays many roles in an ascending scale. First it is said to be the witness alone. In the primitive stages of human existence, the human being is bothered only with the satisfaction of his physical life. He eats when he is hungry, sleeps when he is sleepy and so on. At that time the Self within him plays a quiescent role, as a mere witness. With the dawn of moral consciousness, the *jiva* starts examining each action and judges it as right and wrong and then the Self within enacts the role of guide or mentor who approves or disapproves. This is called the voice of conscience, which, however dimly, is beginning to be heard. In the next stage the *jiva* recognizes this voice to be the voice of its maker who is also its master and sole support. With the dawn of this realization the *jiva* begins to understand that this Self is not merely the supporter and the enjoyer but also the Supreme Lord (*Maheswara*) and then he starts to dedicate the fruit of all actions to him, who is the giver of all fruits—*Upadrashtanumanta cha bharta, bhokta, Maheswara!* The Supreme Lord seated within the heart thus enacts these different roles progressively in the *jiva's* evolutionary ascent to him.

The *jiva* has now reached the stage when through the instrument of its body and senses the Lord consciously enjoys the world of his own creation! Actually nothing changes. Nature creates and acts. Seated within the hearts of all creatures, the Supreme Lord sanctions her operations, witnesses her actions, upholds all her commands and enjoys with his universal delight, her manifold creation—her play of forms of his own Being! But in the lower forms of *Prakriti*, the divine enjoyment is obscured and distorted by the dualities of pleasure, pain, etc. But this is only an illusion. Having once attained the Supreme knowledge, the *jiva* becomes free and is no longer bound to the wheel of births and deaths, even though it might have to continue acting as if bound in its outward transactions with the world. At last the *jiva* comes to the stage when it realises that nothing is in its hands and everything is consciously surrendered at the feet of that Lord of Lords.

The *jiva* becomes truly liberated only when it finally experiences its unity with this eternal and universal *Purushottama*.

THE SEER

"Whatever is born, whether movable or immovable, know it to be from the union of the *kshetra* and the *kshetrajna*," Spirit and matter, the field and the knower of the field. This knowledge can come either through meditation or by hearing of it from others and moulding our minds with faith to what has been heard. But whatever the means employed, the knowledge will carry us beyond death to immortality. True knowledge shows us our highest Self as the Supreme Lord of the action of *Prakriti*, equal in all creatures, not born by the taking on of a body and not subject to death by the perishing of that body. The one who is able to see that which is eternal and immortal within us is known as "the seer". This alone is true seeing and not just the surface observation of the objective world. As we begin to see more and more, we begin to identify ourselves with the eternity of the *atman* and not with the mortality of the body. All this surface movement is seen as the divine becoming of natural existences in the one eternal Being, just as the waves can be seen to be part of the mighty ocean. Then we see that all our actions are the operations of Nature. The Self is not the doer but the witness, Lord and unattached enjoyer of her actions. As the all pervading space is not changed or affected by the forms it assumes, but always remains pure and subtle, so the Spirit even though permeating all bodies and conditions of change, remains the same—pure and immutable.

POWER OF KNOWLEDGE

The true seer is one who sees that all action belongs to *Prakriti* and the Self is the non-doer. It is the spectator and not the actor and therefore it is unconditioned and immutable. Though it dwells in the body, it neither acts nor is it tainted. This

Kshetra Kshetrajna Vibhaga Yoga

Spirit or *kshetrajna* illumines the entire field of Nature or *kshetra* with the splendour of its rays, as the one sun illumines the entire world. In the light of that splendour all knowledge is revealed. Without the sun our eyes, though good, are useless to us. It is only with the coming of dawn that our eyes also open and we can put them to use. So also when the sun of spiritual knowledge dawns in us, our third eye opens—the eye of wisdom—and only then can we discern the truth of existence.

This knowledge has the power to transmute every tragedy into bliss, for everything in the world reflects the three aspects of the Brahman, which are existence, consciousness and bliss. Tragic circumstances are the greatest incentives given to humanity to goad it into discovering itself to be the source of bliss. However obscene, freakish or fiendish the situation might be, it is the power of the Divine, alone which supports it and gives it an apparent cloak of reality. Therefore, even in negative situations there is an underlying bliss, which can be found only when we have utterly and totally accepted it. When we are filled with the power of the *kshetrajna,* we will experience the world as bliss, whatever be the nature of the external situation. This is the meaning of true liberation. Only when the *jiva* has learnt to accept everything as it is without trying to change every situation to suit its own egoistic demands, does it lose its double identity and become a *jivan mukta* or liberated soul. The liberation it achieves is from the trammels of its own ego enshrouded in ignorance, and not from any external object. After casting off the burden of its illusory ego, the *jiva* discovers that its idea of liberty was not a myth at all but only a case of mistaken identity. This idea, which the Lord has given in this chapter, is one that has already been told to Arjuna in the second chapter. But at that time he was not capable of imbibing its full meaning. Having evolved through the teaching of each chapter, he has reached the stage when he is able to realize this great truth, which the Lord reiterates.

> You are not the body; you are not the mind or intellect.
> You are the immortal Brahman, flawless, faultless,
> indestructible and transcending the body.

Thus knowing the difference between the *kshetra* and *kshetrajna* the *jiva* attains liberation. This is the final metamorphosis of the *jiva* when it throws off its cocoon of ignorance and emerges into the sunshine of the eternal Spirit, a beautiful, blissful and radiant butterfly!

ॐ *Hari Aum Tat Sat* ॐ

Thus, in the Upanishad of the *Bhagavad Gita*, the knowledge of the Supreme Brahman, the Scripture of *Yoga*, the dialogue between Sri Krishna and

Arjuna, ends the thirteenth chapter entitled 'The *Yoga* of the Distinction between the Field and the Knower of the Field'.

> O Bharata! Know me to be the sole cogniser of all fields. I consider true knowledge to be the knowledge of the Field and the knower of the Field.
>
> *Chapter 13, Verse 2.*

14

GUNATRAYA VIBHAGA YOGA

The Yoga of the Distinction between the Three Gunas

Aum Sri Krishnaya Paramaatmane' namaha!
Aum Sri Parthasarathaye' namaha.

The thirteenth chapter has shown us that the Spirit is Supreme. It is Supreme Knowledge, the knower of all knowledge, and the object of all knowledge. So then what is the meaning of liberation? Who is it that is to be liberated and from what, when all is Spirit and Spirit alone. Since the Spirit is immortal, how can it gain immortality? Since it has never been bound, how can it liberated? Is liberation and immortality only for the body? This can never be for by its very nature the body is both mortal and bound. So the Indian philosopher never wasted any time in trying to make immortal that which is patently mortal. But the Spirit also is by its very nature immortal and needs no aid to become so, then for whose liberation are we striving?

IMMORTALITY

Immortality is not dissolution into the Absolute but the attainment of universality and freedom of the spirit. It is a status that is unaffected by the cyclic process of creation and dissolution. In the deeper sense, to be immortal is something different from the mere survival of physical death. Immortality is that supreme status in which the *jivatma* knows itself to be superior to birth and death, unconditioned by Nature, immortal, because never having been born it can never die! If we were merely products of nature, we could not attain immortality. The *atman* is eternally divine and immortal and is known as the *jivatma* when it takes on a body. It is because of its identification with this body made of the elements of lower *Prakriti* that it forgets its essential nature. Its liberation comes through knowledge. What this means is that in reality there is no bondage for the *jivatma*. *Maya* is an illusion by which the *jivatma* imagines itself to be bound. Freedom is only a process by which the illusion is cast off and then it realizes that it has never been bound at all. It is something like a chained dog whose master has gone through the process of chaining it entirely by mime. The dog does not realise that it has not been chained at all and will lie there quietly as if chained until the master comes and tells him to get up and go. But even then the dog has become so used to its imaginary chain that it will not get up and discover its freedom unless the master goes through a further pantomime of unchaining it! The case of the *jivatma* is very similar. Hence, the very first verse of this chapter declares that knowledge alone is the secret of liberation.

KNOWLEDGE

The first verse of this chapter thus reiterates once again the nature of the highest and supreme knowledge by which the sages have liberated themselves and attained immortality. Having gained this knowledge, one dons the garb of immortality, which is the nature of the Supreme-*sadharmya*. Such a soul goes beyond the cycle of birth and death, eternally conscious of the Supreme in all his various forms. *Pralaya* is the end of the cycle of eons and is the temporary disintegration of the universal form of existence, but it is only a momentary pause, followed by an outburst of new creation and re-construction, in which all the manifest worlds are born again in a new creation.

Our individual death can also be called a *pralaya* because again it is only a short rest before another birth and another outburst of activity and creativity in another life. This round goes on until the *jiva* experiences its identity with the Supreme and thus reaches the end of its individual, limited existence.

The cosmic evolution proceeds from the unmoving, unknowable, unmanifest macrocosm to the conscious, moving, knowable and manifest microcosm. Human evolution is a return journey from the gross, physical plane of existence back to the unmanifest, unknowable Absolute. In the one case the force is centrifugal and the other centripetal. Knowledge of the modus operandi of the Spirit in the world of nature and the constituents of nature which give rise to all the vast differences which we see, is a must in the progress towards immortality and this chapter proceeds to make these matters clear.

PROCESS OF EVOLUTION

Prakriti or primordial matter is called *Mahat Brahman*, which is the divine womb of creation in which the Lord places the seed of consciousness from which follows the birth of all beings. We can become divine only because we have come from him and we are one with that divinity. We could not become immortal if we were only of mental and physical origin. All existence is a manifestation of divine existence and we ourselves are nothing but this eternal Spirit. All this movement in this world is only the self-creation of the Supreme Spirit. As the Supreme Soul or *Purusha*, he casts the seed of consciousness into the womb of *Prakriti* or nature, which again is only an emanation from his nature. It is he alone in his role as *Prakriti* that develops the divine embryo into the mental and physical forms of existence. Thus, the divine is at once the father and mother of all existences. What we see here are the finite forms of the infinite idea. Every possible type of creation has its corresponding possibility in the unmanifest. The world is the play of the infinite on the finite. The Spirit is the father and *Prakriti* the womb of any form produced in any womb be it human, animal, bird or beast. Both *Purusha* and *Prakriti*—Spirit and Nature—are eternal. The *jivatma*, which takes on a particular form in nature, is also eternal. Even when seemingly bound by nature it is capable of becoming aware of its innate divinity. God has an eternal vision of creation in all its details. Every possible manifestation has a corresponding possibility in the unmanifest where it exists in its eternal cause.

Martin Rees, the cosmologist, said that there are six formulae which are essential for the production of an incredible universe like this. If any one of these was not there, such a universe could never have come into existence. These must have been envisaged to the last detail by that initial intelligence before the Big Bang. In Hinduism, creation is cyclical so a period of *srishti* or creation is followed by a period of *laya* or dissolution after which another *srishti* will appear. So in Hinduism it is said that everything about this universe lies latent in that Supreme Consciousness waiting for the next creation to occur. At that time everything comes out in its original perfection.

REASON FOR APPARENT BONDAGE

What is it then that gives the *jivatma* its semblance of bondage? It is its identification with the modes or *gunas* of nature. They are known as *sattva, rajas* and *tamas*. The *gunas* are the three strands or tendencies of *Prakriti*, which make up the twisted rope of nature. They are the primary constituents of nature and are the bases of all substances. They cannot be said to be qualities inherent in these substances because their emergence is dependent on the *Kshetrajna*. *Sattva* reflects the light of consciousness and has the quality of radiance (*prakasa*). *Rajas* has an outward movement (*pravritti*) and *tamas* is characterised by inertia (*apravritti*) and indifference (*pramada*). It is difficult to give exact English words to these three. Physics describes the three modes of Nature as equilibrium (*sattva*), kinesis (*rajas*) and inertia (*tamas*). The cosmic trinity in Hinduism reflects these three modes. *Sattva* predominates in Vishnu, and contributes to the stability of the universe; *rajas* is prominent in Brahma and leads to all creativity and *tamas* is attributed to Shiva and represents the tendency of things to decay and die.

Identification with the *gunas* of *Prakriti* is what gives the *jiva* the semblance of bondage. When the *jiva* identifies with the modes, it forgets its divine status and uses mind, and body for egoistic satisfaction. This is how the whole game of life is played. Otherwise, there would be no bondage or freedom and no play of the Divine. To rise above bondage we should rise above the three *gunas*—become *trigunatita* as Krishna told Arjuna in the second chapter. If the Spirit associated with *Prakriti* is the cause of the entire manifest universe, then everything and every person should be similar. The dissimilarity arises due to the mixture of the three qualities of *Prakriti* in all things. A person in whom *sattva* is predominant will be mostly contemplative. One who is hyperactive and ambitious, etc. will have a preponderance of *rajas* and one who is dull and stupid will have more of *tamas*. All the three *gunas* are found in everybody. Everyone is at times active and at times dull and contemplative at other times. From the combinations and permutations of these three, all the differences in the world arise. When the *gunas* are transcended, *sattva* changes into the light of consciousness, *rajas* into austerity and *tamas* into tranquillity or *shanti*. Having transcended the three *gunas*, the *jivatma* becomes eligible for immortality.

THE GUNAS

In the second chapter itself the Lord had asked Arjuna to dissociate himself from these three modes of nature. But before we can do so it is necessary to understand what they are. Though these *gunas* make up the whole of physical and mental nature they are not quantitative or physical qualities but qualitative and psychological since the connecting link between spirit and matter is psychological and qualitative. Modern physics has accustomed us to a different view of nature because the first thing that strikes us in nature is the physical and quantitative aspect of her workings. But even the scientists have now discovered that matter is not made up of material substance but is merely a dance of energy. Energy in motion is matter. Matter is not made up of solid blocks of physical substances. Five thousand years before this astounding discovery was made by modern physics, Lord Krishna had explained to Arjuna about the qualitative strands of nature, which make up the entire physical and mental universe. The whole quantitative action of nature has been cast from these qualitative moulds or modes of nature. In the *Gita*, these modes are described only by their psychological effects on man or incidentally on the food we eat and so on. Actually, these *gunas* are products of ignorance and have no existence from the standpoint of the Absolute, just as shadows have no reality in relation to light. The three qualities influence the *jivatma* in three different ways. *Tamas* makes us lazy and inactive, *rajas* makes us passionate and selfishly active, and *sattva* makes us pure and harmoniously active. When the Infinite Spirit involves itself with lower *Prakriti*, it becomes bound by attachment to these three modes of nature. *Sattva* binds by attachment to happiness, *rajas* by attachment to action and *tamas* by attachment to inaction.

The three *gunas* are inextricably intertwined in all cosmic existences. *Tamas* is the principle of inertia. It is a dull ignorance, which suffers all the shocks of life without making any effort at mastering them and eventually leads to a dispersion of all substance and energy. It is driven by the kinetic power of *rajas* and balanced by the harmonizing principle of *sattva*. *Rajas* is a type of half-conscious desire or seeking for happiness, which is the very nature of existence. By itself it would lead to an unstable life of ceaseless activity without any settled result. On the opposite side it is met with the disintegrating power of *tamas* leading to death, decay and inertia. In between it is harmonized and sustained by the positive power of *sattva*, which is subconscious in the lower forms of existences but which becomes more and more apparent with the emergence of the mind. The *jiva* evolves through these three stages. It rises from dullness and inertia, subject to ignorance, through the struggle for material enjoyments to the pursuit of knowledge and happiness. But even in this stage there is a sense of insecurity since we don't know when *rajas* and *tamas* will overcome us. This is the picture of a world governed by the mutually limiting play of the three *gunas*. The *Gita* applies this generalized analysis of the universal energy to the psychological nature of man in relation to his bondage to lower Nature in order to help him shake off the shackles imposed by these modes and attain to the purity of his essential divinity.

WHY THE ATTACHMENT TO THE GUNAS

But how does the Spirit get attached to the three *gunas*? It happens because of the mind's attachment to their effects. We can of course understand how *rajas* and *tamas* can bind but how does *sattva* bind? *Rajas* binds due to its craving for continuous action and *tamas,* through attachment to laziness, procrastination and sleep, but one would think that *sattva* would produce a pure type of happiness? This is true but the *sattvic* mind attaches itself to this very purity and becomes addicted to it; craves for it when it is absent and delights in it when it is present. This is what constitutes its bondage. However great the happiness supplied by *sattva*, it still falls far short of that Supreme bliss which is got by unity with God. By its attachment to this inferior type of happiness, the *sattvic* mind can block its progress to the Supreme. Attachment to anything is bondage, whether it is to doing good and noble acts, or going to places of worship, or reading enlightening literature. All these are very worthy endeavours no doubt and help us to raise ourselves from *tamasic* sloth and *rajasic* hyperactivity but they also create a subtle type of bondage. Insidiously this attachment acts as a block to the final leap into that which is beyond all *gunas*. If *tamas* can be likened to an iron chain and *rajas* to a silver chain, *sattva* can be called a golden one, but a chain is a chain whatever the material out of which it is made up of and the one who wants to attain liberation has to break all three. Even if the *sattvic* man has given up all desire for the fruit of action, there may be attachment to the nature and pure quality of the work done for its own sake. This is actually a blend of *rajas* and *sattva*. Subjection can also be due to the nature of the work which though good in itself is done as a routine, like the many rituals which people keep doing since they have been habituated to this. This is the *tamasic* bond. The bondage can also be the purely *sattvic* bondage of the work, which is done because of its pure quality. Strange as it may seem, this also causes a powerful bond in the virtuous man.

SIGNS OF GUNAS

When the mind is flooded with light and knowledge, as if the closed doors of a house have been opened and flooded with sunshine, when the intelligence is bright, senses sharp and the whole mentality satisfied and filled with brightness, one should know that there is an uprising of *sattva guna*. When the mind is full of unrest and fever, lust, greed and excitement, know that there is an uprising of *rajas*. It is the force of desire, which motivates all personal initiative in action. *Tamas* is born of inertia and ignorance and its fruits are laziness and bondage. The darkness of *tamas* causes delusion and obscures knowledge. In this way it is the opposite of *sattva*. But it is also the opposite of *rajas* for it brings about negligence in action as well as sloth. The essence of *rajas* is *pravritti* or action and the essence of *tamas* is *appravritti* or inaction and the essence of *sattva* is *nivritti* or repose. It must be understood that this is the repose of wisdom and not the sloth of laziness. *Tamas* is the inertia of ignorance as well as the inertia of inaction—a double negative. These three qualities are found both in Nature as well as in human beings. None can be said to be devoid of any one of them. All human beings have the *rajasic* impulse of desire and activity and the *sattvic* touch of goodness and happiness; we all have our full share of *tamasic* ignorance and laziness. But these qualities are not consistent in their action and combination. At one time one predominates and at other times another. Only by a general predominance of one or the other can a person be said to be *sattvic, rajasic* or *tamasic*. But this can never be an exclusive description. The three together bind the imperishable *atman* to the perishable body. The *jivatma* evolves through these three stages. It rises from inertia to ignorance, through the struggle for material enjoyments to the pursuit of knowledge. But so long as we are attached to anything including noble objects, we will be limited and there will be insecurity. The *jivatma*, though ever free, concentrates its consciousness on the results produced by the *gunas* and thus imprisons itself as it were in the outward action of life and forgets its own greater heritage. In order to be liberated it must go above these three *gunas* and return to that power of the divinity within it. "When the seer perceives no agent other than the *gunas* and knows that which is beyond the *gunas*, he attains to my being."

PERFECT ACTION

Transcending these qualities which are the cause of its bondage, the embodied person liberates himself

Gunatraya Vibhaga Yoga

from birth, death, dotage and suffering and wins immortality.

When we hear this advice of the Lord, we will no doubt be compelled to ask whether a cutting off from the *gunas* would not also imply a cutting off from all action, since a man cannot act by himself but only through the modes of Nature. But though the Lord insists on going above the *gunas*, he also insists on the necessity for action. How is this dilemma to be solved? Here we must remember his initial advice on the technique of action. Action should be done without desire for personal fruits. In fact, this has been stressed in every chapter. It is the desire for the fruit of action that is the most forceful factor in the soul's bondage in Nature. The *jivatma* can rise to its full spiritual stature only by abandoning this selfish desire and acting without involvement in the lower forms of Nature, as a faultless instrument of the Supreme. Ignorance is the result of *tamasic* action and pain the result of *rajasic* action. The pain of reaction, disappointment and dissatisfaction due to the impermanence of the fruits it has desired and received, is the lot of *rajas*. But even *sattvic* action, though rightly resolved, should be abandoned, says the Lord, for as long as *sattva* is entangled with *rajas* and *tamas* there is insecurity. This is why the *Gita*, though it insists on doing, action, at the same time insists that the action should be given up to the Lord of all action and the *jivatma* should remain as the desireless instrument alone. The word used constantly by the Lord in many of the chapters is *sarvarambaparityagi*, or the one who has stopped from taking personal initiative in any action. Such a person waits for some sort of prompting by God and then dives in and obeys the divine commands like a faultless instrument. Such a person is a *gunatita*, or one who has transcended the *gunas* since his action has not been initiated by any of the *gunas* which are preponderant in him at the time.

ABOVE THE GUNAS

Arjuna immediately asks for the signs of a man who has risen above the three *gunas*. The Lord has given pen portraits of the enlightened man and the liberated man many times but once again he describes the qualities of the one who has risen above the *gunas*. These are very similar to the *sthitha prajna* and the *karma yogi*. What can we say about the qualities of a man who has no qualities! What can be said of the colour of a clear piece of crystal? In itself it is sheer clarity and brightness but it can dissolve into a dazzling spectrum of colours when the bright light of the sun passes through it. It can also rest in its own pristine beauty. So also is the state of the person who has risen above the *gunas*. She neither desires the presence of the *gunas* nor opposes them. Equality, which is the hallmark of the liberated person, which has been stressed in all the chapters, is the primary quality of the *gunatita*. She initiates no action and is only a witness to all the work which she knows is being done by Nature through her modes—the *gunas*. *Sattva*, *rajas* and *tamas* may rise in her outer mental and physical activities but she does not rejoice when they come nor does she shrink from their operation or cessation. Their play is restricted to her conscious mind and they cannot manipulate her. In other words, they cannot make her dance to their tune. She is the perfect instrument of the divine and responds only to the call of that tune. Her consciousness is fixed on the Divine and from that Supreme state she is unaffected by the powerful movements of the *gunas* of *Prakriti*. She is like the sun shining above the play of the clouds. She watches the *gunas* of *Prakriti* rotating and revolving perpetually, never resting in harmony, even for a moment. She sees the whole of life as a fabric woven by these three strands of *Prakriti* and remains a disinterested witness of the cosmic drama, which Nature enacts for her Lord. Such a person is indeed liberated. She regards sorrow and happiness alike. To her a piece of gold, a clod and a stone are of equal value. Praise or blame, honour or dishonour is the same to her. She makes no differentiation between friends, enemies and well-wishers. She sees only the Supreme in all these roles, donning the threefold cloak of the *gunas* of *Prakriti* and enacting the cosmic drama, so why should she shun one and adore the other?

The difference between the teachings of the *Gita* and other *advaitic* texts is that the picture of the liberated person does not end with the passionless, indifferent and unattached soul, untouched by the modes of Nature, completely absorbed in the bliss of the Brahman. It presents the portrait of the eternal devotee, the *bhakta*, adoring the cosmic Beloved, the *Purushottama*, in and through his creation, in every creature, whether human, animal or divine, constantly engaged in acting for him, mentally engaged in thinking of him, faithful to him and only him through all the vicissitudes of life. Such a person is fully qualified for attaining the immutable Brahman, says the Lord. In the final verse of this chapter, the Lord declares that he himself, the *Purushottama*, is indeed the home of the imperishable Brahman—of immortality, eternal righteousness and infinite bliss! Brahman showers his grace on his devotees through *Iswara*, which in this case is the *avatara* of Krishna. The Lord here has identified himself with the absolute, unconditioned Brahman.

ॐ *Hari Aum Tat Sat* ॐ

Thus, in the Upanishad of the *Bhagavad Gita*, the knowledge of Supreme Brahman, the Scripture of

Yoga, the dialogue between Sri Krishna and Arjuna, ends the fourteenth chapter entitled 'The *Yoga* of the Distinction between the Three *Gunas*'.

> The one who serves Me with an all-consuming and constant devotion, such a one can be said to have transcended the *gunas* and is fit for becoming Brahman.
>
> *Chapter 14, Verse 26*

> Primordial matter is my womb into which I cast the seed O Bharata! From this comes the birth of all beings.
>
> *Chapter 14, Verse 3*

15

PURUSHOTTAMA YOGA

The Yoga of the Supreme Person

Aum Sri Krishnaya Paramaatmane' namaha!
Aum Sri Parthasarathaye' namaha.

In the fifteenth chapter, all the basic ideas of the *Gita* find their fulfilment. It is so important that the Lord Himself calls it a *shastra* or science. The function of the Veda is to awaken the human being to an awareness of the Supreme Reality and because this has been done in this chapter, it is also known as *vedasaara* or the essence of the Vedas. The eternal tree of the universe as mentioned here is also found in the *Katha Upanishad*, *Mundaka Upanishad*, *Atharva Veda* and *Rig Veda*.

THE BANYAN TREE

The chapter begins with a beautiful description of the cosmic tree, which has its roots in the sky and its branches on earth. This is the tree of existence, which has neither a beginning nor an end. Its real form is incomprehensible to the human mind. Its principle is the urge to action, which proceeds without beginning, and without end. Its origin is from above, but its branches and aerial roots project downwards, thrusting their clinging roots of attachment and desire into the world of human beings. The Vedic hymns are its leaves. One who knows this tree is the knower of the Veda. The upside-down nature of the tree implies that the tree of existence has its roots in the Divine, for we are inclined to think of the Divine as being somewhere up in the Heavens above. Infinite is the universe and it emanates from the infinite Brahman. Infinite are the varieties it manifests before us and mysterious the way in which it expresses itself. The whole of existence is a mystery, which cannot be comprehended by any individual.

There is another association connected with this tree with its roots in the heavens. There are seven *chakras* or energy systems in the human body, which lie along the spine. The one at the bottom is known as the *'muladhara'*. The one at the top of the head where the fontanel exists in the baby, is

The Tree of Existence

known as the *sahasrara*. This is the place of the Supreme known as Shiva. The *Kundalini Shakti* or power of the divine mother is supposed to join with the Shiva Shakti found in the *sahasrara*. When this happens, the individual becomes liberated and attains the form of the Supreme. This network of *nadis* or *pranic* currents proceeding from the *sahasrara chakra* to the *muladhara chakra* at the base of the spine resembles a huge inverted tree with its roots on top.

The tree of life as described here is imperishable though it has been previously stated elsewhere that the universe is transitory. Why does the Lord describe it as imperishable? The universe is the manifestation of the one Supreme imperishable reality that is all-pervading and exists eternally in all its splendour and glory. It is immutable. The universe, however, is transitory for it changes as a result of the activity of the three *gunas* but it is finally absorbed into that all-pervading Absolute at the end of one cycle of existence. However, after a long period of *pralaya* or dissolution, it returns to manifestation in exactly the same form as it was before. It is in this sense that Krishna says it is imperishable. It is sustained by that which is eternal. *Poornamadam, Poornamidam* is what the Vedas proclaim. "That is full and this is also full". Here the word 'this' stands for the world and 'that' stands for the Absolute. How can an unreal world come from that which is the Supreme Reality? How can 'the full' project anything but 'the full'? Thus, the world which is a projection of the Supreme is also real though not in the way that our senses see it. Actually the potentiality of everything in the world does not change. The energy does not change. It can never be destroyed. As Krishna said in the eleventh chapter, *Existence can never become non-existent and that which is non-existent can never become existent except in a very temporary sense. The* forms and names are subject to change, decay and destruction but not the energy which comes from the divine itself. Modern physics has found this out thousands of years after the *Gita* has declared it. "Matter is only energy in motion!" Though the forms of matter can change, existence can never change.

The nature of this mysterious universe (the *ashwatta* tree) is beyond our comprehension. We see only the branches, flowers and fruits of this tree and not the divine source from which it has emanated. We sink ourselves in the enjoyment of this glorious tree of life and think that this is supreme. The aerial roots of this tree has dug themselves deep into our minds and hearts and the only those with discernment can know that there is more to this tree that appears on the surface and try to discover the source. At last they realise that the only way to cut themselves off from the charms and temptations of this tree is to cut it with the sword of detachment. The tree grows and feeds through attachment and withers through detachment. Our individual worlds come into existence through the strength and avidity of our desires and when these desires dry up, our worlds also come to an end, even as the cloth ceases to exist when the threads are pulled out and as a plant dries for lack of nourishment. The separate worlds making up our universe are not ultimately made up of substances but of the desires of the individuals that constitute it. The warp and woof of the universe is made up of the desires of the individuals that constitute it. So to cut the root of this tree would mean to cut at the roots or our own desires. We tie ourselves like silk worms into the cocoons of our own desires, which wind themselves round the centres of our egos. Then we complain that we are bound, forgetting that we have bound ourselves up through our own desires and liberation is within our own grasp.

The *Mundaka Upanishad* gives the beautiful description of the two birds sitting on the branch of the tree of life. One keeps pecking at the fruit, now liking one and now disliking another and therefore it suffers. The other bird is only the witness to the cavorting of its companion and remains ever in a state of bliss. A time comes when the bird becomes fed up with this constant seesaw of happiness and unhappiness and turns to the other bird, which has been its constant companion through many lifetimes and then it merges itself into that, and experiences bliss.

In the thirteenth chapter, the Lord calls the phenomenal tree of the world as the *kshetra* or field and the witnessing bird or the Supreme as the *kshetrajna*. When the *yogi* goes beyond the *gunas* as has been said in the fourteenth chapter, he becomes free from desires and attains the highest state of knowledge. This state of the divine Spirit is not extra cosmic though it is supracosmic. The Lord says in mystic language that the Supreme is that where the sun shines not, nor the moon nor the stars nor anything that we can think of as effulgence here in this world. What light can a small candle have when placed before the sun. So also his effulgence is such that even the light of the sun loses all its glory. The divine is the source of all lights. The sun, moon and fire are only fragments of this light of all lights. The darkness of ignorance can only be removed by the light of knowledge. The Brahman is the source of all lights and that is the final abode for all seekers.

All creatures are nothing but that Divine clothed in different humble guises. Every individual soul is divinity clothed in humanity.

"It is an eternal portion of me that becomes the *jiva* in this world of *jivas*," says the Lord. This means that each soul is a spiritual reality that is essentially divine, however partial its actual manifestation may seem to appear in the physical world. We call it a *jiva* because it appears here as a separate living creature in the world of living creatures. We are prone to think of it only in terms of its humanity. But in truth it is much greater than its appearance and is not bound by its humanity. It might have been a lesser manifestation than the human in its previous births and has the potential to become a greater manifestation in its future births.

However, in this world we see an infinite multiplicity of *jivas*. How are they to be explained? Just as we can never cut up space into little bits, so also we cannot cut up the eternal Being into pieces and make up different *jivas*. The space inside many pots is the same as the space outside. For a short while it appears as if the pot space is different from the outside space that is all. This eternal individual or *jiva* is in no way separate from the Lord. The *jiva* is in fact the Lord himself. This *jivatma* takes up different types of bodies and casts them away as and when it is necessary. Whenever it takes on a body, it comes armed with the equipment of the senses, mind and the intellect. Using this equipment the Lord within enjoys the world. When the *jiva* leaves the body, it takes away this equipment as the wind takes away odours! The ignorant are not conscious of the *jiva* entering and departing from this body while the wise are able to discern this movement.

"The brilliance of the sun, the radiance of the moon and the blaze in the fire are all my brilliance," says the Lord.

Expressing himself through these forms, the Lord enables plants to grow and nourish animals and humans.

> I am that *vaiswanara* fire which exists in the bodies of all creatures and digests all types of food through which all beings are nourished.

Every creature knows it has to eat in order to live but no creature knows what happens after the food enters its mouth. This is only the beginning of the story of nourishment. The fire of life, which actually digests the food, is the Lord himself who is the *vaiswanara* fire existing in the bowels of every creature by which the food is digested and sent to all parts of the body in different guises like blood cells, brain cells and so on. The Lord alone gives us the power to function and do our duties—to know and remember as well as to forget. He himself is the Veda and the knower of the Vedas and that which is to be known in the Veda.

THE PURUSHOTTAMA

Krishna now gives us a glimpse of the two realities which we find in the world—the *kshara* and the *akshara*. The first glimpse we have of this reality is in the *kshara* or the mutable and the perishable—the constantly changing face of Nature with its innumerable appearances. It is the moving power of life, the womb of birth and action. It is itself space, Time, and causation—*desha*, *kala* and *nimitta*. It encompasses the multitude of individuals, gods, creatures, forces, qualities, and quantities. In fact, it encompasses all existence. This is the face of lower *Prakriti,* which seems to be operating blindly, totally oblivious of the Spirit within her which is prompting all her action. Her work is a confused ignorant play of the three modes of *sattva, rajas* and *tamas*. Hidden in her bosom, unmanifest in her appearance is the Spirit, the *akshara* the imperishable, known as the *kshetrajna* in the thirteenth chapter, which is the motive power in her action. In the previous chapter, we have been told that *Prakriti* uses her three strands known as the *gunas* in order to bind the imperishable *atman* to the perishable body. But as long as we live in the lower Nature bound by her three *gunas*, we can never know this reality, for the Spirit is hidden by his own veil of *maya*. The *Gita's* message up to this chapter speaks of *maya* as a bewildering, partial consciousness, which is difficult to overcome but can be overcome by the grace of the Supreme Being who is above his *maya*. If the *jagat* or world is *mithya* or non-existent as the Advaitins claim, then the *Gita*'s stress on action would be meaningless, but the *Gita* affirms that the world does not disappear with the dawn of enlightenment but only changes its character. Seen from the angle of the spiritualized vision, we find that the world is glorified into the divinity itself. Everything is Vaasudeva or the Supreme Spirit, as has been said before. The *kshara* is nothing but the *akshara*. The world for the *Gita* is real. It is not merely the creation of the Lord, but the Lord Himself. There are some types of photos of deities which we see in India which don't look very meaningful when we look at them face to face. But when we look at our own reflection in the clear glass and start concentrating on it, the whole picture slowly turns to that of the deity, which it is meant to be. This is quite a strange phenomenon and obviously this is what happens to the vision of the enlightened human when he starts looking at the world after enlightenment. The whole world takes on another aspect.

When we start evolving, we become aware of another Spirit who is neither the *kshara* nor the *akshara* but is pure Spirit alone, eternal and imperishable, inactive in her action, immobile in her mobility. It is the Self of all, unmoved and as if indifferent, as if all these things were totally unconnected with It, only a drama which is unfolding before Its indifferent gaze. This Spirit is timeless, though we see it in Time, unextended, though we see it as pervading space. The more we withdraw from the outward, mutable working of the *kshara*, the more do we become aware of the *akshara* or the imperishable. The *Kshara Purusha* is visible to us since it encompasses the whole of natural existence. It is the *kshetra* or field, which has already been described in the thirteenth chapter. It moves and acts in the immobility and eternity of the *akshara* or the *kshetrajna*, which we have been told is the knower of the field. It is the immobile, non-active, support and witness of the field. These two parts are found within each individual; one is made up of the body, senses and the conscious mind which we all know, while the second consists of the unconscious mind and the embodied soul or *jivatma*. The first part constantly undergoes— change birth, growth, decay and death—but the second part is semi-immortal and this is the part which the Lord says is carried away like the odour from a flower, to another life. We become aware of these two entities as we progress in our spiritual practices, one emerging in front as action and creation and the other remaining behind as the background from which this action emanates and into which it must disappear, as the mighty restless waves sink into the bosom of the silent unchanging ocean. The Spirit in the ever-changing cosmos is called the *kshara*. The *akshara* is the eternal Spirit, unchanging and immobile, the immutable in the mutable. Over and above these two is the Supreme Self or ultimate reality, which has already been said to be the source of life and light and nourishes and supports the whole of creation. The *Gita* exalts the concept of the personal god, who combines in himself the timeless existence of the *akshara* and the temporal world of the *kshara*. But what is that which contains this duality within its oneness. This is the *Purushottama* or the Supreme Person, in the language of the *Gita*. The two realities of the *Kshara Purusha* and *Akshara Purusha* are transcended, comprehended and absorbed in the *Uttama Purusha*. With the dawn of realisation, we become conscious of the power of this immutable Spirit, acting through us and only then are we able to understand our role as the instruments of the cosmic purpose. It is only by putting on a likeness of the divine nature that a unity of this double experience becomes possible.

THE PURUSHOTTAMA

There is finally only one *Purusha*, whose heads are all heads, whose eyes are all eyes, whose ears, all ears. All thoughts are his thoughts and all deeds are his deeds. No one can think or exist except him, the Supreme, the One without a second. As the Veda proclaims, whatever was, whatever is and whatever shall be, whatever can exist anywhere under any circumstances is that *Purusha* alone. Into that *Purushottama* both the *kshara* and the *akshara purushas* melt like ice blocks into the ocean and there is neither the individual nor the world of matter, neither the subject nor the object. There is only one indivisible, oceanic experience of all-comprehensive existence. One, who knows this, is the liberated soul or the *Mahatma*. It is only by knowing him, the *Purushottama*, in all his aspects as *kshara*, *akshara* and *Uttama*, that the soul is released from the three-fold strands of Nature. However, we must realise that the truth of the *kshara* is also the truth of the *Purushottama*. This truth has been alluded to in all the previous chapters but only now is the distinction stated by name. The infinite One has infinite powers from which the miracle of individual personalities emerges from a play of apparently impersonal forces. The mystery of the Supreme Person can only be known through love and devotion. The Spiritual entity within us, the *akshara* or the individual soul offers itself and all it has to the eternal, divine Supreme Person or *Purushottama* of whom it is a likeness. Knowledge finds its completeness in this self-giving, this uplifting of our personal nature to the master of our personality. The sacrifice of action or *yajna karma* thus attains a perfect consummation.

THE KNOWER OF THE PURUSHOTTAMA

O Arjuna! The man of wisdom who knows Me in reality as the Supreme Person knows everything and thus worships Me in all ways!

The enlightened soul, who sees him in all things, knows him as all things and loves him in all things, has only one thing to do and that is to worship him in all things, at all times. Having gained this knowledge there is nothing left for the devotee to do but to offer worship to him—the Supreme One through all her actions—physical, mental and emotional. The *Akshara Purusha*—the immortal, unchanging *jivatma* embodied in the mantle of our present body, makes use of the *Kshara Purusha* or the changing universe with its myriad forms and faces in order to worship the *Purushottama* or the Supreme Person in all ways, and in all things. Every day when the devotee of the *Purushottama* wakes up, she is aware of three things—the immortal Person, her Master—the *Purushottama*, the immortal Self, the *Akshara Purusha* and the external Self or *Kshara Purusha* of his own creation. The eternal devotee uses the eternal creation as the means of worship of the eternal Lord. Everything that she sees or hears or touches or smells or tastes or feels or knows is offered to him, the *Purushottama*.

CONSTANT WORSHIP

The Lord spreads the whole manifest creation before us so that we in turn can offer it back to him in countless acts of self-giving, which knows no limits and suffers no boredom. Because of its very mutability, creation provides us with ever-novel things with which to worship him—the cosmic beloved. Yesterday's flowers are not today's. Every day there is something new and precious to offer our Divine Beloved. Now in this life, now in that, now in this body, now in that, it matters not how or where, the *Akshara Purusha* embodied in the *kshara* keeps on worshipping the *Purushottama*, life after life, using all the means at her command. She keeps offering her love, age after age, birth after birth, through all eternity. She unites the triple strands of divine love, divine knowledge and divine works into every action. *Karma Yoga*, *Bhakti Yoga* and *Jnana Yoga* all blend into one, since Creator, creature, and creation have become one. To know him, is to love him and to love him is to serve him. Knowledge of the Supreme *Purushottama* brings in its wake an outpouring of our entire heart's love and this in turn leads to an outpouring of service for him. The outer form of love is service. *Karma Yoga* is love in action as has been said before.

This is the *Gita*'s way to liberation. This is the *Advaita* of the *Gita*. This is the supreme teaching, which leads us to the heart of the highest mystery of existence. No other knowledge can bring the complete fulfilment of life, which this knowledge gives us. However erudite a person may be, however much he or she might know of the external mysteries of Nature, there remains a thirst in her, which can never be satisfied. This thirst can only be quenched by drinking of the waters of immortality, which is offered in the fifteenth chapter of the *Gita*. Only such a one is complete in body, mind and Spirit, and only such a soul can be called *kritakritya* or one who is completely fulfilled.

ॐ *Hari Aum Tat Sat* ॐ

Thus, in the Upanishad of the *Bhagavad Gita*, the knowledge of Supreme Brahman, the Scripture of *Yoga*, the dialogue between Sri Krishna and Arjuna, ends the fifteenth chapter entitled 'The *Yoga* of the Supreme Person'.

16

DEVASURASAMPATH VIBHAGA YOGA

The Yoga of the Distinction between the Divine and the Demonic Qualities

Aum Sri Krishnaya Paramaatmane' namaha!
Aum Sri Parthasarathaye' namaha.

ॐ

Everything that has to be said has already been said by the end of the fifteenth chapter. It is actually the culmination of the teaching of the *Bhagavad Gita*. The sixteenth and seventeenth are in the nature of supplements and the eighteenth is a grand summing up.

The opposition between the gods and the demons is found in scriptures from all parts of the world. In Hinduism, this antagonism is mentioned even in the Rig Veda. The great epics of the *Ramayana* and the *Mahabharata* also have this opposition between the negative and positive forces of the world. Even today we find this opposition—people with divine qualities and those with demonic qualities. In this chapter, Lord Krishna talks of these two forces, which are apparent to us in the world. Actually they are but two aspects of a single force, thesis and antithesis, and these are known as *daiva* and *asura*—the former moving towards the centre and the latter surging away from it to the periphery of names and forms, one centripetal and the other centrifugal. Some religions refer to these opposites as God and the devil. But the Hindu philosophy considers them to be but two aspects of the same essence. In the Puranas, both the *devas* and the *asuras* have the same father—the sage Kasyapa but different mothers! They actually typify the two impulses in us. We have a strong urge to get to the centre of things and to find out their essence. That is why we have an unquenchable thirst to know more and more. Our love for knowledge is endless. It never gets satiated. At the same time, our ignorance also seems to be never-ending. Though we seem to be seeking for freedom from ignorance, yet at the same time we seem to be working for bondage, because the conflicting urge is also working powerfully in us at the same time. We are like people whose legs are being pulled apart in opposite directions. There is a battle going on everywhere at all times between these two forces, the *daiva* and the *asura*, the divine and the demonic. There is the universal power of integration driving the *jiva* towards the Absolute. At the same time, the psychic, rational and sensory powers keep urging it towards indulgence in the material world. This is the Mahabharata war. This is the conflict we see everywhere, in ourselves, in the streets, in all countries and in the world. These powers struggle, one against the other, and the history of the world is the story of the success or failure of one or the other of these powers. The royal road to evolution lies in co-operating with the powers of integration or the *daivi sampat*. The *asuri sampat* is that which pulls us away from our centres and converts us into objects when we are actually the Supreme Subject!

HOW TO CHANGE OUR NATURES

The practical difficulty when we want to change from the ignorant and shackled beings that we are becomes apparent when we start on the path of *yoga*. We have been told quite emphatically that this transition is indispensable. Liberation means a deliverance from the confining cage of *Prakriti's gunas* and living in the freedom of the eternal, infinite Spirit. This can be affected only through the full development of *sattva guna*. When *sattva* reaches a point when it can go beyond itself, it is capable of entering into its source.

To make this point clear, in this chapter we have been given the distinction between the divine and the demonic natures. The *deva* is capable of self-transforming *sattvic* action and the *asura* is not. The general nature of the human being is a mixture of all three *gunas*. Thus, it would seem that all of us stand an equal chance of proceeding beyond *sattva* into the liberated state. But in actual fact we find that human beings fall largely into two categories—those who have a predominance of *sattva* and turn automatically to knowledge, self-perfection, harmony and benevolence and those who have a preponderance of *rajas*, who are filled with ego, dominant and strong willed, with powerful desires, for the satisfaction of which they try to dominate and put down all who stand in their way. These two categories are the human representatives of the gods and the demons! In order to give Arjuna a clearer understanding of the nature of these two forces, the Lord gives a list of their qualities.

DIVINE QUALITIES

The divine qualities are described first. The first to be mentioned is *abhaya* or fearlessness, since good qualities cannot flourish in an atmosphere charged with the negative emotion of fear. An army has to be guarded from the back as well and it is 'humility', which guards the rear. However many divine qualities we might have, if pride rears its ugly head, all the other qualities become null and void, hence, the Lord's insistence on 'humility'. The remaining qualities are purity of heart, firm upholding of the *yoga* of knowledge, charity, control of the senses, sacrifice, study of the scriptures, penance, honesty, harmlessness, truthfulness, absence of anger, renunciation, peace, an uncritical attitude of acceptance, absence of anger, kindness to all, indifference to sense objects, modesty, a sense of shame in doing wrong, fidelity, intelligence, patience, resolution, purity and absence of malice with humility coming at the end as said before. These are the qualities of the *daivi sampat*.

DEMONIC QUALITIES

Verses ten to twenty give a graphic description of the demonic nature. The normal man is always a mixture of the three *gunas* with one predominating. The one in whom *sattvic* qualities predominate can be known to have *daivi sampat*. The one in whom *rajas* has been carried to the extreme is the *asura*, absolutely selfish, living for personal aggrandizement alone, arrogant, hypocritical, given to bursts of anger, cruel, boastful and devoid of compassion. Even the rituals he performs are for his own enhancement. Does this mean that we are born with certain qualities, which we cannot change? We cannot conclude this, since the *Gita* has been insisting all along that all *jivas* are eternal portions of the Divine. Both *asura* and *deva* have access to liberation as has been brought out many times in our Puranas. Prahlada and Vritra, who were born in the *asura* clan, were two of the greatest devotees of the Lord. A person can be either *sattvo-rajasic* or *rajaso-tamasic*, which prepares him for either divine clarity or *asuric* violence. But we must not take this list to be totally exhaustive. Many beings have both natures intermixed and we find that the *tamasic* man falls into neither category. As the *Mahabharata* says 'Nothing is wholly good or wholly evil.' All we can say is that godlike qualities lead towards liberation and the others lead to bondage. This is the point of the distinction. Just as the twenty qualities given in the thirteenth chapter have to be cultivated by the one who wants liberation, so also the *daivic* qualities mentioned here have to be promoted in us.

GOOD AND EVIL

The *Gita* rises above the ordinary human concepts of morality and takes its stand on a metaphysical ground. What we call good and evil are our human readings of the meaning behind the great drama enacted in the cosmos by these impersonal powers, which alternatively move inward or outward. Thus, we find in the Puranas that at one time the *devas* win and at other times the *asuras*. So also in the human mind we have this two-fold urge within us. The more we move away from the centre, the more we are moving towards what the Puranas call hell, since sorrow is the fruit of this movement. Those who move towards the centre gain heavenly regions. The cosmic forces work perpetually and they work everywhere so that nothing is free from their operations. The evolution and involution of the universe are the workings of these two forces and our human mind cannot perceive why they work in this manner. Our minds are already involved in their operations, and thus cannot comprehend their intentions. The evolution of the *jiva* in Nature is an adventure in which *swabhava* or inherent nature and *karma* or action act as the decisive factors of its destiny. When the *swabhava* is highly *rajasic*, the elements of *sattva* and *tamas* become progressively weak and then the trend of *karma* results in a turning away from the *sattvic* heights into the highest exaggeration of the *rajasic* nature and a full-blown *asura* is born! One can have some idea of the birth of these *asuras* by reading the Puranas. A glimpse into the lives of the great tyrants and despots in the history of the world will also give us an idea of the life and progress of an *asura*. People like Hitler and Mussolini are classic examples of the progress of the *asura*. Once such a strong turn has been taken away from the *sattvic* course, the person is incapable of reversing the process and is plunged into the depths of hell by the very force of the misused divine energy within him. But it must be understood that the energy which propels the *asura* is also divine, just as it is the same electricity which kills a person in the electric chair and gives him heat, light and breeze in different things, like bulbs, fans and so on. Hence, Prahlada the *asura* boy, who was full of *daivic* qualities, told his father who was a complete *asura*, that the might of which he is so proud of, is due entirely to the power of the Lord Narayana, who has allowed him to wield his sword in this mighty fashion. This is as incomprehensible to us as it was to Hiranyakashipu, the father of Prahlada.

All energy, all strength proceeds from one source, which is divine. When it passes through the prism of lower Nature, it gets deflected by the three strands of *sattva*, *rajas* and *tamas* and thus we find the enormous differences in people. The next question is what happens to such a person? Is he damned forever? The *Gita* has emphatically declared that even the vilest of sinners if he resolves rightly should be considered a saint! The demonic nature having plumbed the depths not once but many times now gets an opportunity to take an upward turn since its speed has been checked and then the other truth becomes apparent and propels him in another direction. Just by that one orientation he gets into the *sattvic* path, which leads to liberation. Very often this change takes place by association with good people. Just one word by some noble soul may well lead an *asuric* man to change his ways. Valmiki, the author of the *Ramayana*, was a cruel hunter. The sage Narada met him and changed his destiny with just a few words. Hence, the Hindu philosophy places great importance on *satsang*, or association with the holy.

SHASTRAS

The *asuric* nature is the *rajasic* at its height. It leads to the slavery of the soul. Desire, wrath and greed are the hallmarks of the *rajasic* ego and these are the triple gates to hell, according to the Lord. These three finally fold back into the power of *tamas* or ignorance. The uncontrolled force of the *rajasic* nature when exhausted falls back into the weakness and darkness of *tamas*. To follow the law of selfish desire is neither the truth of our nature nor the law of our being. There is a higher law and a better standard. But where is this to be found. The human race has always been seeking for this just law and whatever it has discovered has been embodied in the *shastra* or scriptures, ethics or rules of conduct. The scriptures expound the rule of the best to be found in social living. All scriptures try to give us certain rules concerning a person's right relations with man, God and Nature. The *shastra* is not a mass of superstition, unintelligently followed by the *tamasic* man, as some people suppose. *Shastra* is the knowledge of the saints gained through intuition and experience, the best standards available to the race. The *asuric* man who disregards the dictates of the *shastra* in order to follow the demands of his own under-developed instincts and selfish desires may get pleasure but not lasting happiness, for true happiness can only be gained by right living, which means living in harmony with the rest of the creation. The law of instinct and desire must be replaced by the knowledge of right action as given in the *shastra* or books of right living.

In its normal aspect, the *shastra* is not the supreme law. Like the laws of Manu, and the Ten Commandments, the *shastra* only provides a rule for the transcendence of our lower nature and develops the discipline, which is essential for all spiritual ascents. It is a means and not an end. There is a vast difference between action according to personal desire and action according to the *shastra*. The latter is the recognised science and art of life, the outcome of man's collective culture, religion and knowledge generally expounded by some great soul in some age or other. It is reiterated by other great souls, age after age. Action, according to the dictates of the *shastra*, allows for the growth of *sattva*. So humankind must perforce proceed according to this. This is the general rule for all humanity. All societies from ancient times down to the present have decreed this. The way out of the *asuric* nature is to follow the rule of the *shastra*. In the beginning it might be followed blindly and with no understanding, in a *tamasic* fashion. But later, when these rules have become a part of the personality, the person will slowly rise from the first *tamasic*, blind obedience into a *rajasic* enquiry and rebellion and then on to the *sattvic* acceptance of such a life, which is based on personal experience and knowledge.

The *shastra* is thus the rule of conduct which man sets up to control and govern his own lower animal tendencies by the use of reason and an intelligent will. This must be first observed and made the guide for our conduct and action until our instincts are schooled and controlled and we are ready for a freer and more intelligent self-guidance. Only after many births of such schooling would an *asura* be evolved enough to follow the highest and supreme law of the divine nature, which gives the maximum liberty to the evolved person. The *Gita* gives the way of rising above the *asuric* tendencies. Chapter 18 verse 59 shows how we are first prompted only by desire, next we come to the state of guidance by law—*shastra* (Chapter 16 verse 24) and finally we act spontaneously as we are guided only by the spirit. (Chapter 18 verse 64).

AVAILABLE TO ALL

Everyone living in a society will have access to some type of *shastra* or other. The human race has always been seeking for some high and just law of action, which can free it from the bonds of its demonic nature, for everyone has a demon lurking within him. Therefore, we find that every culture had its own formula for right living, based on the intuitive experience of its master minds, the sages and the prophets. The *asuric* person leaves this rule in order to follow the animal instincts of his baser nature. Therefore, if he wants to reach the Godhead he has to retrace his steps back to manhood first and that can be done only by following the dictates of the *shastra*, which embody the highest and noblest ideals of the human being. These rules must therefore be observed and followed until his instinctive *asuric* character is schooled and the habit of self-control made part of his nature. Only then would he be ready for the freedom of self-guiding action leading to the supreme liberty of the spiritual nature. The *Gita* itself is known as *dharma shastra* or the code of living in the light of the Spirit. It is also known as *yoga shastra* for it supplies us

Devasurasampath Vibhaga Yoga

with a practical guidance for transcending the *gunas* of nature and developing the discipline, which leads to the highest spiritual enlightenment. But the *Gita* is not an ordinary *shastra*. It is not merely a code of social ethics but of spiritual ethics. It tells us how to lift ourselves from the *asuric* depths into which our demonic natures may have dragged us, and also shows us how to raise ourselves up to the pinnacle of the freedom of the Spirit, which abandons all rules and turns to God alone for its sole law of action and its sole inspiration! But this is a jump, which cannot be made by the *asura*. Hence, the Lord's last words in this chapter are to advice Arjuna to follow the *shastra* when in doubt.

ॐ *Hari Aum Tat Sat* ॐ

Thus, in the Upanishad of the *Bhagavad Gita*, the knowledge of Supreme Brahman, the Scripture of *Yoga*, the dialogue between Sri Krishna and Arjuna, ends the sixteenth chapter entitled 'The *Yoga* of the Distinction between the Divine and the Demonic Qualities'.

> Therefore let the scripture be your guide in determining right and wrong action. You should act in the world only after knowing the rules that are given in the scriptures.

17

SRADDHATRAYA VIBHAGA YOGA

The Yoga of the Three-Fold Faith

Aum Sri Krishnaya Paramaatmane' namaha!
Aum Sri Parthasarathaye' namaha.

The seventeenth chapter begins with a doubt on the part of Arjuna. What is the basis of an act, which does not proceed from animal desires or from scriptural injunctions? Even the rule of desire contains within it a certain force since it proceeds from our primitive origins, which we cannot deny. The *shastra*, on the other hand, is backed by the authority of established rule. But what can be said about that action which is done on the spur of the moment with full faith and belief that we are doing the right thing? We may not always be able to consult the *Bhagavad Gita* or the Laws of Manu before performing some action. In fact, most actions are done spontaneously without previous thought, but with the full faith that we are doing the right thing—that which ought to be done. On what basis do such actions stand, is Arjuna's question.

Some people may not wilfully defy the *shastra* but they may be ignorant of them. What happens to them?

Action, according to personal desire, belongs to the lower stages of life and is dominated by the quality of *rajas*. Action, according to the *shastra*, allows the growth of the *sattvic* element. Humanity must first proceed through these as has been said in the previous chapter. But after proceeding along this path, slowly and perhaps unconsciously we formulate a greater rule, which we try to live up to. The religion we follow, the philosophy we believe in, the social ideas that we try to enforce, will all depend on the relative values or absolute perfection about which we have some vague idea. In proportion to the sincerity in living according to this ideal, we can become living examples of this ideal.

THE BREAK FROM THE SHASTRA

Sometimes there is a freer tendency in the human being, which tends to break away from the established code of conduct and goes in search of a new law, which is considered more fitting. This happens when the existing *shastra* ceases to be a living force and stiffens into a mass of dead customs and superstitions. Then we find that a newer truth and a newer law have to be found by some great individual or *vibhuti* of the Lord. Buddha modified the Vedic ritualism and Christ replaced the ancient Law of Moses. Humanity's search for perfection never stops. Sometimes an individual may revolt against the *shastra*. This revolt may often be the *rajasic* ego seeking recognition and adulation. Even this is better than the dead *tamasic* following of a convention without any right knowledge of the great principles underlying the convention. Most people follow certain customs blindly because all those who have gone before them have followed it. They do not enquire into the meaning underlying it. Sometimes the *shastra* is a living, vibrating force in which case it is the best rule for the average man, but the exceptional man, who has spiritually developed far beyond the rest of his brethren, is not bound by that standard. He is called upon to go beyond, to an absolute perfection and learn to live in the liberty of the Spirit.

FAITH GUIDES US

But this is very often a puzzling and insecure path and unless one is absolutely sure, it would always be better not to deflect from the norm since the

Sraddhatraya Vibhaga Yoga

dangers of losing our direction are great. Hence, it is always necessary for all spiritual seekers to have a guide or *guru* who, having traversed the path himself, is competent to guide the newcomer. But what happens when such a guide is not available? What is the basis of such a person's action? The Lord replies that the basis is to be found in his or her *sraddha* or faith or what he or she thinks to be the truth of her life and existence. Faith here does not mean blind belief but a striving towards an ideal. Even those who have no idea about *Shastras* will have some ideal on which he or she bases their actions. But it must be remembered that even this faith will be coloured by the three *gunas*. If the person is *tamasic*, she will never be able to reach the truth. If she is *rajasic*, she may be carried away into strange paths. In both these cases, her chance for salvation lies in a return to *sattva*, which will impose restrains on her *rajasic* ego as well as on her *tamasic* ignorance. There is a sub-human level of faith, a human level and a super-human level. So the faith on the basis of which we act is not merely a whim of the moment but a judgement, which springs from the very depths of our personality. The faith of each person takes on the quality of our temperament. As our faith so we are, says the Lord. This sounds very much like the modern theory of pragmatism. If a person consists of her faith, then to follow that is to follow the truth, which has shaped her, and therefore there is no other truth for her. She is what she is today by the power of her past will or faith, which in turn creates her future. Thus, we are ever creating ourselves. We are our own makers. To some extent this is true but it is not the whole truth. This is only the truth of our becoming; the truth of our dynamics but it is not the truth of our Being. Beyond our changing personality there is a universal becoming of which ours is only a movement or ripple, and even beyond that is the eternal and changeless Being toward which we are meant to proceed.

TYPES OF FAITH

Through the *yoga* of the *Gita*, we are encouraged to become divine, as our inmost being is divine. Our success in this endeavour also depends on our *sraddha*. We have to make a conscious effort of will to change our natures and existing *sraddha*, which may be *tamasic* or *rajasic*, and make it *sattvic* and finally go beyond that as well. All *sadhana* or *yoga* is an effort to do this. *Tamas* is considered the lowest and *sattva* the highest. The reason for this is due to the degree of reality, which is expressed through their media. In *tamas*, reality is hardly expressed, in *rajas* it is distorted and in *sattva* it is transparent. The sun's rays can be reflected in tar, turbid water and crystal clear water. In *sattva*, even though there may not be a direct contact with reality, there is a perfect reflection of it. In *rajas*, this reflection is distorted as in the murky water and in *tamas* it is hardly seen, as in a barrel-full of liquid tar. Our attitude to every aspect of our life depends on the type of *guna*, which is predominant in us—our personal conduct, our political life, our social relationships, our religious practices and even our choice of food.

GUNAS DIRECT OUR CHOICES

Why do different people automatically veer towards different types of things? *Sattvic* people worship the Supreme Divine, *rajasic* people worship the demigods in order to attain some object of desire, and *tamasic* people worship ghosts and spirits. There are some that undertake severe penances not decreed by the scriptures, torturing their bodies in order to achieve certain selfish or even devilish ends. These penances may appear to be saintly, but are in fact prompted by hypocrisy, arrogance and a desire for power and thus they should be considered demonic. Torturing the body by prolonged fasting or by self-inflicted corporeal punishment comes under this type of *tapas* or austerity.

AUSTERITY OF THE BODY

The Lord then tells us what is meant by *tapas* of the body. The body should be considered as a vehicle for the progress of the *jivatma* in its journey to perfection and should be treated with the respect it deserves. It should neither be pampered nor punished unjustly. Buddha says, "The habitual practice of self-mortification which is painful, unworthy and unprofitable should not be followed." *Tapas* or austerity has been prescribed in order to remove the impurities that may arise in the body due to wrong eating and wrong living. As a machine needs fuel so a body needs food and the type of food one eats is of the utmost importance, for upon that will depend the type of thoughts which arise in the mind.

SATTVIC DIET

Indian thought has always realized the importance of diet in the spiritual life. Many experiments have been done on these lines from ancient times. The result of these experiments is the *sattvic* diet, which is a must for all followers of *yoga*. There is no country in the world in which the major portion of the population gave up meat eating in order to purify their minds and thus gain spiritual heights. Today, many people give up meat eating for health reasons but in India it was given up purely for moral and spiritual reasons, for it was felt strongly that the taking of life in any form was a sin and must be minimized to the greatest extent possible. This was not because they were unaware of the benefits of a vegetarian diet as far as health was concerned but this was not their main consideration. The health of the body though important was given a subsidiary place to the health of the mind and the progress of spiritual evolution. Even today neither western medical science nor psychology has fully realized the importance of food and the effect it has on the health of both mind and body. More than ten thousand years ago the Lord enumerated these properties to Arjuna. The *sattvic* temperament instinctively prefers foods that nourish the mental, vital and physical forces. These foods are bland, naturally sweet and increase longevity, intelligence, strength, health and happiness. Such foods are fresh and not over-cooked or over-spiced. This in fact is the perfect natural diet, which is becoming increasingly popular in the modern world.

RAJASIC DIET

Rajasic people prefer food, which is sour, pungent, hot, and burning, giving rise to pain, grief and disease. This describes the over-spiced and over-rich foods which even doctors now admit have led to all the ills of modern society. Heartburn, heart attacks, indigestion, dyspepsia, constipation and so on are all caused by this type of food. The list is too well known to need enumeration.

TAMASIC DIET

Foods, which are devoid of vitality, over-cooked, stale, polluted and impure, are dear to those of a *tamasic* disposition. For perfect health, food should always be eaten as fresh as possible both after plucking as well as after cooking. The more it is kept, the more it will lose its vital quality and the less likely it is to produce vitality in us. This is a very obvious statement, which is completely overlooked by the modern man in his addiction to tinned, canned and refrigerated foods which no doubt are a part of modern life but whether there are an absolutely essential part is left for each individual to decide for herself. To some extent we may not be able to help our innate tastes but having known and accepted the truth, it is left for each of us to decide what is best for us and whether we are capable of making the effort of changing our diet style, which itself is a *tapas*.

COMPULSORY ACTIONS

The Lord in this chapter divides into three sections those actions which are compulsory for all human beings. These are *yajna*, *dana* and *tapas*, or sacrifice, charity and austerity. These three cover the entire field of our relationships—our relationship with the Supreme, our relationship with society and our relationship with our body and mind. We owe certain duties to each of these three. Hence, these are actions, which are compulsory for all human beings. They have to be performed by all. None can consider herself to be above these.

The categorization of food comes under both *yajna* and *tapas*. The food, which is eaten, should first of all be offered to the deity within us. This is a *yajna* to the Lord manifesting within the body, who has not only provided the food but who alone is capable of digesting and assimilating it, so that it can benefit us. This is a daily *yajna*, which everyone has to perform. This *yajna* can also be made into *tapas* if a *sattvic* diet is adhered to and the food is eaten sparingly. Then it becomes *tapas* or control of the body and the senses, which clamour for exciting and stimulating food rather than for life-giving food.

TYPES OF YAJNA

The Lord has already said that all actions can be considered as a *yajna* or offering to the Supreme. And all actions can be made *sattvic* by two factors—one by giving up the desire for fruits and the other by avoiding fruitless actions! When action is done with a keen desire for the benefits, it can be considered *rajasic*. When the action is done without due observance of the rules by which it should be done, it will become fruitless and thus it can be termed *tamasic*. When the *yajna* or ritual is done with pride and hypocrisy, in order to make a show of one's wealth or for personal gain and aggrandizement, it must be considered as *rajasic* even if it is offered to the gods. The *tamasic* offering to the gods is normally done without faith, just because everyone else does it, with neither concentration nor belief in what is being done and naturally it will not produce any results. Thus, it is fruitless. The *sattvic yajna* is offered to God with full belief in what is being done and full belief in the divinity to which it is being offered. It is done without desire for personal gain. It will be noticed that the more impersonal the motive the more *sattvic* the act will be. Though the *sattvic yajna* appears to be very near to the ideal, it is still not the ideal, though it is a very necessary step in our progress to perfection, since it purifies our mind and will. The highest *yajna* is offered to the Supreme *Purushottama* for the fulfilment of the divine will alone. Here there is neither self nor selflessness, and the *jivatma* stands united with the *Paramatma*. Such actions cannot even be termed as actions unless we say that the Master of the *yajna* is the *Purushottama*, who is offering the works of his energy to himself making the *jiva* as his instrument. In this we find that there is no personal initiative (no *arambha*) and no expectation of benefits (no *sankalpa*).

TYPES OF TAPAS

Tapas is divided into three types—*tapas* of the body, mind and speech. *Sattvic tapas* of the body consists in the worship of the gods, of the noble ones, of teachers and also in purity, uprightness, continence and non-violence. *Tapas* of the mind includes study of the scriptures, cheerfulness, gentleness, silence, self-control and purity and *tapas* of speech is the utterance of truthful, pleasant and beneficial words. Even a harsh truth can be clothed in pleasant terms, which will make it more palatable. *Tapas* of the mind purifies the whole temperament and produces serenity, calmness and love for all.

Rajasic tapas, on the other hand, is done to get honour and distinction from others, with a view to impresses them. Its fruits are fleeting.

Tamasic tapas tortures the mind and body and is motivated by the desire to cause injury to others. Sadistic actions may be called *tamasic*.

TYPES OF DANA

Having dealt with this, the Lord goes on to describe our duties to society. This comes under *Dana* or charity. The *tamasic* gift is offered with no regard to the right time, place or need of the recipient, and is despised by the recipient even while accepting it. Bribes are a classic example of the *tamasic* gift. The bribe is given with a low motive. We despise ourselves and the one who accepts it even as we give it. Coins thrown to beggars and gifts which are offered rudely with no love or respect for the recipient are all example of *tamasic dana*. The *rajasic* gift is given with a view to gain alone. The *sattvic* way of giving is to give due thought to the right time, place and the needs of the recipient. It is given with due regard to the needs of the person. It is given with love and not with a view to the benefits already received or to be received. In fact, the *sattvic dana* is also a *yajna* or offering to the God within the recipient.

The entire universe comes into being and is sustained by the Supreme Lord's giving of himself in a continuous flow of love to humankind. The action of the perfected man will also be such an outpouring of knowledge, love and joy to those around him. The Lord has elaborately dealt with the original question of Arjuna's as to the stand of those who worship with faith but without scriptural sanction. He has shown how every type of action can be considered as worship, if done in the *sattvic* manner. He has also shown how even those so-called pure actions like *yajna*, *dana* and *tapas* can be non-*sattvic* and lead to no spiritual benefit if done in a *rajasic* or *tamasic* way.

Aum Tat Sat

The chapter ends with the *mantra* or formula, *Aum Tat Sat*, which is a triple definition of the

Sraddhatraya Vibhaga Yoga

Supreme Brahman. It signifies the total comprehensiveness of the nature of Brahman in both its transcendent and immanent form. *Aum* stands for absolute supremacy, *Tat* for universality and *Sat* for absolute reality. These two words *tat* and *sat*, point to the fact that God is both outside us and inside us, both far and near. Even this idea is to be transcended in a larger grasp of the Absolute, which enfolds within itself both these, and goes beyond these. *Aum* is the symbol of the triple Brahman as well as the three states of consciousness and is the initiating syllable pronounced at the beginning of all acts of *yajna*, *dana* and *tapas*. These three words when uttered together signify a grasp of the whole, which is both within, without and everywhere. They should be pronounced at the outset of every action in order to remind us that our work should be an expression of the Divine and should be motivated by him, dedicated to him and done for him. If this is our *sraddha* or faith, then it will have the power to create for us the world as it really is, permeated and saturated with Divine consciousness. The Divine is all. It is the Absolute reality and this invocation within our mind at the beginning and conclusion of any *yajna*, *dana* or *tapas* completes it and imbues it with reality. When this *mantra* of mental attunement to the Divine is not there, the action itself becomes devoid of reality and leads to bondage and is called *asat*. God is the completion of everything. Anything done without his remembrance is incomplete and therefore unreal. The Supreme *Purusha* has to be invoked always. This is the *sraddha* or faith, which should dominate our lives at every moment. Only then will all our actions be divinised and provide another foothold with which to reach him—the *Purushottama*!

ॐ *Hari Aum Tat Sat* ॐ

Thus, in the Upanishad of the *Bhagavad Gita*, the knowledge of Supreme Brahman, the Scripture of *Yoga*, the dialogue between Sri Krishna and Arjuna, ends the seventeenth chapter entitled 'The *Yoga* of the Three fold Faith'.

> Foods which promote life, vitality, strength and heath and give joy and satisfaction – which are tasty, succulent, nourishing and agreeable are liked by the sattvic types.

18

MOKSHA SANNYASA YOGA

The Yoga of Liberation and Renunciation

Aum Sri Krishnaya Paramaatmane' namaha!
Aum Sri Parthasarathaye' namaha.

The eighteenth chapter begins with Arjuna's last and final appeal to Lord Krishna to tell him the difference between *sannyasa* and *tyaga*. Both these words mean renunciation and both topics have been exhaustively dealt with in the previous chapters, but since people even from those times have misunderstood these words, Arjuna wanted further clarification.

The frequent harping of the *Gita* on this crucial distinction has been justified by the subsequent history of India and the constant confusion regarding these two similar yet different attitudes and in answering Arjuna, Lord Krishna sums up the entire teaching of the *Gita*.

In the previous chapter, the Lord has already stated that acts of sacrifice, charity and austerity should never be renounced. But since even these can come under the sway of the three *gunas*, only the *sattvic* type should be followed. In the third and fourth chapters, he has extolled *Karma Yoga* or inaction in action while in the fifth, he has praised *Karma Sannyasa* or action in inaction. So what is his final word on the subject? This is Arjuna's question for on that answer relies the entire teaching of the *Gita*. Krishna has always insisted not on renunciation of action but on the renunciation of the desire for the fruits of action. This is both *sannyasa* and *tyaga*.

Tyaga is the mental renunciation of the fruits of action and *sannyasa*, the physical renunciation of action and therefore of life in the world since one cannot live in the world without acting as has been stated before. The *Gita* does not approve of the renunciation of action but on the renunciation of personal desire in the action. The *Gitacharya* (teacher of the *Gita*) insists that the liberated soul can and must remain in service even after liberation. This theory is Krishna's great gift to the world. He is totally against all renunciation of action but gives us the method of converting *karma* into *nishkama karma* or desireless action. Another idea which the *Gita* gives is that the *tyagi* is one who has stopped taking any personal initiative in action and waits for the Lord to give the commands and makes himself into a perfect instrument. The second idea he gives is that the *sannyasi* is one who has given up all expectations of the results of his action, leaving everything into the capable hands of the Lord, who is indeed the doer, enjoyer and giver of the results of the action.

TYAGA

Indian thought from those times right up to the present day has misunderstood the meaning of these words and has extolled non-action or *sannyasa* as the highest spiritual state and condemned action to an inferior position since they suspect that action is the culprit, which forges us to the chain of *karma*. They assert that even those actions, which are insisted on by the *Gita*, like *yajna*, *dana* and *tapas*, should at best be considered as preliminary to the supreme inaction of *sannyasa* or non-action, which is the only way to self-realisation. This immediately cuts the ground from under the feet of the majority of the world's population who would find it impossible to take to a life of *sannyasa* in its conventional form. The glory of the *Gita*'s teaching is that it brings *sannyasa* out of the forests, mountains and caves of classic thought into the hearth and homes, offices and factories of daily life. It insists that real *sannyasa* has action and living in the world as its basis and not a flight to the forest. True *sannyasa* is renunciation of all expectation—*sarvasamkalpa sannyasi*, as has been reiterated over and over again. Therefore, it does not preclude all action. On the contrary, it can be practiced only in the midst of activity. Again *tyaga* is not the physical renunciation of action but refusal to initiate or instigate any action—*sarvarambaparityagi*. *Tyaga* according to the Lord is the mental renunciation of personal initiative. In this sense, *tyaga* is more important than *sannyasa* since it is a pre-requisite to it. The doubt now arises as to how any action can be undertaken without initiative. There are three requisites in renunciation—renunciation of the fruit, relinquishment of the idea that we are the agents of the action which automatically cuts the bond of attachment to the action, and finally the relinquishment of personal agency which comes with the realisation that the Lord alone is the author of all action.

RENUNCIATION

"No initiation or instigation of action, no expectation or anticipation of the fruits but full participation in the drama of life!" This is the core of the teaching of the *Gita*. The wise man whose doubts have been dispelled has no aversion to disagreeable actions and no attachment to agreeable ones. He reiterates that *yajna, dana* and *tapas*—sacrifice, gifts and penance—should not be given up but it must be remembered that even these are coloured by the *gunas*. The abandonment of any of these three due to ignorance is declared to be *tamasic*. One who relinquishes these three through fear of physical suffering is *rajasic* but one who performs them with a deep sense of duty, without attachment either to the action itself or its fruit, is indeed *sattvic*. Sattvic renunciation is to withdraw not from the action but from the demand of the personal ego behind it. It is to do the work as dictated by the strong faith or *sraddha* of the person that has been guided by the rules of correct and acceptable living as dictated by the *shastra*. Of course it is always possible to delude oneself that we are abiding by the *shastra* and that God demands the death of the infidel. This of course arises from a total misconception of the idea of God. When God is thought of as a vindictive monster who demands blood and vengeance, obviously the action is done by an *asuric*, demonic ego who has no conception of the nature of the Godhead. The Law of Karma will automatically take care of such offenders.

The Lord has given many pen portraits of the different aspects of the evolved soul—the *bhakta*, the *Karma Yogi*, the *Sthitaprajna* and as *Gunatita*. All of them have one thing in common. They have realised that all action is instigated by the Lord alone and done by his *Prakriti*, so the only thing that is left for them to do is to accept the role of a faultless instrument and perform the action as perfectly as possible. The one who initiates is the Lord and the one who acts is his *Prakriti*. So where does the actor come? As has been said by the Lord to Arjuna, his only duty is to make himself into a perfect instrument. This is why the *Gita* insists on action. Only in the faultless performance of an action can we perfect ourselves as instruments. That is why we are not asked to renounce actions but only the desire for the personal gain to be got from it. There is no harm in liking and appreciating the work we are doing. In fact, if we did not find the work to be desirable and rewarding we could never do it with the zest and enthusiasm, which is expected of the *Karma Yogi*. But personal motivation is to be completely given up. All motivation and initiative comes from God and we really don't need to know what the motivation is or what the outcome will be. All we are expected to do is to throw ourselves heart and soul into the work which has been placed before us with no anticipation or expectation. This is the *Sthitaprajna*, the Karma Yogi, the enlightened soul who, is a walking God for he has emptied himself of all

Moksha Sannyasa Yoga

personal ego and has been filled with divine initiative and divine glory.

When it is done for the good of all, *lokasamgraham* it yields enormous results. Of course the *yogi* does not do it for the sake of even these good results. In fact, she has no way of knowing what is good and what is bad in the ultimate sense and what the world considers as good and bad may not be seen as such in the eyes of God. So it is not her business to conjecture on these points but to get on with the action as *kartavyam karma*, or that action which has to be done and is the best possible at that particular moment. Success and failure is in the hands of the Supreme and he will relegate these according to his omniscient will and purpose. In the end all action has to be given up, not physically by inertia or immobility but spiritually to the Master of our Being, who is the Lord of all works and by whose power alone all action is accomplished. It is the universal *Shakti* or motivating power of the Lord that acts through the instrument of our individual personality. The mental transference of all our works to him and the dedication of the fruits to him are the real *sannyasa* and the real *tyaga*, according to the *Gita*.

The next doubt, which might occur to us, is whether there are any prohibited actions. To this the Lord gives an emphatic reply. Any action can be done so long as it is done without any personal motivation in order to gain some selfish results. Negative actions can be easily located when this method is applied. No amount of euphemistic thinking can make us believe that slander, theft and murder can be condoned for it is pretty certain that these actions are done only for some personal and selfish benefit. Sometimes people do some violent actions for the sake of their religion or for the sake of their country or so they say. They may sincerely believe this. But ultimately this is also selfish since in so doing they are causing pain and death to many innocent people. The case of the modern suicide bombers come under this category since their motivation is to cause injury and pain to others under the delusion that they are working according to the dictates of God. Moreover, they are guilty of the heinous crime of taking their own lives. So when in doubt as to the quality of the action, ask yourself what your motivation is and whether you can renounce the fruits.

The Lord further elucidates correct action by saying that there should be no attachment to pleasant, successful or lucrative work and no aversion to unpleasant and non-profitable work. The wise person puts aside the doubts and hesitations of the normal desire-ridden individual and follows the highest ideal of her nature, which is the will of the Lord within. She does not hanker for the fruits of heaven or the hereafter as the religious person does nor does she crave for the benefits of this world as the materialistic person. Her will is totally subjugated to the will of the Lord within. Since she expects no personal benefits from her action she is above the Law of *Karma*, which decrees three types of results—pleasant, unpleasant and mixed.

CAUSES FOR ACTION

The Lord enumerates the five causes or requisites for the accomplishment of any action as given by the philosophy of the *Samkhya*. The first is *adhishtana*, which is the foundation of all action and is made up of the mind, body and intellect. Next comes the *karta*, the individual or doer of the action, *kaarana* or the instrumentation of nature, *cheshta* or the different kinds of movements, which are necessary to perform the action and finally *daiva* or the unseen universal power, which is the deciding factor behind the success or failure of any action. These five together make up the efficient cause of all the types of actions that a person undertakes. The one who thinks of her limited, individual personality as being the doer is deluding herself. It is the *Shakti* of the lord that does the action and the individual should consider herself to be merely an instrument in the hands of the universal energy. Such a person is a non-actor even though she may do all actions. As the bow in the hands of Arjuna is guiltless so Arjuna in the hands of the Lord has no claim to doership and cannot be praised or blamed for the work of destruction. Gandhari, the mother of the Kauravas, at the end of the war cursed Krishna and not Bhima or Arjuna as being responsible for the destruction of her sons. Krishna merely smiled and accepted her curse. This work of destruction was needed for humanity to move forward to another creation of the kingdom of *dharma*. The Pandavas were the chosen instruments for the furtherance of this universal cause. At the end of the war, far from having got any personal gain, the Pandavas had lost almost everything they held dear, including their brilliant sons. Therefore, it is not action which binds us to the wheel of *karma*, but the knowledge or intention with which the work is done. This is what makes the important spiritual difference.

Daivam is the non-human factor that underlies all human effort. It is the all-seeing will that is at work in the world. In all human actions there is an element of luck, fate or destiny or whatever we might call it which is also the force of the accumulated acts of one's past life. We can plant the seed but we need not necessarily see the fruit of that tree. *Daivam* is a cosmic necessity, the resultant of all that has happened in the past which rules unnoticed.

MECHANICS OF ACTION

In the mechanics of action, the three things, which impel us are knowledge, the object of knowledge and the knower. The agent of the action and the organs of action are the constituents of the action. The knower and the agent are one and the same. This agent is the individual who takes in various bits of information through her senses and decides that she knows enough about the matter to act upon it. Knowledge of the object is that which she has previously gained by the mind and which impels her with a desire to possess it. What we must understand is that this knowledge is also coloured by the three *gunas*. It is because of the element of the *gunas* in them that there are differences in the way we know things and in the spirit in which we do the work.

TYPES OF KNOWLEDGE

Lord Krishna goes on to differentiate between the three types of knowledge, the three types of action, agents and intellects that constitute any action. *Sattvic* knowledge sees the one, indivisible whole in all the differences. It sees the imperishable Being in all becomings. The principle of the *sattvic* person's action is related to the total purpose of existence. The *sattvic* actor reflects the divine will and grows slowly into a faultless instrument in the hands of the Divine. *Rajasic* knowledge is that which sees only the multiplicity and is incapable of discovering the true principle of unity. This knowledge is a jumble of various types of learning put together in order to make some sense out of the confusion in the mind. It promotes restless action with no firm governing law. *Tamasic* knowledge is a lazy, narrow-minded and obstinate way of looking at things. It sees nothing beyond what it wants to see and regards its knowledge as infallible and clings on to it despite every effort made by others to disabuse it of its obstinacy.

TYPES OF ACTION

Sattvic action is done in the clear light of reason without any personal bias or initiative and without any expectation for personal benefits. At its highest culminating point it becomes that action, which is solely dictated by the Spirit within us and not by our own intelligence, however lofty it might be. Such an action is totally free from ego and even from the limitation of the best opinion, noblest desire or loftiest mental ideal. In their place will be the complete assurance of an infallible power that instigates the actor from within. *Rajasic* action is that which a person undertakes with a view to some gain alone. It is done with great strain and an inflated sense of ego in order to achieve the fruits of personal desire. This may often be masked under a cloak of patriotism or religious fervour.

Tamasic action is undertaken with no idea of how the work should be done or one's own ability to accomplish the task, a mistaken idea of its fruits, and with no consideration for others. In other words, it proves to be of no use either to the doer or to others. It is a waste of effort from beginning to end. It is quite different from *rajasic* action, which may well bring name and fame to the agent who has done it with effort and determination to succeed.

TYPES OF AGENTS

Now the Lord examines the three types of agents. The *sattvic* doer is without ego and free from passionate attachment either to the action or to its benefits. Her mind is not elated by success or depressed by failure. She has a pure and selfless enthusiasm for the work on hand, however small or trivial it might appear to others. This is because she is fixed in the knowledge of the divine purpose of her action and the scorn and praise of the world has no effect on her. It can neither deter her nor encourage her for she knows no law but that of the divine. She strives to become the perfect instrument. In her all personal ego slowly become obliterated. The free agent does his or her work as an instrument of the Universal Spirit for the maintenance of the cosmic order. He may even perform violent acts without any selfish motive but only because it is his ordained duty. What matters is not the work but the spirit in which it is done. When an action is done with joy and totally unselfconsciously, it becomes a labour of love and is not felt as an obligation or a pain.

The *rajasic* doer is passionately attached to the gain to be got from the action and thus negligent of the action itself. She thinks that any means can be employed to gain the desired ends and cares little as to who she injures so long as she gets what she wants. Greedy, impure and violent she jumps with joy at success and slumps in despair at failure.

She might force herself to do unpleasant things and feel that she is doing something great but there is something vital missing from this type of action.

The *tamasic* doer is lazy, procrastinating and obstinate in her stupidity. She does things in a purely mechanical fashion, totally uninterested in what she is doing and makes little or no effort to do a good job. She follows the most vulgar opinion of the herd and takes foolish pride in her wrongdoing. Narrow, brute-cunning replaces intelligence. She has an insolent contempt for her superiors and a total lack of sincerity. She is slow to act, easily depressed and offended and gives up the whole enterprise at the slightest provocation. The action is done with suffering and with the thought that she is doing something disagreeable, and this takes away from the value of the act, however noble the act may be.

TYPES OF INTELLECT OR BUDDHI

Having thus given a brilliant analysis of the three types of knowledge, action and of the agent of action, the Lord goes on to clarify the different types of intelligence and firmness with which the actor works. It is the *buddhi* or intellect, which chooses the type of action and decides what is right and what is wrong—*dharma* and *adharma*. The *sattvic* understanding immediately assesses what should be done and what should be avoided with regard to the right place and time. This assessment is made not from the point of view of personal gain but from the point of view of the ultimate liberation of the Spirit. In other words, the intelligence of the *sattvic* doer immediately gauges the merits of an action on the spiritual scale—whether it will fetter her to the chains of *karma* or whether it will release her.

Rajasic understanding, on the other hand, misinterprets what is right and what is wrong action and what should be done and what left undone. The *rajasic* intellect is fully capable of making a right judgment but her reason is a slave to desire and is capable of distorting the truth so as to serve the selfish purpose of the ego. She assesses everything through the highly coloured glasses of personal gain so that even *adharma* is justified if it helps her to gain the fruits of her desire. Greed, anger and desire are the hallmarks of the *rajasic* intellect—the triple gates to hell as the Lord says.

The *tamasic* intellect is enveloped in ignorance and sees everything as being just the opposite of what it really is. It persists in its wrong understanding and insists that it is right. No amount of advice or persuasion can deter it from the senseless path of its own ignorant choice. It dwells on the fears and depressions of the mind, which make it weak and cowardly. The actions to which this intellect urges the doer will naturally be of very poor quality and may not even have any result.

TYPES OF DETERMINATION.

Sattvic firmness engages in those activities, which produce spiritual evolution. Despite all the difficulties on the path, the *sattvic* doer will continue with her *sadhana* with great determination. *Rajasic* determination, on the other hand, assiduously goes after the first three *purusharthas* or goals of life—*dharma, artha* and *kama* corresponding to virtue, wealth and pleasure. These three are firmly pursued by the *rajasic* person for purely selfish reasons.

The firmness with which the deluded mind clings to sleep, fear, worry and pride can be called

Moksha Sannyasa Yoga

tamasic. Even when someone points out a way to get rid of her fears and worries, the *tamasic* person will not take it; for she derives a perverse pleasure from them.

TYPES OF HAPPINESS

Happiness is the universal pursuit of humanity. It may be pursued in an obvious manner or in an indirect way. Pain is an exception, which we accept when we have to. The type of things which bring happiness to a person will depend on his dominating mode. When *tamas* predominates, we get happiness from sloth and error. When *rajas* prevails, we get happiness from wealth, power, pride and glory. Happiness of the *sattvic* person lies in the fulfilment of the higher mind and spirit and not in the acquisition of wealth and relations. The *sattvic* nature, which seeks the happiness of the higher mind, does not depend on external incentives but only on its own inner serenity. But this has to be achieved through a strict self-discipline, which may mean an apparent loss of our habitual pleasures in the beginning but which in the end will put an end to all sorrows.

As has been said before, *sattvic* firmness does not balk at the strict discipline entailed in following the path of *yoga* for it knows that despite the temporary discomforts the end will be blissful. The *rajasic* person, on the other hand, derives her happiness from the keenly felt joys of the senses and body, which are like nectar to her in the beginning but which eventually leave her worn out and unhappy. She is left with the proverbial drop of poison in the dregs of the cup, which she has emptied with such gusto, leading to disappointment, disgust and disease. This is because these pleasures in themselves are not what the Spirit in us truly demands from life. *Tamasic* happiness is derived from sleep, sloth and inertia. Nature has endowed it with a smug satisfaction in its own vulgar joys and trivial pleasures.

SWADHARMA

Up to now the discussion has been on the effect of the *gunas* on the mind and on actions. The development of the mind from the lower natures of *rajas* and *tamas* to *sattva* and from there to the freedom of the Spirit is the goal of evolution, and the goal of the *Gita*'s teachings. Though these are the general behavioural patterns according to the differences in the *gunas*, yet there is also a law of variation for each individual according to her *swabhava* or inherent bent of mind. The *Gita* has already mentioned this factor in the second chapter and Arjuna was asked to follow the *Kshatriya Dharma*, which is his *swadharma*. The law of one's own nature is preferable to the rule of another's nature, says the Lord, for in that way

Moksha Sannyasa Yoga

we will be following the natural bent of our personality. This *swadharma* is of four kinds, outwardly depicted in the four castes or social orders of the old Indian social culture. This type of social division exists even today in all societies even though they may not be so clearly demarked. Actually, the four castes typify the four fundamental types of natures found in humanity. The Indian social system decreed that the work and function of each person in a society should be decided by the prevailing bent of his or her nature. These four types or castes were known as Brahmins, Kshatriyas, Vaishyas and Sudras. The differences in their natures are due to the different proportions of *sattva*, *rajas* and *tamas* in their makeup. It must be noted that though these names are the names of the four castes, in the *Gita* they infer the quality of the person's disposition and not to the caste alone. These verses in the *Gita* pertaining to castes have been stressed by certain fundamentalists, as giving divine sanction for the caste system. The present caste system is a rigid thing fixed by birth alone whereas the ancient system of *chaturvarna* or caste depended on the natural bent of the mind. The economic and social division was only an indication of this basic nature. We cannot possibly suppose that the *Gita* advocates that a man should follow his parent's profession regardless of the bent of his own mind. The *Gita*'s words refer to the ancient system when it existed in its ideal purity. When the Lord enumerates the work of the Brahmin and the Kshatriya, he does not actually classify the types of jobs they should do, but describes their mental qualities and suggests that they should do the work, which is in conformity with their disposition!

THE CASTE SYSTEM

The ancient system or four-fold classification had a social, economic, cultural and spiritual aspect. It was based on the four functions of social life, which exist even today—the intellectual and spiritual, political, economic and service and manual labour. These are the basic needs of any society, which give rise to the four-fold division of society on which the caste system was based. The Brahmin administered to the spiritual needs of society, producing and preserving the best in knowledge and wisdom, the Kshatriyas to the work of government, politics, administration and war, the Vaishyas to the work of production and business and the Sudras to the work of hired labour. The classification of society into these groups was for the constructive, co-operative, wholesome existence of society. It represented a blend of spiritual power, political power, economic power and manpower, which are absolute necessities for social solidarity and a wholesome existence. This system was not confined

Moksha Sannyasa Yoga

to India alone but is found in some form or other in the life of all ancient societies. These four functions are inherent in the life of all normal communities even though the original clear-cut divisions no longer exist. In India, along with the economic division, a cultural standard was set up for each class, a set of customs, education, discipline and family ideals and there was a constant endeavour to keep up to these ideals. Even to this day, this endeavour exists and is successful to a large extent, and this is the reason why the Indian cultural heritage has remained intact through the passage of centuries of time. Finally in India, this system had a profound spiritual significance. The *swabhava* or inherent nature of the individual was to be the guide and deciding factor of her *swadharma* or rule of conduct and action in life. This *swabhava* was the principle of divinity working within the individual to promote his or her spiritual evolution as has been mentioned in the *Gita* and this is why the *Gita* places its seal of approval on the system. This is the reason why the Lord says that it is better to follow our *swadharma* even though apparently inferior, than to follow the *swadharma* of another which may appear to be superior. Let us take the example of Arjuna. His *swabhava* or nature had made him fit to lead the life of a Kshatriya ruler and warrior and even though he might have considered the ascetic life of a Brahmin to be superior, it would have been wrong for him at that moment to renounce his *swadharma* and take up another. This would have been contrary to the rule of his nature and therefore contrary to the cosmic law of spiritual evolution, which proceeds step by step. This is the ideal of the *varnashramadharma* or allocation of duties according to caste as expounded by the *Gita*.

SWADHARMA AND SWABHAVA

Thus, we see that in its ideal state, this four-fold division is absolutely essential for the harmonious running of any society but in practice, heredity soon took the place of mental makeup and the son of a Brahmin came to be called a Brahmin even though he had nothing of the typical traits of the Brahmin in him. This was an inevitable evolution because the internal signs are not easily apparent and birth is a handier criterion for classification. The lack in characteristics was generally made up by education and training. The importance of following one's *swadharma*, which the *Gita* emphasizes, is due to this inner truth of nature, which gives rise to its spiritual importance. In fact, it lays very little stress on the external rule. It emphasizes the individual and spiritual value of this system and not its communal, social or economic aspect. Just as we find that the *Gita* accepts the ancient Vedic view of sacrifice but gives it a profound spiritual significance, so also it accepts the caste system but gives it a completely novel orientation. What the *Gita* is concerned with, is the synchronization of a person's outward life to his inner growth and not with the upholding of the Aryan social order. This can clearly be seen when we look at the verses forty-one to forty-eight, which deal with castes. The Lord describes the functions of a Brahmin and a Kshatriya not in terms of his work in society as priest or warrior or king but purely from the standpoint of his psychology. The characteristics of each type are due the admixture of the three *gunas* in him. For instance, the one in whom *sattva guna* predominates is a Brahmin. His qualities born out of his nature are purity, honesty, self-control, forgiveness, etc. The professions offered to the Brahmin of teaching, religious ministration etc. are only the outer and most suitable fields for his inner characteristics. So it is the *swabhava*, which should point out the way for our *swadharma* or profession. The *Dhammapada* says, *"Not by matted hair, nor by lineage, nor by birth is one a Brahmin. He is a Brahmin in whom there is truth and righteousness."* Power corrupts insidiously and the ancient Brahmins who knew this, refused to accept direct power but since they possessed knowledge, they directed the rulers through persuasion and love and stopped them from going astray.

Bravery, courage, shrewdness, rulership, generosity, etc. are the inborn qualities of a Kshatriya and the fields in which these qualities can best be displayed are government, politics, defence, etc. *Rajas* mixed with *sattva* is the mixture in the makeup of a Kshatriya and to expect such a person to sit silent and mediate would be to go against the law of his nature. It would thus lead to his downfall for he would be an utter failure in meditation and would be unable to fulfil the commitments of life, which nature had best suited him for, and by following which he would have evolved in a natural manner.

The Vaishya is one in whom *rajas* is predominant and is mixed with *tamas*. This provides a natural propensity for business. Agriculture and trade are the jobs most suited to a Vaishya temperament. The *Shudra* is one in whom *tamas* is pronounced and is mixed with a little *rajas* and this makes him fit for service and manual labour of all types. Devoted to one's own duty the human being can attain the highest perfection, regardless of the type of work she does. The feet are as important as the head and hands and the efficient running of a society depends on the efficient working of all its members.

It must be kept in mind that society can never give identical opportunities for all people to rise to the highest station in life for everyone differs in their natures and abilities. All that society can do is to give everyone equal opportunities to achieve the perfection of human life. It makes little difference whether we dig the earth or do business or govern the state or meditate in the forest. The Varnashrama rules recognise that different people contribute to the general good in different ways. Society is a functional organisation and all functions which are essential for the health of society are to be regarded as socially equal and acceptable. Democracy is not an attempt at uniformity but at integrated variety. Though all people do not have equal capacities, they have a unique function in society and have to be given equal opportunities.

PRACTICAL GUIDANCE FOR LIFE

The *Gita* is an extremely practical gospel. It does not fool us with vain hopes. There is no hard and fast rule of conduct, which is applicable to every human being regardless of her calling, station and aptitude in life. If such a dogmatic rule did exist, there would be very few who would be able to fulfil its exacting standards. It would be an unjust God indeed who cast each person in a different mould and yet expected all to follow one adamantine rule of conduct in order to evolve. Each one has to evolve from where she stands and the natural bent of her mind should be her best guide.

If she follows this faithfully, she will evolve, regardless of what the action entails. It is unwise to attempt work which is beyond our capacity and aptitude. By following one's duty faithfully, one worships the Lord from whom all beings are born and by whom all these is pervaded and thus attain perfection.

"Work is worship!" is the keynote and wonderfully encouraging message of the *Gita*. Whatever be the natural born qualities in us, we can attain perfection provided we offer that work, however menial it might be to the Lord who created us, for he is our hope, our goal and our salvation. He is willing to accept whatever gift we give, provided it is given with love. Though the world may make a mockery of our efforts, though we may be despised, stoned, persecuted or crucified, there can be no fall for us if we are faithful to our ideal. This is one of the key-points of the *Gita*'s teachings and it has to be briefly summarized so that is can be remembered.

SUMMARY OF THE FOUR NATURES

There are four broad types of natures, each with their characteristic functions. The choice of profession and therefore of action in the world must be decided with due consideration to this innate nature. If this is done, that work which is conducive to our nature can be oriented towards

God and made an effective means for liberation. It may be pointed out that modern society is not such a simple one and very often forces us into certain moulds from which there seems to be no escape. This is so only if we follow the rule of the herd in a *tamasic* manner. If we make use of the innate capacities of reasoning, which each person is endowed with, we can discern what is best suited for us. If we have the courage to follow that, regardless of whether it brings us more money or less, we will find that we will progress spiritually. The difficulty in modern life seems to be that the Vaishya or business mentality seems to be predominating and even the choice of profession is decided not according to our inherent mental inclination but to the amount of monetary benefit it would bring. If one succumbs to this temptation and goes against the law of our nature, then naturally it would be spiritual suicide, for our life would be a waste as far as spiritual evolution is concerned.

STICK TO PRINCIPLES

If, on the other hand, we have the courage to stick to our principles and carry on according to the bent of our mind, then we will find that the truth of the *Gita* becomes obvious. Such an individual will be a living soul, who will not only evolve faster but will also have a greater capacity for service to society. To perform our duty in unity with the Spirit within us and as a conscious instrument of the Divine, is what is known as *Karma Yoga* and this is a perfection which humanity is capable of. To unveil the immortal within us is the purpose of life and for that each *jiva* has a force, which guides it through its apparently uncertain but actually inevitable growth to fullness. Our *swadharma* is our personal law of action as determined by our *swabhava*. It is embedded in our very genes and makes us what we are.

FROM MAN TO GOD-MAN

When we scrutinize the characteristics of the four types, we will find that they are not really fundamental divisions of mankind but are actually the stages of self-development in our progress from man to God-man. The soul in its journey from beast, to man, to God, starts with a load of inertia and ignorance, which are the *samskaras* or tendencies of his animal origins. These can be got rid of, only by toiling for society and these are the Sudras whose nature is bound in *tamas*. When that *tamas* is mixed with *rajas*, we find the Vaishya driven by his instinct for acquisition. When the *rajas* is mixed with *sattva*, we get the Kshatriya with a burning ambition to lead, rule and command. When the *sattvic* mind predominates we find the Brahmin with his desire for the highest knowledge and the highest truth. The *Gita* stresses that quality and capacity are the basis of functional divisions.

Mr Gerald Heard in his book on *Man the Master* says, "It would seem then, that there have always been present in the human community four types or strata of consciousness."

"*Sreyan swadharmo vigunah!*" Better is one's own law though imperfectly carried out than the law of another carried out perfectly.

It is no use employing our minds in tasks which are alien to our nature. We are born into this world with our *swabhava*, which has been given to us in order to give us guidance on our behaviour. By worshipping the Divine with the type of work as determined by the law of our Being, we can get beyond the limitations of the three *gunas* and the four-fold law in this life itself, for in the eyes of God there is no distinction. *Naishkarmya* is a state which transcends all work. It is not a withdrawal from work.

HOW TO RECONCILE SPIRITUAL WITH MATERIAL LIFE

In the next fifteen verses, the Lord summarizes the whole outline of the gospel. They have to be considered carefully, for they contain what the Lord himself considers to be the central theme of his teaching. The first difficulty, which faces a person on the spiritual path, is how to reconcile life in the world with all its problems, with the life of the Spirit. How to act in the world, yet live in the highest Self? The *advaitic* way is the ascetic path, which appears to be the safest. Regard the world as a snare and an illusion and give it up as soon as possible. The *Gita* recognizes and accepts the existence of this path but considers that this is too facile a solution since it cuts the knot without loosening it. The *Gita* accepts *sannyasa* as one of the ways of solving the problem but certainly not the only way or even the best way. The conventional meaning of *sannyasa* is the total renunciation of life in this world. This might be the fitting way for one who has the mentality of a true Brahmin but what happens to the remaining three castes? Are they to be debarred from liberation? The *Gita* solves this by giving a novel interpretation of *sannyasa*, which the Lord says is as much an inner state of mind as an outer giving up of material goods. The first step to an inner *sannyasa* has to be the mental withdrawal from the objects of the senses. We must arrive at inner *Naishkarmya* or inactivity. This inactivity or non-participation of the mind combined with the activity of the body is known as *Karma Yoga*. Inactivity of the mind merely means non-involvement with selfish motives. Non-initiation of any activity (*sarvarambaparityagi*) and no expectation of fruits (*sarvasamkalpa sannyasi*) can be said to be inactivity, as has been reiterated many times. We have been told that there are two selves in us, the *daivic* and the *asuric*, which are always struggling for possession. The first step to non-involvement is the conscious withdrawal of the intellect from the objects of the senses but this in itself is not a permanent state. The mind craves for some form of attachment. Having detached itself from the *kshara* or world of creation, it must attach itself to the poise and serenity of the *Akshara Purusha* within it. But to divorce the *akshara* from the *kshara* is not the whole truth of our spiritual nature as the *Gita* has been insisting all along. *Kshara* and *akshara*—Nature and Spirit—are in the end one and the same. A perfect spirituality makes us one with the *Purushottama*, which contains both Self and Nature.

STEPS TO ACHIEVE UNION

What are the steps to achieve this? First we must practice inner silence. At the same time, we must regard all actions as being done by the Lord's *Prakriti* with her three-fold *gunas*, and then make an offering of these actions to the *Purushottama*. We should abandon all personal initiative in the action and become divine instruments alone. The enlightened intellect, which has thus freed itself from the coils of lower Nature and fixed itself on the Supreme, finds it very easy to practice *Karma*

Yoga, which is divine love translated into action through the medium of the human body.

In the beginning stages of *sadhana*, it is best to live in secluded places and eat light food while meditating, until one begins to display all the qualities of the *sthitaprajna* as mentioned in the second chapter, such as a perfect equality in all things and towards all creatures and equanimity within. This should not mislead us into believing that the Lord is advocating the classical form of *sannyasa*. These are only the outer preparations for the inner *sannyasa*, which is better described as *tyaga* in which the ego disappears in the silence of the Supreme Self. All Nature reflects the power of the Divine and all action is a reflection of his action through the channel of the individual body. Having attained this wisdom, there flowers in the devotee a great and perfect love for the Master of her being, which cannot be contained within herself, and overflows in a constant flow of love towards all creation and expresses itself by loving and unselfish action. This is the final breakthrough. By this she comes to know him integrally for she becomes one with him. This is the union of the lover with the Divine Beloved, which confers the highest knowledge, since unity is the foundation of integral knowledge. This knowledge is the inevitable portion of the highest experience. The knowledge of the One who eternally becomes the many, and knowledge of the many, which in their apparent divisions are still the One, is the integral knowledge, which makes us capable of liberated action. This is the culmination of supreme *bhakti* and the core of supreme *jnana*, leading to desireless action or *karma*. Now it becomes evident how action continues in the liberated life for it is quite consistent with the supreme spiritual experience. The Lord is quite vehement on this point.

> Having recourse to Me alone, he continues to perform action and by My grace, he will attain the imperishable and eternal abode and status.

HIGHEST RELATIONSHIP

> Surrendering all action to me, regarding me as the Supreme and resorting to steadfastness in understanding, do thou fix thy mind constantly on me.

> Thus fixing thy thought on me, thou shall by my grace cross over all difficulties. If however thou wilt not listen thou shall perish.

> If out of conceit, you desist from fighting, Nature will compel you to fight.

The human being is free to choose between freedom and bondage. However, if we foolishly believe that we can resist the will of God, we will come to grief for it is our ego which thinks thus.

It is Arjuna's lower nature that has caused the confusion. Now that the truth has been pointed out to him he should act, not for some selfish end, or helplessly as a tool of Nature, but as a conscious instrument of the divine.

Verses fifty-seven to sixty-two, though spoken to the protagonist of Kurukshetra, are applicable to all of us, and provide a universal rule for all those who are ready to ascend above the ordinary mentality of the limited ego, to the highest spiritual consciousness. These words express the most complete and intimate relationship possible between the human being and God. They contain the concentrated feeling that comes from the outflow of religious experience based on direct knowledge, leading to adoration. The devotee directs the whole of her existence, will, intelligence and heart in a continuous outflow of love towards him, for now she knows that she, as the personalised entity, does not exist. Only he, the Lord, exists. It is an unreserved giving of herself to that from whom she has come and in whom she lives. What can she give but herself? What has she got to give but that which has been given to her by him? Thus the *Gita* declares *bhakti* or adoration of the Supreme to be the crown of knowledge.

BHAKTI—THE PINNACLE OF KNOWLEDGE

The remaining verses are not addressed by an impersonal, indifferent Absolute but by the sole friend, lover and most intimate Being in our life, not just in this life but also in all the lives that have gone by and all those that are yet to come. This is not the usual relationship established between the so-called religious person and her chosen deity, in order to satisfy the limited desires of the ego. The individual, who surrenders here, is the one who has divested herself of her personalised ego and melted into the divine. Such a one has no desire, for she has found the fulfilment of all her desires in the Lord of her heart and soul. It is this spiritual being who enters into an ecstatic relationship with the Supreme beloved! It is the state achieved by the *gopis* of Vrindavan, who forgot their bodies, who forgot their minds, who forgot every other worldly consideration and recognised only the Lord as their eternal Beloved, ever ready, ever waiting for them to come to him out of their own volition, without any desire, without any expectation, without any thought of reward, purely because they could not exist apart from him even for a minute, even for a second. Their entire Being was bound up with him and existed only in him! Nothing and nobody—no earthly bond— could restrain the mad impetuous rush of their beings towards him, their Lord, their Master, and their Beloved! The Divinity who demands and receives this total surrender is not the limited deity of our religious misconceptions, but the

Purushottama, the original, transcendent and immanent Spirit of all existence. It is he, the Absolute, but it is also he, the sole friend and lover, who is the object as well as the subject of this most complete surrender.

STAGES TO ATTAIN THIS STATE.

This state is accomplished in stages. The *Purushottama* veils himself and appears as if subject to the law of *Prakriti*'s three *gunas*. It appears as if there is an ascent towards him, in which the first step is the *dharma* of *tamas* or inertia, the second step, the *dharma* of *rajas* or activity and the third step, the harmonic *dharma* of *sattva*. In each of these steps there is an attempt to follow one's own limited personal standard of virtue and ethics. Each step is recognized and supported by the divine since the *jiva* knows no other rule but that of its own *swabhava*. How can God disown that which he himself has created? But even the last step of *sattva* is only temporarily satisfying, since it is not founded on the whole truth of existence. In fact, the life of the human being is a mixture of all these three *gunas*. The best human knowledge is but a half knowledge and the highest human virtue is but a thing of mixed quality. The reason why we try to be good is not clearly understood even by the doer. The reasons are very often selfish, though we may cloak it even from

Moksha Sannyasa Yoga

ourselves. The perfect fulfilment of the *sattvic* nature is only an illusion, for neither the nature of the world nor our own nature is made up wholly of *sattva*. Therefore, our path lies beyond the three *gunas*.

Arjuna's refusal to persevere in his divinely appointed work was due to his ego alone. It sprang from a confused mixture of *sattva*, *rajas* and *tamas*. The desire of not to cause injury was no doubt *sattvic* but it was mixed with *rajas*. It was not repugnance against the causing of injury to everyone but only from his abhorrence at causing injury to his own people. It was also *tamasic* because he was frightened of the sin that might accrue to him. All these doubts, as has been mentioned before, would not have occurred to him if the antagonists had not been related to him. Even now, as Krishna knew well, if he persisted in casting down his arms, he would be helplessly compelled to take them up again due to the propulsion of his nature, which would irresistibly force him to battle in order to protect the *dharma* which he had upheld for so long and which was going to be destroyed in front of his eyes on the battlefield. If he was thus compelled by Nature alone and forced to act through her instigation, what virtue would he get out of it? He had desisted because of his ego's prompting and if he acted due to Nature's prodding, where was the virtue in either of these acts? Both action and non-action would have been due to the force of Nature and not due to his conscious volition and that would have meant a double victory for the ego, for he would have been only a helpless tool in the hands of Nature. Here Lord Krishna was calling on him to become a living and conscious instrument in the hands of the Divine.

LIFE IN IGNORANCE

The life of the ordinary person is on an ignorant and half-enlightened level of the development of the Spirit concealed within her, the secret of which she is either ignorant of, or has not completely mastered. She conducts her life as if she were a separate entity who has all freedom of thought, will and action. It is the headstrong, *rajasic* ego, steeped in the delusion of its separateness that thinks in this fashion. So long as we are mounted on the wheel of this body, mind and intellect and consider ourselves to be this physical and mental entity alone, separate and individualistic, selfish and dissatisfied, we are indeed helpless victims in the machinations of nature.

> The Lord abides in the hearts of all beings, O Arjuna, causing them to revolve helplessly as if mounted on a Ferris wheel.

We live in our own make-believe world, in which we play the role of a hero, strutting and bowing to the applause of an audience, consisting of ourselves, on a stage of our own making! The truth is that as long as we believe this, we are but puppets in the hands of Nature—dancing to her tune and being manipulated by the puppeteer from behind the screen of *maya*. We think we know everything and that we are the sole proprietors of this body and sole agents of our destiny. We believe that everything related to us is entirely within our control! Even in the midst of our posturing and acting we might be struck down dead! This is how sure we can be of our make-believe structure. This stage, this physical edifice on which we pin our hopes and which we think is the basis of our personality may be felled at any moment. Even the bravest hero, the greatest millionaire, the strongest wrestler or the cleverest scientist cannot be certain of the moment of his death and yet we claim that we have freedom of will and mastery over our destiny. The mind and intellect on which we pride ourselves may also fail us at the moment of our greatest need. The number of mental asylums and psychiatrists found in every society is proof of this. Ignorance of our real Self is the root cause of our bondage and as long as we are ignorant and believe ourselves to be physical and mental entities alone, we will be in bondage to Nature.

Our freedom is only pale shadow, our knowledge, only a partial ray and our will only a deflection of this Spirit who is the master and soul of the universe. It is he, seated in the chariot of our hearts, who has been manipulating us through all our inner and outer actions during the period of ignorance in which we had been mounted on a machine of the wheel of his lower nature.

The truth is that both in ignorance and in knowledge, we have our existence in this world only because of Him—the Divine. His will is the sole agent in us as well as in the whole universe. As soon as this knowledge dawns on us, we can climb down from the giant wheel of Nature's machinery and become free agents. We think we are asserting our rights and establishing our greatness by enforcing our individuality and reiterating our mortality. The Lord declares that it is only by renouncing our individuality and surrendering our mortality that we can achieve the heights of universality and immortality, which is our natural heritage. We have thrown away the real and clung to the unreal. We have clutched the empty shell of the body and called it our own, without tasting the sweetness of the kernel within, which is the very stuff of which we are made of. The Supreme is the innermost self of our existence. Our life is a shadow of his life and our powers are all derived from him. This truth will not alter even if we forget. There will be no compulsion to yield to this divine will. God wants our free co-operation. Only then will things begin to happen effortlessly. We become transparent crystals for his light to pass through.

When we enter into this innermost Self of our existence, we will come to know that we are one with that Spirit and Godhead whom all Nature serves. To live consciously and integrally in this knowledge and this truth is to escape from the ego and step down from the wheel and thus break free from the veil of *maya*.

GOAL OF ALL DHARMAS

All other *dharmas* are only a preparation for this *dharma* and all *yoga* is only a means by which we can come to an integral union with Him—the Master of our Being. The crux of the spiritual problem, which is so difficult for the normal mind of the human being to apprehend, is due to our complete belief in our limited egos and our complete ignorance of our radiant existence, which we can enjoy when we are liberated from the confines of the ego. We are all hard-boiled individuals. We are loath to surrender our individualities even if we are promised the state of immortal bliss. We cover the naked truth of our inherent weakness with the frail cloak of our egos and brandish our sword of pride to fight for our non-existent individual rights! How can we ever contemplate a state of absolute surrender if it means a surrender of our cherished egos! But this is just what the Lord demands.

> In Him take refuge with every aspect of your being and by His grace you shall come to enjoy the supreme peace and the eternal status.

We must become conscious of God on all the planes of our being. The *gopis'* love for Krishna is the symbol of integral love on all planes of existence from the physical to the spiritual.

SECRET OF SECRETS

> Thus has this wisdom more secret than all secrets, been declared to thee by me. Reflect on it and then do as thou wish to do.

At the end of the discourse, Krishna leaves the decision of whether to act or not to act in Arjuna's hands. God does not coerce the human being to co-operate with him. He does not compel us to do anything. The final surrender should be with the fullest consent. We should choose to go to him out of our own free will. In the meantime, he waits patiently for the conscious turning of our will to him.

Krishna is only Arjuna's charioteer. He is ready to obey his commands. He uses no violence since he bears no arms. He influences Arjuna through his unconditional love alone. The easiest path is to surrender to him but this is a decision which Arjuna should make for himself. He should not act from a blind belief in Krishna or some form of authority. Only then would he be able to redeem himself and be the redeemer of his society.

The greatest *yoga* is to withdraw from all the perplexities and difficulties of our life and take refuge in the Lord seated within us and turn to him with our whole being. Surrender to him our body, mind, intellect and senses. Then that divine power will take hold of us and fill us and lead us through all the doubts and difficulties and perils that beset our lives to the eternal status, which is our natural abode. Arjuna was most beloved by the Lord and so to him was given this great secret. It is only the rare soul who can be admitted to this mystery for only such a one is near enough to the Godhead to understand and appreciate this message. It is only after having gone through the practice of the various *yogas* of the previous seventeen chapters and even up to the previous verse of the eighteenth chapter that we would be ready to receive this supreme secret. Had it been given at the beginning of the discourse, its impact would have been lost, for its meaning would have been incomprehensible to us and to Arjuna in that state of mind. Only that *jiva* which has been burnished in the fire of renunciation, sharpened on the stone of action and drenched with the love of the Divine is capable of understanding and following this message given so simply and firmly in verses sixty-five and sixty-six. The meaning of these verses can only be hinted at. Their actual import has to be a revelation within each individual, the flowering of her personal spiritual experience—a secret between her and the divine *guru*. All the teachings and disciplines of the previous chapters were but a preparation for this final consummation.

> Listen again to my supreme word, the most secret of all. You are well loved by me and therefore I shall tell you that which is good for you.
>
> Fix your mind on Me, be devoted unto Me, worship Me and prostrate unto Me. I give you my solemn pledge that you shall attain Me for you are indeed dear to Me.
>
> Surrender all your duties to Me. Take refuge in Me alone and I shall absolve you from all sins and lead you to eternal freedom.

It is as if Krishna is telling us through Arjuna of his love and eagerness to take us to him. He is ever waiting with open arms for us to run to him. The union of the personal God and the devotee is a two-way process. It depends as much on our running to him as on his coming to us. His love is pressing on our hearts and waiting for us to open them and let him in.

CONTRARY ADVICE

Till now Krishna had been insisting on the practice of a well-built system of *yoga* by following our *swabhava* and doing our *swadharma* and now at the end he seems to be telling us something quite contrary to this.

Abandon all *dharmas* and give yourself to the Divine alone. That is all you need to do for that is the highest *dharma* and the highest duty and the highest religion. For he is the Spirit whom all Nature serves and we ourselves are soul of this Soul, spirit of this supreme Spirit—our body is his image, our life, his movement, our mind, a mirror of his consciousness, our senses, his instruments and our action, a means of fulfilling his purpose. The following of all other *dharmas* is only a prelude leading to the knowledge of this supreme *dharma*. This is the only duty, which is obligatory on the *jiva*. All other duties are only meant as a preparation for this and once that has been accepted and decided upon by the *jiva*, it can abandon all other *dharmas*. For this surrender itself will aid us in the attainment of him who is in himself the Supreme *Dharma*! Having surrendered allow him to do what he wills with your life and do not be perplexed when his ways seem to differ from the established ideas of the world for his way is the way of perfect trust and perfect love and perfect knowledge. The one who cares nothing for merit or sin, the one who sets aside all conventional ideas of obligations and duties and serves him as his sole support, is the greatest.

FINAL WORD

This then is the supreme word—that in essence the Spirit is eternally free and therefore has no *dharmas*. But the embodied soul takes upon itself the burden of its own life and thus inherits the burden of duties imposed by the world. It fails to realise that the world is conducted by the Godhead according to fixed laws and will continue on its way with or without help from it. It has to find its path through the maze of lower *Prakriti*'s web of *maya* before final realisation dawns after many births. During its journey from ignorance to knowledge, it has to experiment with many *dharmas* based on the prevailing view of right and wrong, sin and virtue, like and dislike, pleasure and pain, joy and sorrow. The soul has to traverse the path of *dharma* as given by its own *swadharma* based on its own *swabhava*. The path it takes will be directed by its physical, mental, vital, emotional, intellectual, ethical and spiritual mentality. This in turn dictates the forms of conduct, rules and standards, which a just society imposes on it. The Spirit or Godhead transcends all these *dharmas*. The *jiva*, which casts away the different cloaks of its false identity with these various aspects of its

Moksha Sannyasa Yoga

personality and comes to realise its identity with this free Spirit, finds that it can transcend these values. If we surrender our egos completely and absolutely to this Spirit within us and accept only his guidance, it will bring with it the absolute and inevitable perfection of our nature to be enjoyed in an absolute freedom. This is the way offered to the chosen person, to those who are closest to him, those who have completely surrendered their egos as Arjuna had done and those who have none to call their own, except him. To such a one the Lord makes a solemn promise—the promise made by God to humanity!

> Surrender your ego, which is a myth of your own making, together with the duties imposed on you by that ego, to Me the Lord seated within the chariot of your body and I will carry you through the dreary desert of your life (as I carried Arjuna through the gory battlefield of Kurukshetra). Do not grieve at the happenings of this world which you cannot understand for I give you My absolute assurance that I Myself will lead you beyond sorrow to the highest abode.

The Lord sits within our body. Seek refuge in him alone with your entire being. Surrenderg to him, bow and prostrate to him for by his grace we will attain supreme peace.

This dialogue between Arjuna and the divine charioteer is a secret, esoteric and most intimate conversation between the human being and God.

Arjuna is only the immediate cause for this message, which is meant for the whole of humanity. We are all dear to him and all of us can reach him if we follow this advice.

Krishna then goes on to say that this doctrine should not be spoken to one who has no devotion to him or speaks ill of him. This message is not easy to understand. Only someone who has the heart and will of an Arjuna can understand and appreciate it.

He continues to say that those who teach this doctrine with devotion to others will undoubtedly go to him. In fact, there is no one who does greater service to him and to humanity than the one who teaches this to others. Those who study this sacred dialogue are actually performing a *jnana yajna*—a sacrifice of knowledge. Even those who listen to this discourse with faith will be liberated and attain the world of the liberated.

This is the final word of the *Gita* and the Master lovingly turns to his disciple and asks, "Has this been followed by you O Arjuna with single-pointed concentration? Has your delusion been destroyed?"

"Destroyed is the illusion of my mind. My doubts have vanished and I stand firm to do Thy bidding," says Arjuna.

Arjuna decides to do his appointed duty bolstered with self-confidence and self-knowledge.

Karishye vachanam tava, is what he says. "I am ready to follow thy bidding and thy will."

The Sufi poet says, "May my will always be thy will O Master."

The whole *yoga* has thus been revealed and Arjuna is the chosen soul, the *vibhuti*, who now stands ready to take up the divine action. Sanjaya, the enlightened Prime Minister of the blind king Dritarashtra, to whom the discourse is being narrated, as has been said before, utters the last verses of the *Gita*.

O King

says Sanjaya,

Blessed am I for by the grace of the sage Vyasa I have heard this soul-stirring discourse by Krishna, the Lord of *yoga*, and I stand enthralled. Whenever I think of this holy discourse and recall that wondrous form of Krishna, I am thrilled again and again.

Wherever there is Krishna, the Master *Yogi* and Arjuna, the wielder of the bow, there will be prosperity, victory, glory and righteousness!

The whole teaching of the *Gita* is *yoga* and Krishna is the *Yogeeswara* - the Lord of *Yoga*.

Sanjaya gives a hint to the blind king about the outcome of the battle for where Krishna and Arjuna stand united there can be only victory! Krishna and Arjuna stand for the *jivatma* and the

Paramatma, man and God, seated together in the chariot of the body. When man and God stand united, when the individual works in union with the Divine, when he becomes the living, conscious instrument of the Divine, there can never be a defeat for him! When Arjuna, the embodied soul, the *jivatma* becomes the bow in the hands of the divine archer, then there can be no doubt that victory, auspiciousness and righteousness will prevail!

> *yatra yogeswara Krishno,*
> *yatra partho dhanurdhara,*
> *tatra, sri, vijiayo, bhuthir*
> *dhruva nithir mathir mama*

ॐ *Hari Aum Tat Sat* ॐ

Thus, in the Upanishad of the *Bhagavad Gita*, the knowledge of Supreme Brahman, the Scripture of *Yoga*, the dialogue between Sri Krishna and Arjuna, ends the eighteenth chapter entitled 'The *Yoga* of the Liberation and Renunciation'.

> He who performs his duties at all times with mind surrendered to me, he attains the Eternal and Imperishable abode by My grace.

SUMMARY OF THE GITA'S TEACHINGS

Nitya Yoga: The Yoga of Constant Communion

Aum Sri Krishnaya Paramaatmane' namaha!
Aum Sri Parthasarathaye' namaha.

ॐ

When we read the *Gita*, we might wonder why Lord Krishna keeps reiterating certain things. This is because the *Gita* is more than anything else a handbook of practical spirituality. It is not like the Upanishads or Puranas, which you might read to understand certain things about spirituality. It does not contain *mantras*, which have the power to grant us spiritual merit just by mere repetition. If Lord Krishna has repeated many of his ideas over and over again, it is only to ensure that someone sometime may realise that he or she has to put his advice into practice. Many people pride themselves on being able to chant the *Gita* by heart. No doubt this is very good but if one does not practice even one of the *Gita*'s teachings, any amount of repetition is not going to give you any benefit except that of sharpening your memory. It is with this knowledge that one should read the *Gita* and then adapt its teachings to suit our special needs, for each of us is special—special to us as well as to the Lord. He has given any number of hints to suit every type of character. These hints should be taken up and moulded into our character and acted upon so as to enable us to reach the highest goal of union.

The *Gita* is a very special book. It is an intimate personal discourse between the human being Arjuna and Krishna—the incarnated godhead. The teaching of the *Gita* is not just a general spiritual philosophy or ethical doctrine to be contemplated upon but a practical application of ethics and spirituality in human life. It is a gospel of divinity to be experienced in and through our humanity.

God's love for the human being is shown in every line of the book. Krishna tries from all possible angles to uplift his dear friend Arjuna and through him, the rest of us, from the quagmire of ignorance in which we are all wallowing into the

Summary of the Gita's Teachings

light of perfect freedom and knowledge. God has not made this creation and left us to struggle as best we can and make our own way back to freedom. He is with us every moment and keeps telling us to listen to him, who is the indweller, who is instigating us all the time. Like an FM radio station the sweet, loving, insistent voice of God is continuously broadcasting to us but since we have not tuned into the station we are unable to hear this voice. Methods to suit every type of personality are given by Krishna in order to tune in to this divine broadcasting station. Of these the three foremost methods or *yogas*, which are simple and easy to practice, are known as *jnana yoga* (*yoga* of wisdom), *karma yoga* (*yoga* of action) and *bhakti yoga* (*yoga* of devotion). By using these, each one of us can lift ourselves out of the lethargy into which we have fallen and rise up to the divine heights within us.

First of all he gives us, through Arjuna, the *yoga* of wisdom, which is here called *Samkhya Yoga*. In this we are asked to find out the nature of the person behind the personality, which is what we normally see every time we look into the mirror. We are asked to go beyond the three outer casings, of the body, mind and intellect, and discover the reality within which is known as the *atman*. When the *atman* relates itself to the outer casings, it is known as the *jivatma* or the embodied spirit. In itself the *atman* is eternally free since it is the Brahman itself. It only observes the play of its own *Prakriti* in the external circumstances, which enfold the *jivatma* in a cocoon of ignorance. *Prakriti* has three modes known as *gunas* or strings, which are called *sattva* (harmony), *rajas* (kinesis or action), and *tamas* (inertia). These are really psychological strands and they make their way insidiously into the human system as well as the physical world. These are the strands that bind the boundless, eternal entity called the *atman* to the mutable, transient physical body, mind, and intellect equipment. These *gunas* exist in the external world, and project their tentacles on the human system and make us slaves to their characteristics so that we also begin to act as they act, forgetting our essential divine, free nature. The one who knows the nature of these *gunas* will not be frightened of them. Even though they act on us, we will be able to observe their play both on our own personality as well as on the external world and laugh and think to ourselves, "This is the play of the *gunas* on the *gunas*—'*guna guneshu varthante. Iti matwa na shadjate.*' Thinking in this fashion we will not be bound. A person who is wise to the nature of the *gunas*, is known as a *gunatita*. This is what Krishna says about the *gunas* and the method of going above them. Unless we transcend the *gunas* we will never become free agents. The moment we understand their

Summary of the Gita's Teachings

workings, we become free from their stranglehold. Then only will we understand that we are not creatures of the world alone but that our basic nature is divine. This thought will sustain us through all our relationships with the external world.

Next we come to *karma yoga* or the *yoga* of action. Since we are born in this world, it is incumbent on us to act since this is an action-filled planet. No one can remain here without action. Even for the upkeep of our body we need to act. But as we know, the Law of *Karma*, which is a universal law of justice, decrees that every act must have its equal and opposite reaction. This is Newton's third law of motion, which has its reflection in the human being. However, in the human being it is not just the act which will give a reaction but the intention by which the act has been committed. The intention is the cause which brings about the effect, which we ourselves have to accept since we are the ones who had the intention. This is not a moral law but a law of nature which will ensure that universal justice is meted out to all under all circumstances, without any discrimination. Everyone however wise or stupid must come under this law. All the causes which have been started by us through our actions need not necessarily come to fruition in this life so it is imperative that we take another life in order to experience the effects of the action which we ourselves have done in this life. The machinery of cause and effect, which we have set into motion in this life will have to be completed by us in some other life since this is a natural law which cannot be gainsaid by anything, not even the death of the body that started it. Hence the belief in Hinduism in reincarnation. Nature does not like any loose ends. Every cause has to have an effect if not in this life then in another. Does this mean that the human being is condemned to rotate eternally from life to life?

The generally accepted notion is that any action will perforce bind us to this wheel of cause and effect, which is known as the *samsara chakra*. We must not think that only negative actions will bind us. Positive actions also have effects which will bind us. We have to take on a body in order to enjoy the effects of a positive action or intention as well as to be punished by the effects of a negative action. Thus, the idea arose that *sannyasa* or total renunciation of action was the only way to get off this Ferris wheel of birth and death and attain to the Supreme State.

Krishna totally blasts this view. He says that this is a false view, which has arisen due to our misconception as to what constitutes bondage. He says that what binds us to the wheel is not the action as such but the desire for the fruits of the action. Our desire is usually a selfish demand that we must be the sole enjoyer. If we make such a

Summary of the Gita's Teachings

demand, Nature will see to it that we get it if not in this life then in another. So the first advice he gives about the technique of action, which he calls *Karma Yoga*, is to give up the fruits of action—*sarvasamkalpa sannyasa*. Nature has given us one right and that is to do our duty but she has not given us the right to demand the wages or fruits of action. The result of the action depends entirely on another cosmic law over which we have no control. We think we are in control over the results and hence we get disappointed when things do not turn out the way we want it. Actually we are never in control of the effects of the action. But very often we get the expected results and hence we are lulled into a belief that the effects depend on us. Many examples can be given to show that even though we may perform an act perfectly, it need not follow that we will get the expected results. Thus, Krishna says the first rule about action is that we should do it without expectation of any selfish benefits—*sarvasamkalpa sannyasa*. Of course the act itself should be done to the best of our ability but we should then relax and allow Nature to take her course which might be either failure or success as we see it. This type of action is known as a *yajna* or offering to the Supreme. Nature herself does everything for the secret Self within her. Rains fall, grass grows, flowers bloom and trees bear fruits. She does it as a *yajna* and so should we do all our actions as a *yajna* or offering to the Supreme both outside us and inside us without expecting anything in return. The Vedic idea of *yajna* is given a deep spiritual and individual meaning by Krishna. Another point to be remembered is that since we have given up all expectations, we will not be disappointed or elated at whatever happens. This is known as *prasada buddhi*. Any result that we get from the action, either good or bad, is accepted as *prasada* or leftovers from what has been offered to God. This means that it has been blessed by God so we are not to judge whether it is good or bad. This equilibrium of mind in the face of dualities is something which Krishna insists as being the foundation of enlightenment.

The equilibrium of the mind should be accompanied by an equality of vision. This means that we see everything as aspects of God. When we practice this for some time, this attitude turns to one which sees the face of God in everything both good and so-called evil, both beautiful and so-called ugly. This is called equality of vision. This naturally leads to the state where we do not judge anything. We leave all judgements to God since we do not know the *karmic* events which have led to a person's behaviour. We see only the present action and not the *karmic* causes which have led to this act. This does not mean that we do not recognise negativity when we see it. We not only

Summary of the Gita's Teachings

see it but we should also take the appropriate action which is called upon. We see the accident and take the person to the hospital and render what help we can but we do not make judgements on the driver. Such things are left for that impersonal Law of *Karma* which will see to it that everybody gets whatever he or she deserves, nothing more and nothing else. But this is not our problem. Our problem is only to render aid when we can.

Having cut the ground from under our foot about the end product of our actions, Krishna proceeds to do the same with the start of the action. He says that all action proceeds from the same source, which is the *Prakriti* of the Lord. She is the sole actor while the *Purusha* is the sole witness and by his very witnessing, he is also the instigator of the action. Therefore, we should act with the attitude that we are not the doers of the action. We should allow ourselves to be mere instruments in the hand of the Lord, who will instigate his *Prakriti* to make us act in the correct possible way. The word he uses for this is *sarvarambaparityaga*—not instigating or initiating. Thus, the enlightened man does not initiate or instigate any action nor does he expect any fruits from it. The *yogi* waits for the Lord to prompt him from inside and allows himself to be used by the divine as a mere instrument. Secondly, though he has no expectation of personal rewards, he will fully participate in whatever work is on hand. This has to be done to the best of our capacity. This is all that we are expected to do. This is the core of the *Gita*'s teachings. No initiation, no expectation but only full participation in the drama of life.

The purpose of the *Gita* is to fashion a God out of this mortal clay—to unveil the divinity within the humanity. For this it makes use of a three-pronged weapon like Lord Shiva's trident in order to attack the enemy, which is within us, as the Lord reminds Arjuna. This enemy is the ego and desire is its stronghold. This desire lurks in all the three aspects of the human personality—the body, mind and intellect. Therefore, the *Gita* advocates the triple *yogas* of *jnana* or wisdom, *karma* or action and *bhakti* or devotion. These three are aimed at routing the enemy from the three personality angles of the intellect, body and mind. When the body has been subdued with the practice of *karma yoga* and the intellect submerged in the *atman* through the practice of *jnana yoga*, the heart overflows with love for the Divine so that there is no place in it for love of the world. This is the final victory over the enemy. Then is the divinity fully revealed and the purpose of the *Gita* fulfilled.

The *Gita*, unlike other religious texts, does not say that this state of union can be achieved only after shedding the body. It insists that this state can and will be achieved even while living in this

Summary of the Gita's Teachings

world and inhabiting this body, for what constitutes bondage is the desire of the mind for the fruits of action and not the action itself. He who is free from this desire is a *jivan mukta* or liberated soul. He or she is compared by Krishna to the lotus leaf, which lies on the water of the pond and still remains totally dry. All the waters of the pond cannot wet this leaf. Water drops glimmer like diamonds on it but cannot wet it. The drops simply roll off without making the slightest change on the leaf. Thus, the *jivan mukta* though living in the dirty pond of the world is not affected by it. He keeps his own personality intact and unsullied.

It is a mistaken belief that spirituality and materialism cannot go hand in hand and that the *yogi* will be a misfit in normal life. The teacher of the *Gita* insists that God-realisation, instead of abolishing the law of the world, transforms it into a reign of divine wisdom. God and the world do not and cannot deny each other since the world is an integral part of the Divine. Each one of us can rise at our own pace out of our lower animal being into the full blossoming of our spiritual nature, which is our true nature. The result is an integral union of the individual being with the divine being which is the condition of the perfect spiritual life as well as the perfect worldly life. This union is to be achieved through the practice of the triple *yogas* of *jnana*, *karma* and *bhakti*, meant to divinise the three aspects of the human being's outer personality.

The last *yoga* which he takes up is *bhakti yoga* or the *yoga* of devotion. In this the intellect is to be constantly dwelling on his perfection, the body to be constantly performing action for his sake and the heart to be ever flowing with adoration towards him. The mind has to be conditioned to recognise him in everything—in the mountains, in the rivers, in the seas, in the stars and in the stones! This is the essence of the *Vibhuti Yoga*. This triple *yoga* of the *Gita* is not something to be practiced at special times and places but it is to be made into a constant communion with the Divine Beloved at all times. The mind which has been conditioned to notice only the differences in the world has to be re-conditioned to see him alone in everything and therefore to act for him and to adore him in all things. The *Gita* is not satisfied with a lukewarm love, which grudgingly allots a small portion of the lover's time for the beloved. It demands nothing less than a twenty-four hour affair! The Lord is an exacting as well as an exciting lover! He demands constant contact with him at all times—walking, sleeping, dreaming, breathing, laughing, talking, eating or sitting! The prize offered to such an extraordinary lover of God is that she becomes one with God! The personality takes on the likeness of that with which it is obsessed! If we are infatuated with the world, we become worldly and the one who is enamoured by God becomes God-like. This then is our greatest *dharma* and as we have seen at the end, our only *dharma*. Each of the eighteen chapters of the *Gita* gives us different *yogas* by which the mind can be made to achieve this state of divinity.

Established in union with the Self within, one should act and such an action is a *yajna*. When Arjuna acts in union with Krishna, even the act of battle becomes a *yajna*. There is nothing trivial in the eyes of the Lord, so every action, from our grandest endeavours to the most trivial function of our daily lives, can be turned into a *yajna*. He accepts everything if offered with love. The *Gita* holds out hope of liberation not only to the great and noble soul but also to the poor and the weak. The Lord does not set the same values on our actions as the human being does. What is acclaimed as great or glorious in the eyes of the world may well be deemed worthless in his eyes. The worth of an action is judged by the amount of unselfishness that goes into it. If it is done as a *yajna* or offering to the Almighty, even the most petty and insignificant action can be acclaimed as a sacrament.

Yajna, *dana* and *tapas* are what constitutes a person's *dharma* according to the Lord and these are obligatory on every human being, whether she is a *karma yogi* or *sannyasi*. These are incumbent on all of us by virtue of our being a human being and a denizen of this planet earth. *Yajna* is the work we owe to the world. As has been said, any action done for the sake of the Lord, who is both transcendent and immanent, is a *yajna*. Watering a plant, feeding the hungry, planting a tree, keeping our environment unpolluted and clean are all part of the universal *yajna*, for he is immanent in all creation. *Dana* or charity is what each of us owes to society, which upholds us and *tapas* is austerity, which is what we owe to ourselves.

Faultless performance of one's *swadharma* is the supreme *yajna*—the greatest offering or worship of the Lord! This is the universal *dharma*. Action, which is based on this, is the action, which is determined by our inner nature. To follow this is to follow the law of our own development. To deviate from it is to end in confusion, retardation and error not only in our spiritual life but also in our social life. The spiritual evolution of the individual as well as the stability of the society depends upon the correct performance of the various duties (*swadharma*) by the members of society.

Having said this much about the importance of *dharma* in all the preceding chapters, in the sixty-sixth verse of the eighteenth chapter the Lord of Kurukshetra makes a dramatic reversal of all his former statements and tells his disciple to

Summary of the Gita's Teachings

surrender all his *dharmas* to him and have recourse to him alone and he would carry him across the ocean of life to the shores of immortality. How are we to interpret this? We have already seen that our *dharma* is decided for us by the amount of dependence we have on other things—on family, Nature, nation and society. But the perfect person has no such dependence on anything. She has nothing to gain or lose in the world, nothing to know or learn, nothing to wish for or desire and therefore nothing to be done as a matter of duty or obligation. Having surrendered all her *dharmas* into the capable hands of her Divine Charioteer, she has gone beyond all *dharmas*. She has to go on performing her *swadharma* as an example to others but not as an obligation, for she has none. She wants nothing and expects nothing, though she may still be prepared to give her all, if called upon to do so. To know God, to act for him and to adore him, this alone is her *dharma*. She faithfully follows this triple *yoga* of the *Gita*. It is not a *yoga* reserved for special times and places but it has to be practiced at all times and in all places. It is thus the *yoga* of constant communion. She touches the Lord at all times and in all places, and in all things. She is never parted from him. She sees her Beloved in every face, meets him in every glance, in every word and in every act. What *dharma* is left there for such a person? She wants nothing and expects nothing, for all her wants are perfectly fulfilled by him, in whom she reposes her very being! The whole world is her storehouse and the universe her home and the Lord of the cosmos her only friend and benefactor. She has no dependence on anyone! Like a child reposing in the arms of her mother, she rests in the arms of her beloved, secure in the knowledge that all her wants will be fully taken care of and that she has nothing further to do. She is perfectly fulfilled and absolutely secure in the knowledge of her love for the Divine and his for her. She is like the lotus flower in the muddy pond of the world—untouched and unpolluted! Thus being in constant communion with him, she has no *dharmas*, for the Lord of all *dharmas* is her private charioteer, who is directing the fiery horses of her inner life and attending to every detail of the battle with divine foresight and infinite power! In constant union with the *Paramatma* within her, she sits in the chariot of her body and is swiftly borne through the gory battlefield of life, unscathed and unafraid, for the Divine Charioteer has given his solemn word to absolve her from all sins and to take her to the goal of complete liberation!

> *Ananyath chintayantomam*
> *Ye jana paryupasathe*
> *Thesham nityabhiyuktanam*
> *Yogakshemam vahamyaham.*

"I shall personally attend to all the needs of those who worship me with the *Yoga* of constant communion."

Thus, in the Upanishad of the *Bhagavad Gita*, the knowledge of Supreme Brahman, the Scripture of *Yoga*, the dialogue between Sri Krishna and Arjuna, ends the concluding summary entitled 'The *Yoga* of the Constant Communion'

ॐ *Hari Aum Tat Sat* ॐ

GLOSSARY

Aum Sri Krishnaya Paramaatmane' namaha!
Aum Sri Parthasarathaye' namaha.

adambitwam	without boasting.
adharma	non-righteousness
adhishtana	the foundation for all action—body, mind and intellect
adhyatma	same as the *atman*
adhyatma jnana nityatwam	constantly pondering on the nature of the Self
adibhuta	the world of physical nature
adidaiva	the secret soul in nature, which shapes the ends of all action
adiyajna	the divine to whom all actions are to be offered
advaita	philosophy of non-dualism

advaitic		pertaining to the philosophy of non-duality
agni		fire
ahamkara		ego
ahimsa		non-violence
ajna chakra		psychic centre in the middle of the brows
akarma		non-action
akasa		space
amanitwam		without false pride
ananda		bliss
apas		water
apravritti		inertia
archanam		doing *puja*
artha		one with lots of complaints
asat		non-existence
Ashwatta		peepul tree
asuras		demons
atman		soul
atmanivedanam		total surrender of oneself
Aum Tat Sat		triple definition of the Brahman. *Aum* stands for the totality, *Tat* for the transcendent and *Sat* for the existence in all of us.
avatara		incarnation

Glossary

avyakta	unmanifest
bhakti	devotion to God
brahmacharya	celibacy
buddhi	intellect
chakra	wheel
chakras	energy whorls lying along on the spine
cheshta	different types of movement used in action
chit	consciousness
chitta	the super-conscious mind
daiva-m	the unseen universal factor which shapes the ends
daivi sampat	divine qualities
damba	a boastful person
dana	charity
dasyam	taking the role of a servant
desha	space
devas	gods
dharma	cosmic law of righteousness
dharmakshetra	field of righteousness
dhr	uphold; protect
dukha	sorrow
dwesha	dislike
grihastashrama	state of being a householder

gunas	the three strands found in nature: *sattva, rajas, tamas*
guru	Spiritual preceptor
iccha	like
ishta	favourite form of God
jagat	world
japa	constant repetition of the mantra (name of god)
jati	birth
jiva	embodied soul
jivan mukta	liberated soul
jivatma	embodied soul
jnana	wisdom
jnana bhakta	devotee, who is also a sage
kaaranam	instruments used for the action
kala	time
kama	pleasure
karma	action
karmaphalatyaga	renouncing the fruits of action
karmic	pertaining to *karma*
karta	the individual who does the action
keertanam	singing the praises of God
Kritakritya	totally fulfilled
kshetra	field
kshetrajna	knower of the field (*atman*)

Kundalini Shakti	psychic power of the divine mother coiled up at the bottom of the spine
laya	dissolution
lila	play or game of the Lord
lokasamgraham	for the good of all
maani	proud person
mahabhutas	the great elements five in number
mahatma	noble soul
manana	contemplating
manas	mind
mantra	incantation
maya	Illusory power of the Lord
mithya	non-existent
muladhara	the name of the *chakra* situated at the bottom of the spine
naishkarmya	state of being unaffected by the effects of *karma*
niddidhyasana	practice
nimitta	cause
nirvana	state of beatitude
nishkama	without desire
nitya	constant
padasevanam	worshipping the feet
pancha-mahabhutas	five great elements: space, air, fire, water and earth

poorna	state of fullness; plenum
Poornamadam, Poornamidam	That is full and this is also full
prakasa	radiance
Pralaya	end of a cycle of existence
pramada	indifference
prana	life-current
pranayama	method of controlling the breath
prapti	total surrender to God
prasad	leftover food, which has been offered to God
prasada buddhi	acceptance of everything as a gift from God
pravritti	movement
prithvi	earth
purusha	man
purusharthas	the four goals of life: *dharma, artha, kama* and *moksha*
Purushottama	the Supreme person
rajas	quality of kinesis or action (one of the *gunas*)
rajaso-tamasic,	mixture of *rajas* and *tamas*
rishis	seers of the Vedas
sadhana	spiritual practice
sadharmya	nature of the Supreme
sahasrara	name of *chakra* on top of the head

sahasrara chakra	the psychic spot on top of the head
sakhyam	taking the role of a friend
samadhi	a state of super-consciousness
samsara chakra	the wheel of cause-and-effect
samskaras	inborn tendencies carried over from past lives
samvada	dialogue
sannyasa	total renunciation of the world; fourth stage of life
sannyasin	monk
sarvabhutahite rathaha	delighting in the welfare of the world
sat	existence
sattva	quality of harmony (one of the *gunas*)
sattvo-rajasic	mixture of *sattva* and *rajas*
shareera	body
shastra	spiritual book
shrishti	creation
shudra	the fourth caste; labourers or those who render physical service
shunya	state of nothingness; void
smaranam	remembrance
sraddha	faith
sravana	listening

sthitha prajna	man of steady intellect; enlightened man
sukha	joy
swabhava	natural born qualities
swabhava	inherent nature
swadharma	personal law of right behaviour
tamas	quality of inertia (one of the *gunas*)
tamasic	pertaining to the *guna* called *tamas*
tapakshetra	field of austerity
tapas	austerity
tatwa jnanartha-darshanam	knowledge of the Self
thandava nritta	cosmic dance of Shiva known as Nataraja
tyaga	inner renunciation of the fruits
Uttama	supreme
Vaishya	the third cast in the Hindu caste system; tradesman or farmer
Vaiswanara	Lord as the fire of digestion in the stomach of all creatures
vanaprastha	living in the forest as a prelude to the final renunciation of life
vandanam	obeisance
varna	caste
varnashram-	allocation of duties according to

adharma	caste
vayu	air
vedasaara	essence of the Vedas
vibhutis	extraordinary manifestations of God
vijnana	scientific knowledge
vikarma	special action
yajna	Vedic ritual involving a fire ceremony
yajnakund	space made with bricks to light the fire for the ritual.
yatra	journey
yoga	any attempt to attain union with god
yogashastra	practical application of *yoga* (*Bhagavad Gita* is known as *yogashastra*)
yuj	to unite
yukta	one who is united

APPELLATIONS OF KRISHNA

In the Sreemad Bhagavad Gita

Achyutha	the one who never falls or fails (his devotees); the unshakeable one
Aadideva	the first of the gods; the unseen witness of all events

Aja	the Unborn
Akshara	the Imperishable one
Anaadi	the one without a beginning
Ananta	the one without an end
Anantabahu	the one with endless arms
Ananta rupa	the one with endless forms
Anantaveerya	the one with unlimited valour
Aprabhava	the one with incomparable glory
Aprameya	the immeasurable one
Arisudana	the slayer of enemies
Avyaya	the immutable one
Bhagavan	the blessed one with eight divine qualities
Bhavan	the holy one
Bhutesa	the Lord of all beings
Deva	the shining one; a god
Devadeva	God of gods
Devavara	best among the gods
Devesha	Lord of gods
Dharmagopta	the custodian of *dharma*
Divyam	the effulgent
Govinda	protector of all *jivas*; the chief of herdsmen
Hari	the remover of sorrows
Hrishikesha	Lord of the senses; one with curly hair

Isa; Iswara	God
Jagannivasa	the abode of the universe
Jagatpathi	the Lord of the universe
Janardana	the one who removes the sorrows of birth and death; the agitator
Kamalapatraksha	The lotus-eyed one
Keshava	the one with thick hair
Keshinishoodana	the slayer of the demon Keshi
Krishna	the enticer; the one who is dark in complexion
Madhava	consort of Madhavi or Mahalakshmi
Madhusudana	destroyer of the demon Madhu
Mahabaahu	the mighty-armed one
Mahatman	the great-souled one
Mahayogeeswara	the great Lord of *yoga*
Mahayogi	the great *yogi*
Paramam	the transcendent one
Parabrahman	the supreme, transcendent Brahman
Param Dhama	the supreme abode
Parameswara	the supreme god
Paramnidhanam	the supreme refuge
Pavitram	the pure one
Prabhu	the splendid one
Prajapati	Lord of creatures

Purusha	the pure witnessing consciousness
Purushapurana	the ancient person
Purushottama	the supreme person or spirit
Sahasrabahu	the thousand-armed one
Sakha	friend
Sarva	the all-encompassing one
Sri Bhagavan	the blessed and auspicious one
Vaasudeva	the son of Vasudeva; the omnipresent being
Varshneya	belonging to the clan of the Vrishnis
Vedidavyam	the supreme knowable
Vishnu	the all-pervading one; the harmoniser in the trinity
Vishwamoorti	the one whose form is the universe
Vishwaroopa	the one with the cosmic form
Vishveshvara	god of the universe
Yadava	descendent of King Yadu; belonging to the clan of the Yadavas
Yogi; Yogin	the one who is ever united with the supreme
Yogeeshwara	the Master *Yogi*

APPELLATIONS OF ARJUNA

IN THE SREEMAD BHAGAVAD GITA

Anagha	the sinless one
Arjuna	the pure one; the white one
Bhaarata	descendent of the King Bharata
Bharatasattama	most virtuous among the descendents of Bharata
Bharatarshabha	bull of the Bharatas
Bharatashreshta	best among the Bharatas
Dhananjaya	conqueror of wealth
Gudakesha	one who has conquered sleep; the curly-haired one
Kapidwaja	the ape-bannered one
Kaunteya	son of Kunti
Kireetin	the diademed one
Kurunandana	joy of the Kurus
Kurupraveera	hero of the Kurus
Kurusattama	noblest among the Kurus
Kurushreshta	best among the Kurus
Mahabaho	the mighty-armed one
Pandava	the son of Pandu
Paramtapa	scorcher of foes
Partha	the son of Pritha (Kunti)
Purusharshabha	bull among men
Purushavyagra	tiger among men
Savyasachin	the ambidextrous one

List of Characters in the Sreemad Bhagavad Gita

According to Order of Appearance

Dritarashtra	blind king of the Kurus; father of the Kauravas
Sanjaya	the king's companion and narrator of the *Gita*
Duryodana	eldest of the Kauravas
Dronaacharya	preceptor of the Kauravas and Pandavas
Drupada	father of Draupadi
Drishtadyumna	brother of Draupadi; Drupada's eldest son
Arjuna	third among the five Pandavas
Bhima; Vrikodara	second among the Pandavas
Yuyudhana; Satyaki	heroes of the Yadava clan
Virata	king of the clan of Matsyas
Drishtaketu	king of the clan of Chedi
Chekitana	ally of the Pandavas
Purujit	ally of the Pandavas
Kuntibhoja	adopted father of Kunti, mother of the Pandavas
Shibya	king of the clan of the Shibis
Yudhamanyu	ally of the Pandavas
Uttamaujas	ally of the Pandavas.